The Adventure Racing Manifesto

If you're not hungry, you're carrying too much food.
If you're not thirsty, you're carrying to much water.
If you are warm, you have too many clothes.
If you're not wet, scratched, and bruised, you took the long way.
If you are not frightened, you have too much gear.
If you are not tired, you're going too slowly.
If you are not drop-down sleepy, you're getting too much rest.
And if you finish the race on schedule, it was too easy anyway.

THE THRILL OF VICTORY, THE AGONY OF MY FEET

Tales from the World of Adventure Racing

Neal Jamison
Maureen Moslow-Benway
Nic Stover

BREAKAWAY BOOKS
HALCOTTSVILLE, NEW YORK
2005

ISBN: 1-891369-54-7
Library of Congress Control Number: 2005920864

Published by Breakaway Books
P.O. Box 24
Halcottsville, NY 12438
(800) 548-4348
www.breakawaybooks.com

FIRST EDITION

Contents

Acknowledgments

We each would like to thank our contributors for sharing their stories. Without them this book would not have been possible. Additionally, we'd like to thank adventure racers everywhere, for reminding us just how much is possible when people dare to dream, work together, and soar to new heights.

Maureen: I would like to thank my husband, Bob, who is my number one fan and biggest supporter. Fifteen years ago, we had our first date—a long bike ride through the foothills of Tennessee—and since that time, we have logged literally tens of thousands of miles together on this journey we call life. I would also like to thank my three children, Matthew, Connor, and Mikaela, whom I love more than life itself. They have each brought me innumerable joys and, in many ways, have shown me what's truly important in life. I'd also like to thank my family, especially my mom and dad, who have always been there for me. Additionally, I would like to thank my friends and training partners—Billy, Steve, Tony D, Brian, Mallman, Barbekka, Chris, Jamie, Wayne, Caroline, Lee, Paul, Jeff, Deb, and many others. From the rocks and roots of West Virginia, to the jungles of Borneo, you guys have been with me through thick and thin. I'd also like to recognize my former employer, Booz Allen Hamilton, for sponsoring my Eco-Challenge teams. I couldn't have worked for a better company, nor had a better boss and co-workers. Thank you Larry, Marcia, Holly, Marilyn, Christine, and Sarah—you're the best! Finally, I would like to thank my teammates in this endeavor—Garth, Neal, and Nic. Co-editing this book has fulfilled a dream of mine and there's no way I could have done it without you.

Neal: I need to once again thank Garth and Breakaway Books for allowing me to do what I love, and for continuing to put out some of the best sports-related books in print. To Nic and Maureen: Thanks for coming to my aid and helping me put together this great collection. To Suzanne, my wife: You read and edited these stories when there were certainly other things you would rather have been doing. You know this will not be my last writing project, and thanks for putting up with me anyway. To Evan: May stories like these someday show you that there is nothing you cannot accomplish. Learn from what these athletes have done. Remember to enjoy the journey on the way to the finish line. Then cross the finish line and keep on running.

Nic: I wish to thank my mom, Susan, for her continuous support of whatever I choose to do; my father, David, for always encouraging me to never close any doors and make good choices; my grandmother Jane (Mimi) for her spirit and support; my sister Kate for proving that life isn't always perfect but you can still make it through; my childhood ski instructor John Spencer, who continues to teach me more about life than skiing; all my friends who read my tales of adventure and pretend they like them. I can't say thanks enough to my employer, Tamarack Resort, for having the vision not only to support adventure racing but also to allow me so much time away from my work. And special thanks to my girlfriend, Jen Garretson, for showing me how to try new and exciting things and, most importantly, to believe in myself.

Foreword
A Lifetime of Adventure

Brian Metzler
Editor, *Adventure Sports*

Although I had heard of adventure racing before, my first exposure to the sport came in the spring of 1998 when I was invited to attend the Presidio Adventure Racing Academy near San Francisco. I received an enormously long gear list and was told to be ready for a wide range of weather. The night before the trip, I packed my bag and wondered what the heck I was getting into.

It didn't take long to find out. Upon arriving at the academy, I talked with adventure racing luminaries John Howard, Ian Adamson, Robyn Benincasa, and Robert Nagle. They spoke about crazy, weeklong races in places like New Zealand, Madagascar, and Malaysia. Then for the next three days, under the direction of Navy SEAL/adventure racer Duncan Smith, the thirty or so attendees, myself included, were put through a skills camp and simulated adventure race.

Although I had participated in a wide variety of sports like trail running, mountain bike racing, triathlon, skiing, and mountaineering, the three-day camp was one of the most thrilling experiences of my life. And while biking, hiking, paddling and navigating our way in and around the Marin Headlands was a lot of fun, that wasn't the half of it. It was what adventure racing represented that intrigued me the most—namely the notion of pushing my physical and mental limits within a unique team dynamic.

While sitting around a campfire on the last night of the camp, we were entertained with numerous exciting stories from these legends of the sport. Tales about surviving scalding desert heat in Mexico, trading villagers duct tape, rain jackets, and socks for a warm meal in Ecuador, paddling native wooden boats in Malaysia, and trying to avoid grizzly bears in British Columbia. I felt like I was listening to eighteenth-century explorers as they made their way across North America for the first time, all the while realizing I was in the company of world-class athletes highly proficient in a wide range of outdoor sports like whitewater paddling, navigation, mountain biking and rappelling. I also came to realize that the sport of adventure racing was much more than an athletic event—more a quest for adventure among people with rich personalities and great ambition.

Soon after leaving the camp, I participated in my first adventure race. It was a short, three-hour race, but it was really cool—unlike anything I had ever done. It combined some of my favorite sports—sports that I was good at. However, it also forced me to rely on my teammates when it came to sports that I was not so good at, or situations in which I was uncomfortable or had not yet experienced.

From that experience, I learned that adventure racing is a unique sport that requires numerous challenges to be overcome—some physical, some mental, and others still very spiritual. I was also inspired by the idea that the sport comes to life through the development of team chemistry among the unique people who are attracted to the sport. Not only is adventure racing greater than the sum of its sporting disciplines, an adventure racing team is greater than the sum of its athletes because the dynamics of the sport drive people to accomplish more than they think they can—both on the racecourse and in real life. I drew upon this inspiration when I was charged with launching *Trail Runner* magazine in 1999 and *Adventure Sports* magazine in 2003.

With this wonderful book, Neal Jamison, Maureen Moslow-Benway, and Nic Stover have created a medium for the voices of these great athletes to be heard—many for the very first time. They have collected a wide range of essays, allowing people to share stories about themselves and their experiences. For centuries, books have passed along the greatest adventure stories for many to learn from and enjoy. In much the same way, these editors are passing along the fascinating stories of the everyday adventurers of our generation. It's a must-read book for anyone who loves adventure, has ever competed in an adventure race, or is itching to try it for the first time. As you read through this book, you will sympathize and suffer, daydream and wonder. And you will yearn to have similar experiences of your own.

Introduction

Adventure racing is one of the most exciting and fastest-growing sports in the world. There are literally hundreds of races around the globe, with new races cropping up just about every weekend. These races incorporate a number of different athletic disciplines, but most commonly, they include trail running or hiking, mountain biking, paddling, and navigating with a map and compass. Additionally, the vast majority of adventure races require competitors to compete in teams, usually composed of three to five racers. To make things even more interesting, most race directors require that each team have at least one member of each. Adventure races can be divided into three different categories, depending on their length. Sprint races are the most popular and the fastest-growing segment of the sport. These races usually last three to eight hours, and for the most part speed is more important than skills. Mid-length races usually last anywhere from twenty-four to sixty hours, and although speed is still important, technical skills and team dynamics start playing an increasingly important role. Finally, expedition races are multiday, nonstop events that run anywhere from four to twelve days and usually incorporate a wide range of athletic disciplines. Needless to say, these races require strong technical skills, physical endurance, mental fortitude, and good team dynamics in order for participants to be successful. There are, however, other factors that can come into play. Adventure racing is a sport full of rules—and breaking the rules often results in time penalties. Some of the rules of the sport include mandatory gear—pieces of equipment that (often for safety reasons) must be carried, forbidden areas of the course (such as roads that may not be traveled or private property that may not be traversed), well-hidden checkpoints that must be located and reached by a certain time, dark zones (sections of the course that may not be navigated at night), and so on. Teams who break one or two of these rules or get stopped by a dark zone can find themselves hours, or even days behind the leaders.

Considering all that is involved, it is no surprise that adventure racing lends itself to great stories. After all, it is a sport that combines nonstop, action-packed activities such as mountain biking, mountain climbing, paddling, orienteering, and trekking in some of the world's most beautiful places. In addition, since adventure racing is a team sport, there is an incredibly interesting human interaction not seen in other endurance sports. This human dynamic is greatly intensified due to competition, stress, physical exhaustion, hunger, and, of course, competing egos. Consequently, in many of these tales, there is an inevitable amount of conflict, fatigue, hallucinations, pain, and despair. But just as importantly, there is an equal, if not greater, amount of courage, selflessness, determination, joy and even humor.

Writing this book was almost an adventure race in itself, with a small share of agony and thrill along the way. Despite the geographic distance that separated us, we came together as a team of adventure loving co-editors to compile some of adventure racing's most compelling tales. At the beginning of the project, we came up with a "dream list" of contributors. Naturally, these included some of the biggest names in the sport—Ian Adamson, Robyn Benincasa, and Robert Nagle, just to name a few. However, we also wanted to include lesser-known racers who had equally interesting, if not more compelling tales to share.

As the contributors' stories materialized, we realized that we were on to something great! For example, we could not help but feel David Kelly's raw fear as we read of his encounter with grizzlies in the Alaskan brush. We felt ourselves tense up as solo racer Caroline Brosius paddled alone among dozens of alligators in a remote Florida swamp in the dark hours of the night. We could almost feel what it must have been like for Terri Schneider to be covered in leeches and bat guano in the jungles of Borneo, and we could not help but shiver as we read Chris Rumohr's account of being stranded on a West Virginian mountaintop during a raging electrical storm. We chuckled at Cathy Tibbetts's tongue-in-cheek tale of what it is like to be a middle-aged woman on a team full of testosterone-crazed young males, and we were inspired as we read what it was like for Rob Harsh to successfully guide a blind mountaineer through one of the world's toughest races.

These are just a few examples of the stories we hope will entertain, fascinate, and perhaps even inspire you. As you journey with these contributors through jungles and rivers and over mountains and seas, you will notice that they are also taking you on a journey inside themselves. It is there, inside the heart of the competitor, that you will explore the bonds of blood, sweat, and tears that have been formed on racecourses all over the world. You will be awed by what you read, and will find yourself questioning, *What would I do in that situation? Could I handle it any better or would I have folded up and headed home long ago?* Ultimately you will discover that these spectacular athletes are not much different from you. They are men and women with strengths and weaknesses, hopes and dreams. They are athletes who are not afraid to constantly test themselves and push beyond those mental and physical barriers that exist, more often than not, only in the mind.

When we first started out, our reasons for participating in this endeavor varied. For Neal, it was the logical next step after finishing a similar book about his true passion, ultrarunning. Neal had the knowledge and talent to get the book published; all he needed was a little help. Maureen stepped in, providing veteran experience and a wide variety of contacts she had met in her years of adventure racing. In 1994 Maureen watched the very first Eco-Challenge and immediately knew that she had found her calling. Expedition racing seemed to be the pinnacle of everything she loved—the outdoors, physical challenges, teamwork, travel and adventure. Sprint races led to multiday events, which ultimately culminated in her successful completion of the 2000 and 2001 Eco-Challenges in Borneo and New Zealand. Similarly, Nic Stover joined the co-editor team, bringing some fresh ideas and a new list of contributors. In 2002 Nic became inspired to party less and train more while lying hungover on the couch watching the Eco-Challenge. Nic decided then and there that he was going to one day complete that race. All he needed to do was get into shape, learn the necessary skills, buy the gear and find some compatible teammates. Two years later, with a number of successful sprint and multiday races under his belt and racing on a sponsored team, Nic is well on his way to accomplishing that goal.

Throughout the process of producing this book, all three of us have gained an even greater appreciation for the sport of adventure racing and for the athletes themselves. Ultimately, our hope is that as you read this book, you will not only gain a better understanding of what it takes to be an adventure racer, but you will realize that you can be an adventure racer too. We hope you take the experiences and lessons learned herein, and apply them to your life. In short, we hope you enjoy reading these stories as much as we enjoyed assembling them.

Neal Jamison, Maureen Moslow-Benway, Nic Stover

The Original Adventure Race:
Alaska's Mountain and Wilderness Classic

Photo by Tony Di Zinno

NAME: ROMAN DIAL
AGE: 44
RESIDENCE: ANCHORAGE, AK
YEARS ADVENTURE RACING: 22

I was a young alpine punk, arrogant and stupid. I left my partners and stormed out of the Alaska Range with little more than my skis, stove, and bivy sack—no map, no compass, no tent and no partner. It was late March, winter still, and the road was fifty-five miles away across the north slope of the Alaska Range.

The time alone humbled me as I hurried past nervous caribou and a pack of wolves at the base of Mount Hayes. The rumpled landscape offered straightforward navigation: Keep the tall mountains—thirteen-thousand-foot Hayes and Moffit and eleven-thousand-foot McGinnis—to my right and the vast interior flats of central Alaska to my left. No map needed for that.

After my second night, huddled in the lee of a boulder on the open tundra, I woke to a blizzard. I moved tentatively across complex topography through a confusing maze of drainages leading to a high bench. My arrogance had leaked away, my stupidity apparent. Luckily, I stumbled upon a cabin poking through willows and found a map inside. The road was just five miles away. I marched there quickly, crossing the mighty Delta River on a thin ice bridge.

At the road I clocked myself—fifty-five miles in so many hours. It was my second trip leaving a tall mountain after a climb of mixed ice and rock up an unclimbed route. It was the second time I'd left a camp with little food and big distances. The first time had been skiing roped to a partner across a series of glaciers. It was on a route parallel to this one, but deeper in the glacial gut of the range. This time I had been alone on the tundra, big country tugging at my gaiters, sometimes walking and other times skiing.

I wondered, "Which way is faster? Only one way to tell," I answered myself. "A race." It would be a race on a scale likely never seen before— 150 miles across raw Alaskan mountains, glaciers, and rivers. Point-to-point. Carry all you need, do whatever it takes. It would be a free-form adventure race across pure wilderness.

That was 1981. I was twenty years old.

The following October on my twenty-first birthday, I met George Ripley on the University of Alaska campus. A wilderness and climbing guide from the coastal town of Homer, he was attending a mountain and wilderness guides meeting. George had left photocopies of something he called "The Alaska Mountain and Wilderness Classic: An Overland Footrace from Hope to Homer." Rushing through the words I found his idea of a race—150 miles across the Kenai Peninsula south of Anchorage, no roads, no vehicles. Start and finish with all that you need, carry all your gear and food.

The route covered about fifty miles of trail, then a wilderness of mountains, brush, bogs, and boulders. It was a summer race, but it skirted the huge Harding Icefield, forty miles long and twenty miles wide.

"I have an idea for a race," I told George Ripley during a break in the meeting.

"Yeah, what's that?" Barely listening, his attention drifting to a blonde wearing Vibram boots and a wool sweater.

"It's a wilderness ski race across the Alaska Range from highway to highway, 150 miles, any way you want, but it has to be off-road."

"Sure, kid. I'll tell you what. You come do my race and then we'll do yours," and with that Ripley moved off in pursuit of Vibram and wool.

August 1982 rolled around and the "second annual" Wilderness Classic was approaching. I'd been training with my girlfriend (later wife), Peggy, as my pacer. Shouldering a pack I chased after her up and down hills, through mud and brush for hours. Afterward we downed ice cream by the pint. To prepare my gut I ate race food two weeks before the event. I also wondered about my competition. Reading Ripley's race materials, I discovered that he and the acclaimed mountaineer Vern Tejas, who would later become the first person to climb Mount McKinley solo in winter and also climb all seven of the continental summits (Everest, McKinley, etc.) three times, attempted the inaugural race. However, neither George nor

Vern finished the "first annual" Wilderness Classic. In fact, nobody had, so the "second annual" would be the beginning.

I hitchhiked to the race start in the sleepy town of Hope, Alaska carrying a small pack simplified and stripped down for the race. My "sponsors" at Apocalypse Designs in Fairbanks had modified my bivy sack by sewing a piece of raw insulation into its inside top. I had three pounds of butter and forty bars—this was pre-Clif, GU, and PowerBars—so they were Bear Valley Pemmican, Carnation Breakfast, and a variety of Hershey and Cadbury chocolate. I also had jerky and Pilot Biscuits. As per race rules, my pack held everything needed for the 150-mile distance. I also had a pair of cross-country racing skis, poles, and glacier "sandals"—the soles of cross-country racing ski shoes I'd strap to my feet for skiing. My planned route would go over the Harding Icefield in hopes of avoiding the bears, bad brush, and big rivers other racers following the lowland route would have to negotiate.

When race day dawned, ten of us lined up with our toes in tidewater. Wilderness Classic rules stated we could take any route we wanted so long as we didn't use roads, motor vehicles, or pack animals. I was the only one planning a high glacier route. Another adventurer, the legendary fifty-five-year-old Dick Griffith, carried a small inflatable raft in his pack, but none of us at the start knew this. Others took big packs and partners with bewildered looks in their eyes. Someone shot a popgun and we were off.

I had never covered more than 120 miles in a single trip. I was intimidated. And after the first forty-five miles in thirteen hours I was crippled. I wanted to drop out, as I was sure everyone else had. But I was wrong. Twenty-seven year old Dave Manzer caught me slogging painfully along the trail. Breaking free of a self-pitying limp, I hurried to keep up, dropping my pain like a bad habit as we talked about our lives.

He was strong and smart and best of all, a gifted storyteller. We agreed to travel together until our routes diverged some thirty miles later. Together we entered the "hills of confusion," a series of knobs covered in alder brush and mountain hemlock rising above quaking bogs of sedges and sundews. I tried to link together game trails and marshes until Manzer would pull out his compass and point out we were drifting off course. This went on for about five hours, when somewhat abruptly we busted free of the brush and strode easily across a crusty gravel bar. It was midafternoon and only a few miles up valley we could see the mile-wide

Skilak Glacier, dropping off the Harding Icefield and snaking down in broken drops for nine miles before calving its bergs into a brown lake. The Skilak River drained the lake and hurried by the crumbling banks of the gravel bar.

The river was titanium gray with glacial silt. A hand in its icy flow disappeared from view only inches beneath the surface. We could hear the acoustic crack of big rocks bouncing along the unseen bottom. Two-foot waves rose up and curled over. The far side was a hundred feet away. We had no boat. The two "safety personnel" wore the only life jackets. They had no boat. We could not wade across the river since it was over ten feet deep. We had to swim wearing a backpack and rain gear, with no wet or dry suit and no PFD. I had never swum across a river like this before.

A cold wind coursed down the valley, chilling us with its icy message from the Harding. We built a driftwood fire and waited as three more racers showed up. Ripley was one of them. He told us how blisters from the first fifty miles had stripped half the field only one-third of the way into the race. Then Richard Callaghan, a fireman from Homer, and Dick Griffith arrived. Eyeing the swift water, we all hid behind wilderness wisdom: "Let's wait until morning, when the flow will be lessened due to less melt from the glacier." The truth was we needed to psych ourselves up.

Dick, with more than twenty years on us young ones, pulled a red hat with purple Viking horns out of his pack, pulled it over his white hair, and ridiculed us for letting him catch us. Then he proceeded to pull out his secret weapon: a five-pound vinyl raft and two tiny oars. We were shocked. Dick wasn't going to swim across the river; he was going to row across it! "And not only that," Manzer whispered, "he's likely to float the last twenty miles of the Fox River as well." That bear- and brush-infested valley would later take us fifteen hours of bushwhacking. Dick would float it in five. This man had pluck and wisdom born of years of travel through the wilderness.

Our jaws slack, Dick dangled the raft before us admonishing us "kids" that "Old age and treachery beat youth and skill any day!"

Dick rowed his little "packraft" across the Skilak and waited as the four of us swam. Manzer nearly drowned when a rope tied to his waist got tangled around his legs. It would not be the last time water threatened to kill him in a Wilderness Classic.

Once across, I left the others and pushed onward for the Harding Icefield, wrestling my skis through thickets of alder then scrambling up rubble-strewn slabs that in years to come would be named "the cliffs of insanity." Later I learned that Manzer and Ripley pulled ahead of Griffith and Callaghan and that Callaghan would lose his glasses crossing another river and get charged by a sow grizzly with two cubs. He'd drop out at a cabin where a pilot in a floatplane was visiting two-thirds through the race. I too would drop out of the race many times, but, lacking a pilot's convenience, never would I be able to leave the race. I would be forced to finish.

I was alone and scared. Crossing the Harding would require skiing forty miles in a single day, or risk spending a night out with nothing more than a foam pad and an insulated bivy sack. While I had crossed many glaciers, never had I been on such a huge expanse of ice, and never alone. I looked hard at my ambitions as the ceiling of clouds dropped and spit icy rain. I turned back from the ice and decided to take the lower route, even though I didn't have a map for it. Consequently, I had to catch my "competition."

Not long after my turnaround, I spotted two racers picking their way along an alpine lake. I hurried over to find Ripley and Manzer. The three of us traveled together the next forty miles as a team, sharing time in the front, stories from the past, and food from our dwindling stocks. Often George led the way along game trails while Manzer charted our progress on his maps using compass triangulation. I'd never seen either skill practiced before and was impressed with their bushcraft.

At the most terrifying river crossing, a swim across the Killey River at the bottom of its three-thousand-foot deep canyon, hemmed in by alder-clad cliffs of rotten schist, I slipped on slimy rock at river's edge. Catching myself, my pinkie folded back on itself and became dislocated. I held it up to Manzer, his eyes wide at the finger's wild angle. "Pull it!"

He did, and the joint popped back to normal. I was glad it wasn't my shoulder or leg. There were no bubble-wrapped radios in our backpacks. GPS had yet to be invented. But we knew where we were. We were fifty miles from the nearest road. He offered his hand and pulled me to my feet. We swam the river, climbed through the bear tunneled brush on the far side, racing once again.

On George's thirty-fourth birthday, we stayed in a cabin and feasted on ptarmigan I'd stoned, bread, cream cheese and marmalade George had carried, and Hamburger Helper we swiped from the cabin. This was more than a race and more than a trip. Based on the way we received according to our needs and contributed according to our abilities, it seemed to me a good way to behave in general. It also seemed that what you carried in your pack was not near as important as what you carried in your head and in your heart. This event and the lessons learned would color my life for the next twenty years.

After three days of traveling together, George decided to split from us and take a route he thought might be brush-free and faster than the Fox River Valley that Manzer and I were headed for. Losing George made the wilderness seem bigger and less friendly—I was happy to still be with Dave.

I enjoyed traveling with Manzer. His style differed from mine. He was a self-proclaimed "bush hippie" who had lived for several years in log cabins in the Yukon Territory. He had made long trips there in winter using snowshoes, skis, frame packs, and sleds. "Work trips" he called these epic trail-breaking adventures that lasted for more than a month. In summer, he canoed whitewater rivers, working the rapids in the lonely wilderness of the midnight sun for weeks at a time. Because I was an alpinist, someone who moved fast, light, and boldly up the steep faces of the Alaska Range, I thought his methodical, cautious style was a bit exaggerated. He carried extra food and a shelter. He built nightly fires by dripping candle wax on dry tinder. He had a stuff sack full of miscellaneous items, like clevis pins, needles, rope, and even pliers. My feeling was that the probability of gear going bad was so small during a race, why bring that along? But when his rain pants ripped and I watched him sew, I finally understood the meaning of "a stitch in time saves nine."

He traveled heavy, with a wooden spoon and a cook pot. He'd cook himself a hot meal over a small campfire before crawling into his orange plastic tube tent at night. Carrying nothing but bars and butter, I salivated over his hot food. I offered to thicken his glop with butter. Together we shared and were more than the sum of our parts.

During the day, even though Dave's pack was noticeably heavier than mine, he still moved quickly, swinging his big feet in long strides across the tundra. As I limped along behind, Dave would wait, never showing impatience, and always being helpful and heartfelt. Rather than rub my nose in my weakness, he showed compassion.

Moving first along bear trails in the Fox River Valley, Dave followed close behind me with his small, pen-sized flare guns loaded for bear. It was nerve racking. We wanted neither to leave the trails nor to walk on them. We wished for a boat like Dick's. Finally, after a day and a half, we broke free of the brush and entered the mudflats of upper Kachemak Bay. We had reached the thirty-mile beach that led to the finish line. Finding no other footprints in the sand, Manzer and I congratulated ourselves on winning a footrace without having to run a step—thank God. We agreed we would cross the finish line together, winning as a team.

My face painted white in zinc oxide as war paint, I hustled to keep up with Manzer's speed-hike pace on the shores of Kachemak Bay. This was in the days before Vioxx or even ibuprofen. Pain was something to be managed, like food, something to be negotiated, like rivers and brush. Pain was something conversation could ease, something the thought of imminent victory could erase. I confessed to Dave that I had never won a race, and he to me likewise. It was then that Ripley ran up behind us, grabbing me by the shoulders and shaking me free of complacency.

"You boys better get a move on it! Dick Griffith is just a half hour behind!" Chafed and blistered, Ripley ran by us barefoot and naked from the waist down—and smiling.

I looked at David. "I guess we gotta run now!" I took off in pursuit of George, my skis—unused, but by race rules still needed, since I'd started with them—flapping on my pack.

After fifteen miles, George stopped to put on his boots, and I never looked back, winning the first adventure race ever in six days, ten hours, and thirty-four minutes. Dave Manzer came in a half hour later, George an hour after Dave, and Dick Griffith, the fifty-five-year-old adventurer, three hours later. He'd caught us young bucks less than half his age with his secret weapon—a five-pound inflatable packraft with paddles.

There were no other finishers.

At the event banquet, one after another Manzer, Dick, and I got up and said how this was the most intense adventure of our lives, but never again, never again would we race.

We were wrong. Instead, I became addicted to the Wilderness Classic and the approach it instilled. That first race changed my view of wilderness. No longer was it a single trail, river, or glacier trip. It was a full panoply of landscapes linked by what I carried on my back and the experiences in my head. I even applied the racing style to normal trips and coached Peggy on how to tape her feet, travel light, and share gear with me. We once crossed the Gates of the Arctic National Park on a three-week, three-hundred-mile trip through the Brooks Range, carrying one sleeping bag and one packraft between us. Her pack weighed twenty-five pounds, mine thirty-five: we were essentially racing. Indeed Peggy was always part of the Wilderness Classic, supporting me at home, training with me, working the races we organized, and finishing two races—she still holds the record for fastest female time in the event's twenty-five-year history. Throughout the 1980s I did not work summers so I could better train for and later organize the Wilderness Classic. Later in the '90s and even now, when it looked like the Classic needed a new route, I stepped forward to offer one.

Each year I discovered more. Like every adventure racer, I found out early that weight kills speed. Indeed, like every mathematician (I have two degrees in math, a B.S. and M.S.), I first applied a linear equation to model weight vs. speed: Every pound on your back reduces your mileage by one mile per day. With more data, the true nonlinearity of the relationship revealed itself—miles traveled per day is a constant divided by pack weight, and the constant is something that differs for everyone. After the typical tunnel vision that weight alone matters, I realized that "handling time" is important, too, and that the lightest gear often takes the longest time to make work properly. I made up rules for myself: *Never stop for just one thing*; *each piece of gear needs to serve more than one purpose*; *memorize the map and always keep it close at hand*. As a biologist and natural historian (I also have two degrees in biology, a B.S. and Ph.D.), I studied the habits of big game to best find their trails. I learned to paddle white water in a packraft, to shuffle-run, to pound down water rather than carry it. I found that eating substitutes for sleep, but that only sleep can heal my injuries and wash away the downturns in my mood swings. I discovered that sharing food and watching my partner's health is more important than hoarding my food or proving what a stud I am. All this I experienced in the early 1980s, before there was an Eco-Challenge, a Raid Gauloises, or any other adventure race for that matter. And I gave up relationships with my family. I gave up money and academic advancement. I gave up everything but racing, preparing for races, and thinking about races. But the adventure, the stimulation, and the winning were worth it. Even now, my oldest friends are either dead or former climbers and racing partners.

My family and I share holiday meals with Griffith, Manzer and I still hunt together annually, and Ripley calls me long distance.

And so twenty-two years, fourteen Wilderness Classics, three Idita-sports, five Eco-Challenges, a Raid Gauloises, a World Championship AR, and an X-Games later, I raced with my seventeen-year-old son, young Roman, in the 2004 Classic. Unlike any of the other racers we used mountain bikes to save our feet on the first sixty miles. We rode for fifty miles on mining roads and ATV trails, then hiked and hellbiked to the Talkeetna River, where we loaded our bikes on our four-pound packrafts and paddled twenty miles. Then we stripped cranks, derailleurs, and chains to hellbike through a deep canyon to reach a second thirty-five-mile float to the finish. Dick Griffith, who at seventy-seven years old has finished more Classics than anyone, was there, too. We finished sixth, covering the 160 miles in three days, four hours, and fifteen minutes. Young Roman wants to return next year, without the bikes.

To me, the Alaska Mountain Wilderness Classic represents the essence of adventure, where it takes brains, guts, and luck not only to win, but simply to finish. Nearly everyone in Alaska has heard of the race, despite having never been televised (and hopefully it never will). For a quarter century, this race has shown hundreds of people their true nature. They've learned that they are made of much stronger stuff than they knew. It's been as much a part of my life as anything else I've ever done, sending me down a life path, propelling me to race well in the Eco-Challenge and other races, providing me with skills and techniques I've used to do trips around Alaska and the world with family, friends, and teammates. It has provided me with long-lasting friendships and insights into myself and the land and people. First me, then Peggy—and now my son—have uncovered our inner strength and determination from the Classic. It is this self-discovery that has changed me forever, indeed defined who I am. Perhaps my son will find himself there as well.

Eco-Challenge Utah 1995
Adventure Racing Comes to America

Photo by Tony Di Zinno

NAME: IAN ADAMSON
AGE: 40
RESIDENCE: BOULDER, CO
YEARS ADVENTURE RACING: 20

One of the seminal events in adventure racing history was the 1995 Eco-Challenge in southeast Utah. This was Mark Burnett's first foray into the realm of event production and he produced the race under license from Raid Gauloises, essentially replicating the Raid in an English language incarnation in the United States. This Eco-Challenge was the first time such an event was held on U.S. soil, so for most American athletes this was a completely new experience.

Our team captain Robert Nagel and I met through some internet newsgroups in the early 1990s, including the Dead Runner's Society, ultrarunning and triathlon lists. Our team name *Eco-Internet* was a hybrid of the *Eco-Challenge* and our primary mode of communication, the internet. One of the main challenges we faced was our geographic separation since we were scattered between Boston and New Zealand. Fortunately our internet savvy saved us a great deal of time and effort as we were able to coordinate logistics and share training schedules via e-mail, something that was quite rare in 1995. Since much of our team training was done via the net, we referred to ourselves as a team with very strong fingers.

The original team consisted of Robert Nagle, Kathleen Judice, Rod Hislop, Andrew Hislop, John Howard, and myself. Jo Risk and Angie Guistina were our support crew. As with the majority of teams, we were plagued with injury. Rod came to Utah all the way from Australia but was not able to start due to severe patella chondromalacia, so we substituted Kiwi adventure racing legend John Howard (winner of the first Raid in 1989) at the last minute.

Observing competitors during race registration and check-in was a novel and intimidating experience, with dozens of buffed athletes strutting around in matching uniforms oozing confidence and draped in shiny new, high-tech gear. In contrast, our team was a ragtag bunch with a pile of well-used and grubby equipment and no discernible uniform. It would quickly become apparent, however, that most of the teams were completely inexperienced despite their bravado and bold predictions for the outcome of the race.

Day 1

The early morning start was spectacular, with 250 people and 150 horses coursing through the mist on the high desert savanna and funneling quickly onto a dirt road. The first leg was twenty-five miles of "ride and tie" (three horses shared among a team of five athletes) through the shimmering desert. The hot conditions spread the teams out by between four and eight hours by the first transition point. We started conservatively with a race strategy gleaned from ultrarunning: Start slowly and taper off. Unfortunately one of our horses got confused about who was supposed to ride whom, and in the process landed a hefty blow to my groin, which left a neat horseshoe imprint on my inner thigh and blood in my urine.

Undaunted by our little sojourn in the desert, we cruised in to the first transition point in seventh place. After a fast changeover to our heavy packs, which contained wetsuits, food, water, and clothing for the next three days, we followed the San Rafael River into the Black Box Canyons. We were about an hour down on the leaders, but quickly gained the lead by that afternoon. The terrain for this twenty-mile section included frequent river crossings interspersed with boulder-hopping, sandy washes, and thin scrub trails. The trail became narrow and dark once we entered the canyons, and on several occasions we were forced to swim through very cold pools and climb over automobile-sized boulders.

A compulsory dark zone caught us before we could get through the lower canyon, so we suffered through an extremely cold and uncomfortable six-hour "sleep." We used garbage bags and space blankets from our emergency equipment and spooned together for shared warmth. This is definitely in the spirit of team, since you have to roll over simultaneously, or lose valuable heat. Kathleen was particularly susceptible to the cold, so we sandwiched her two guys to a side. I wondered at the time what her husband would think of her sleeping in such a way with four strange men.

Day 2

At 4:00 A.M. we resumed racing with the several other teams who had arrived during the night: Southern Traverse, Swiss Army Brands, Hewlett Packard, Gold's Gym, and Nike-ACG. The next canyon leg through the lower Black Box started with thirty headlamps bobbing though the early dark hours across the river and around the adjoining four-wheel-drive road. We led the charge, followed closely by Southern Traverse. Before long we were ahead of the other four teams, who apparently had left the trail and disappeared across the river. As the sun was rising, we reached checkpoint (CP) 5 in first place, closely followed by Southern Traverse and Swiss Army. Another four hours of river wading, boulder-hopping and pushing through extremely dense floodplain scrub led us to CP6, where teams were again closely bunched. This was the start of a very long and difficult running and hiking section of over ninety-five miles though the San Rafael Desert. Most teams hiked with thirty-pound packs stuffed full of food and equipment required for the next section. John, however, had skillfully taken his knife to all of our gear before the race, and our packs were considerably lighter.

One of the most difficult aspects of this race was the 1:100,000-scale maps, which made the land navigation challenging. We managed to lose an hour by trying to take a direct compass course rather than follow a circuitous four-wheel-drive road. This put us on top of a butte with hundred-foot cliffs down to the CP and we had no option but to retrace our steps and scramble down some steep rocky slopes to rejoin the trail.

The course from CP6 ascended two thousand feet to the San Rafael Swell through Black Dragon Wash, and was a desert in every sense of the word. There was no water available for another thirty miles, and the temperatures soared from below freezing at night to over a hundred degrees during the day. Our luck was beginning to run out with Andrew suffering from a crippling knee injury and Kathleen from exhaustion and dangerous hypothermia. Other teams were suffering as well, many with ugly foot blisters and abrasions, a condition the race doctors were calling "hamburger feet."

Day 3

By dawn on Day 3, the top six teams were well into the desert and everyone had run out of water. There was a permanent water source marked on our maps at "Well Spring" about five miles short of CP8, so we made a huge effort to find it en route. Southern Traverse passed through early that morning, followed by Swiss Army and Nike-ACG. We shared water with Hewlett-Packard at the well, despite the rotting carcass of an unfortunate animal that had slipped and drowned in the tempting water. Although we used liberal quantities of iodine purification tablets, the tainted water caused us considerable gastric distress.

Injury, exhaustion, and lack of food and good water forced us to make a safety call at CP8, with Andrew and Kathleen withdrawing. It was extremely difficult for everyone, although for Andrew it was a smart choice since he was racing again in the 1995 X-Games adventure race in Maine (his team went on to win). It was a relief to get Kathleen some medical help and see the end to her suffering and of our hard work keeping her on the move. This left John, Robert, and myself to make a dash through to CP11, the next team assistance (TA) point. We were now eleven hours down on Southern Traverse, but by running the flats and down hills and with help from a navigational error made by Southern Traverse, we were back into the lead.

Day 4

By 3:00 A.M. we were within four miles of CP11/TA2 with the other top teams spread out in the desert behind us. Navigation was proving to be difficult, with no moon or stars, and endless stretches of dunes and knee-high desert scrub to negotiate. At this stage we took a tactical break so we could rest up and wait for dawn. Nike-ACG didn't rest, and woke us up at 5:00 A.M. as they stumbled over our prone bodies. They had been following in our footsteps, and in turn had been chased by Hewlett Packard who had followed their headlamps bobbing and weaving through the desert obstacles. Their arrival reenergized us, and we quickly got up and chased them down the trail. By the next transition point, we were an hour up on the other two teams, both of whom had made slow progress in their sleep-deprived mental fog.

Our trusty support crew of Angie and Jo were waiting for us, with diathermic lances (for popping blisters) and cold pizza (for popping in our starving mouths) at the ready. In an amazing frenzy of activity we were stripped and bundled up in warm sleeping bags. After several days of near-uninterrupted progression, our metabolisms rapidly plummeted, dragging our core body temperatures down with them. We had slept a sporadic two hours in the last four days, but with the sunshine and activity we were surprisingly awake and alert. Cameras and microphones crowded our hectic camp as we were fed and massaged. Our crew attended to our feet as we studied maps for the next section and got our climbing gear and mountain bikes organized. We carefully checked our equipment: flares, smoke bombs, first aid, climbing rope, jumars, etriers, daisy chains, carabiners, harnesses, food, water, clothing, maps, bike spares, inner tubes, and sundry other racing necessities. Thirty minutes after arriving, we were on our bikes and racing again.

Our pace was fierce with a fast rolling pace line for the first thirty miles on hard-packed dirt road; then we slowed as we hit a long sandy climb to the top of Horseshoe Canyon. After dropping off our bikes, a short one-mile trot to the canyon rim provided spectacular views down to the river on the valley floor. The ropes course was a stunning 450-foot overhanging rappel, then a 180-foot vertical and overhanging jumar ascent, a 100-foot Tyrolean traverse, another short ascent, followed by several more traverses and rappels to the valley floor. We knew from the race instructions and maps that this would be the make-or-break point in the race, since any team that got through the dark zone would have a significant advantage over teams forced to stay behind. With this in mind we put in a big effort to get through the ropes section, knowing we could relax once our feet touched solid ground. It took us three hours of solid climbing, but we made it through a dark zone cutoff giving us a twelve-hour lead over the other lead teams who were caught at various points along the ropes.

Knowing we were now unchallenged, we took an unhurried lunch break with the climbing director, Jay Smith, and made our way down the canyon toward the Green River. Horseshoe Canyon was a magical wilderness with tracks of mountain lion, bighorn sheep, deer and bear lacing the sandy river floodplain. The going was difficult since the canyon sides were sheer and the undergrowth extremely dense. After six miles, Horseshoe Canyon joined into Green River Canyon where we crossed the swift flow of the river with the help of an inflatable boat. Six more miles of boulder-hopping along the canyon walls and riverbanks found us at Mineral Bottom and TA3.

By this stage our feet were throbbing and painful from blisters and cuts caused by our damp and chafing footwear, so it was a relief knowing we would soon be starting on a water section wearing open sandals. Since

moving water was specified as a dark zone, we were able to relax and prepare for our first good night's sleep of the race. Our crew prepared for us
a magnificent candlelit dinner with fresh food, silverware, candelabra,
and fine Australian red wine. This was a surreal and fitting juxtaposition
to the physical hardships of racing. We dined to the strains of Vivaldi
echoing around the canyon walls and to the amused faces of intrigued
bystanders floating around the periphery of our happy camp. We eventually retired to the luxury of our sleeping pads and drifted off into a satiat-
ed and slightly inebriated slumber.

Day 5

Day 5 dawned cold and clear with mud underfoot from an overnight
drizzle. We executed our packing and gear-checking routine on a soggy
groundsheet, loaded the truck, and jogged the mile to the water. Our
guide, Michele, was waiting with the boat on the riverbank along with a
plethora of television cameras and event officials. It was quite confusing
with the blinding lights and babbling questions from the media. Our
ever-competent support crew, however, got us organized and loaded in
the raft despite the confusion. We donned our life jackets and with whis-
tles, car horns, and shouts of "good luck!" paddled off into the inky black
depths of the canyon.

Andrew and Kathleen had rejoined us for this section since it was a
"null zone" in the national park—no racing allowed. Any team taking
more than forty-eight hours, however, would have the additional time
added to their race time, so we paddled solidly for the fifty-six-mile stretch
to Spanish Bottom. Little did we know it at the time, but we were the only
team to paddle that section. All other teams were motored down to help
them make the time cutoffs. With Andrew and Kathleen back in the boat,
we felt like a complete team again, and enjoyed the ride down the river,
sharing stories and marveling at the spectacular canyon scenery.

A strong weather front moved in by midday, causing gusty winds and
black clouds to boil up over the horizon. Unfortunately it was mostly a
headwind, although we were able to use our tent fly as a sail for some
stretches due to the serpentine nature of the river. We reached Spanish
Bottom by midafternoon, the final checkpoint before some of the biggest
rapids in the lower forty-eight. The race staff was delighted to see us since
they had been waiting for several days with the expectation that at least a
dozen teams would have already passed through. Rather than push on to

the next section, we took advantage of our substantial lead, relaxed, ate, and fished in the river. Michele had a unique fishing method that consisted of throwing bread onto the water and then trying to whack the fish with a spade as they came to the surface to eat. Fortunately for the fish, our skills were substandard; they ended up well fed rather than well fried.

Day 6

We squandered the opportunity of pulling another day ahead of the rest of the field by sleeping in and making a leisurely 11:00 A.M. departure down the much-hyped Cataract Canyon. This is classed as "big water" with twenty-six rapids over thirteen miles, including three-story haystacks and sixteen raft-swallowing stoppers in high flows. We were in a heavily loaded six-man raft, so it was fortunate for us that the water was only moderate with the biggest waves cresting at ten feet. Our strong paddling crew and experienced guide helped us get through the waves unscathed, and we arrived on Lake Powell in time for a late lunch. Jay Smith and his crew were above the CP rigging thousands of feet of rope for the jumar ascent to the canyon rim, but fortunately for us they were not yet complete, so we got to spend another night relaxing, eating, and sleeping.

Day 7

The thousand-foot jumar ascent up Sheep Canyon was tough, but incredibly spectacular. We started up once the course reopened at 8:00 A.M. and made good progress, arriving at the top in just over an hour and a half. We checked in at CP14 and after a quick bite to eat took off on a slow run for CP15 and CP16, the top of the notorious Black Hole in Whites Canyon. This was another desert section with scant vegetation clinging to the red sand amid the towering sandstone buttes and mesas. We arrived at Fortknocker Canyon, the location of CP15, to find it vacant, so we decided to continue into Whites Canyon to see if we could locate CP 16. To our surprise an official vehicle came bouncing along the track toward us. An Eco-Challenge staff member greeted us with a cheery wave and the news that we had just run a leg that had been deleted from the course. Apparently the race officials did not think the other teams were capable of making it through under the ten-day cutoff, so they were being diverted directly to the final canoe leg. John was extremely disappointed that we weren't going to experience the Black Hole, but Robert and I convinced him it would be more pleasant to accept a ride back to the lake and go for a little paddle instead.

After several hours at TA4 waiting for the race organizers to let us continue, we packed our bags and glided off in the late afternoon sun toward Bullfrog Marina and the finish, fifty miles farther down Lake Powell. We arrived at CP18 to find it unmanned, so we pushed on toward CP19. The storms that had been following us down the Colorado River finally caught us just as night fell, and we spent the next several hours fighting through headwinds and fatigue. Exhaustion eventually won out, and we found a small rock ledge under which to take shelter and rest a couple of hours.

We awoke before dawn to the crash of thunder and brilliant flashes of lightning that bounced off the surrounding cliffs. Rather than sit in the rain, we clawed our way along the cliffs to try and find some shelter from the elements. At times we could barely see the bow of the boat as we crashed through waves and vicious squalls. At one stage we pulled along the base of a cliff and clung like climbers to the sheer wall as fifty-knot winds lashed us with spray and bounced us against the cliffs with each passing wave. We finally pulled out of the water when our hair started standing on end due to the static electricity from too-close-for-comfort lightning bolts.

After jumping ashore, we hid under our upturned boat (although in retrospect this really offered no protection at all from the lightning) and struggled to keep our gear from blowing away in the ferocious wind. We later learned that the wind had turned over a seventy-five-foot houseboat at Bullfrog Marina, and uprooted campers' tents, rolling them across the desert like tumbleweed. The whole episode was thrilling and more than a little frightening, but by dawn it had blown itself out and we continued toward the finish at Lake Powell. We finally reached the finish after seven days, one hour and thirty minutes to the finish-line cheers of Jo and Angie and race director Mark Burnett. A day later Hewlett-Packard was the first complete team home, with Nike-ACG second and Southern Traverse, Swiss Army, and Gold's Gym tying for third.

We didn't know it at the time, but Eco-Challenge Utah was the start of a global change in the landscape of adventure sports. It was also the birth of reality television. Mark Burnett got his start in this event and used it as a springboard to thrust adventure racing and later *Survivor* into the consciousness of the American and international public. The following year, Discovery Channel's Eco-Challenge British Columbia left an indelible mark, giving the sport a flavor and presence that has endured for ten years. We felt fortunate to have completed most of the original course, an opportunity not afforded other teams. Today we look back at the inaugural Eco-Challenge with fond memories of the challenge and excitement of the emerging new sport. Few people at the time imagined that adventure sports would develop into a high-profile media spectacle with professional teams and substantial prize money, or that Mark Burnett would shape reality television into a new genre of mass entertainment and become one of the most influential figures in international media.

Welcome the Pain

NAME: DON MANN
AGE: 47
RESIDENCE: VIRGINIA BEACH, VA
YEARS ADVENTURE RACING:
  IT ALL STARTED IN 1974...

Photo by Harry Gerwein, courtesy of Don Mann

Before I became a Navy SEAL, I did a lot of bicycle racing and running. The first race I ever ran was the 1979 Boston Marathon. I finished in 3:44. I guess you could say I caught "the fever," because I ran thirty marathons and a few ultra-marathons within the next thirty-six months. There was no such thing as adventure racing back then. That was even before we had triathlons. Then triathlons came about with the 1978 Hawaii Ironman. Twelve people did that first Ironman, and nobody knew about it. Fifteen people did the Ironman in 1979, but it was still not very well known. We finally got wind of it on the East Coast where I was living at the time. I was really excited about this new sport. Here was a sport where we could bike, run, and swim all in the same event! There were three different things to train for: I got to go to the pool, got to run, go to ride bikes . . . talk about fun! So I flew out to Hawaii to race in the Ironman in 1980. When I got off the plane, I went to a local bike store to find out where the race was. They didn't even know what I was talking about! Nobody knew about it. Of course the Ironman didn't get popular until Julie Moss came defecating and vomiting across the finish line in 1982. And then, *boom!* The growth in the sport of triathlon was really something to witness. As a Navy SEAL, I was also involved in what you might call multisport adventure events, but they were a little bit more serious. Fun, but serious. But more about that later.

Then came adventure racing. First there was the Raid Gauloises. At that time, adventure racing was mainly just for extreme athletes. But then Mark Burnett came along with the Eco-Challenge. He pretty much took the front page off the Raid package, put an Eco-Challenge cover on it, promoted it ingeniously, and the rest is history. The Eco-Challenge did so much good for the sport, because it brought it right into everyone's living room.

My start in adventure racing (we didn't call it adventure racing back then) was as a Navy SEAL. Consider a typical SEAL mission: It all starts with an exhilarating skydive in the middle of the night with full gear. We have to be completely self-sufficient for a week. We're going somewhere we've never been before. We jump into the ocean, inflate a boat, take the boat up to shore. When we get to the shore, we deflate the boat and hide it, and sink our parachutes. Then we start hiking. We hike for three to five days, navigating our way up and over the mountains, through good and bad weather. It might be in any country of the world. Finally we locate our target, whatever that may be. Sometimes we free the good people. Other times we kill the bad people. Bottom line is we do whatever we came there to do. Then we have to run and prepare for the extraction. Sometimes the extraction is a long dive. Sometimes it's a long swim. But it is always difficult. The reason SEAL training is so arduous (and so adventurous) is that SEALs are the only service that come from the Sea, Air, or Land. In the sea we swim, dive, pilot rubber boats, cigarette boats, and big patrol boats. In the air we jump, parachuting low altitude from helicopters, or jumping from thirty thousand feet without oxygen. On land we run over all types of terrain. We navigate, rappel, climb, then run some more. We train in the desert in temperatures of up to 140 degrees. And we train in the subarctic. We train in the jungle, desert and urban areas. Everywhere you might have an adventure race, a SEAL has been there, done that.

SEAL missions also involve teamwork. On a SEAL mission, you're out there with six to fourteen people on a team. It's a small group, and everybody has a very specific job to do. Everybody has a responsibility. At the same time, however, everyone has to be an expert at many different disciplines, or the mission might fail. So we train hard, and we constantly test people. Trainees go through close to a year of screening during SEAL training, and if they make it, then they're on the team. This is very similar to adventure racing. In adventure racing you try out your teammates, you practice with them, and you train with them. You test your teamwork at weekend events and short races. You really have to try them out before you are ready to spend ten days racing with them. SEALs have a saying:

The more sweat and tears put into training, the less blood shed in war. That works for SEAL training, but it also works for adventure racing. The more sweat and tears you put into training, the less blood shed at race time. You have to make sure that your team works well together and is able to carry out a mission. There's no *I* in *team,* as we always say.

As a training officer at SEAL Team 2, I loved training people. I loved pushing people hard. I had a couple of nicknames on the SEAL team. I was a warrant officer so one of my nicknames was Warrant Officer Man-slaughter. The other one was "Don Manniac." In SEAL training, you have to push people hard to find out if they have what it takes to succeed. You don't want somebody quitting on you out there when someone's life might be on the line. As I rose through the military ranks, I found myself sitting more and more behind a desk. It was a lot of fun training the guys and working with them, but I didn't go through SEAL training just to sit behind a desk. So when I heard about adventure racing, it was just what I needed to fill my need for adrenaline.

This guy called me up one day and said, "Hey, there's this new sport. We're getting an American team together to enter this race called the Raid Gauloises, and we've been looking for a team captain." And he asked if I'd consider it. He explained the race and the training to me, and it sounded like a blast. I said, "You know, it sounds really exciting. I can't imagine anybody putting a race together like that, but I don't think I can get the time off from work." He said, "Well, I already talked to your commanding officer. He said you can have the time off, if you can make it fit your schedule." Needless to say I made it fit, and that is how I got into adventure racing.

This new team was being put together in Chicago. They were sponsored by NBA superstar Michael Jordan and a couple of other very prominent athletes. There were these two guys, excellent athletes, Mike Sawyers and Mark Davis. Their goal was to be the first two black Americans to finish the most difficult race in the world. These two guys had a lot of sponsorship money and they were training all over the country, learning to backpack, learning to hike, learning to navigate and paddle and all that. Now all they needed was a team captain to help pull things together, train them, and get them through the race. Well, they didn't call me Don Manniac for nothing. I was ready for this adventure.

I trained with Mike and Mark, and we selected the rest of our team out of trial and error. It was Julie Lynch, fellow SEAL Eric Liebermann, Mark,

Mike, and myself. And together we went to Patagonia to race under the name Team Odyssey. Our team number was 23: Michael Jordan's famous number.

We went to Patagonia that year for one reason and one reason only: to win. It was a mistake that many people made when they raced their first adventure race back then. Fortunately, it is not like that anymore. People now get into racing for more than just the desire to win. A lot of people now get into it for the experience. Our goal, however, was winning, and it was a goal we would come far from reaching. We gave it a good shot, but we had some accidents along the way.

The race started out with a long paddle, and Mark and Mike were having such a hard time with it. Eric and I took turns pushing them and pulling them in a tandem so they did not have to paddle. We finally got through that first section, then came the first accident. We were on top of a twelve-thousand-foot mountain when Mark accidentally pulled a rock down, which created a small avalanche of rocks. A large rock came down and landed on Mike's hand. The impact severed the majority of Mike's hand. I was able to render first aid to Mike and Eric radioed for a medevac. We set off our beacon. The beacon signal went from Argentina all the way to Paris, France. Paris radioed back to Argentina, who got the helicopter to this one little section of that mountain. We got Mike medevaced out just before a big storm set in. Any later and he might not have made it out.

Mark felt terrible about the accident. Mike was his cousin, and he was so upset and depressed that he was in no shape to continue the race. It was very pathetic. I saw Gerard Fusil and tried to explain our predicament. I said, "Gerard, I can't let Mark continue on this race, because he's not thinking right." We had a long way to go, he was slowing us down, we were not going to finish if he stayed with us. He wanted out, and we wanted to let him out. He was mentally handicapped at that time, after seeing what had happened to Mike. Gerard said, "Don, I'm sorry, you have to take him with you." I warned Gerard, "Then I'll see you again soon, because he'll be medevaced out too before long." I just knew that having Mark continue was asking for trouble. Three hours later, we had a glissade down this huge mountain. Eric went down first. He lay down on his backside and just flew down the icy slope. Once he got to the bottom, he looked like an ant. It was so far down. Julie went next. I was still at the top trying to talk Mark down the slope. I said, "Mark, you're going to have to do this. You're going to have to get down." I told him to make sure to watch out for the rocks on the right-hand side. Steer clear from them. I went next, and I couldn't stop, it was just ice, probably three hundred yards straight down. Then Mark stood up, and just before he sat back to slide, he fell and began tumbling and falling down the mountain. Before he even got to the bottom I asked Eric to break out his radio and set off another beacon. We knew it was going to be bad. He reached the bottom, and he was all beat up and banged up. He also had some injuries to his head. Mark was out of the race at that point.

Mark and Mike were both phenomenal athletes in their own right, but they were not good adventure racers. It was a real struggle on my part, trying to get these two great sprinters, basketball players, and wrestlers through the toughest race in the world. They both had basic training in adventure racing and the disciplines involved, but basic training is just not enough.

Now that Mark was gone, the three of us had a lot of energy and adrenaline stored up. We took off running, and we just flew! We went so fast, we passed twenty-seven teams in the next two days and we were having a blast. We were really running. We ran for about three days. We had so much bundled-up energy and we just kept going and going and going. At one point, we were going through a night section. We were trekking along, carrying a big deflated rubber boat on our backs. We were walking through a really thick jungle section and there were lots of bamboo trees cut short about knee-high and they were really sharp. We were trying to keep from falling because if we fell, either we were going to get stabbed or we were going to puncture the boat. This section was made even more difficult due to the fact that we were down to just one headlamp. Eric was carrying the boat right behind Julie, and I was following him. I stopped to use the bathroom and when I tried to get going again, I noticed my foot was stuck. I was in quicksand. I was thinking, "This is kind of embarrassing; I can't get my foot out of here." I looked up just in time to see Julie's light disappearing into the darkness ahead. I wanted to catch up, but the more I pulled on my foot, the more stuck it got. I had trekking poles, but they were no help. I was actually sinking! My right leg was in up to the knee, then before I knew it, my left leg went in. By now Julie and Eric were completely out of sight, so I call to them, "Julie, Eric, come back here."

They came back to help me, and I said, "You're not going to believe it, but I'm stuck in quicksand." They both started laughing. Before long we were all laughing so hard none of us could do anything to keep me from sinking. I was in up to both knees now, and all we could do was stand there laughing hysterically. Finally Julie grabbed my belt to keep me from sinking farther, and Eric and I reached underneath my right knee and pulled with all our might. They finally got me out of there, and we continued on to finish the race. In that race, there were seventy teams, and we finished unofficially in twenty-first place.

You might wonder how I could be up to my knees in quicksand, in the pitch dark, and find that a laughing matter. It is because I know that it could have been a lot worse. When you compare an adventure race to a Navy SEAL mission, things can definitely get worse. In an adventure race, the worst that is going to happen is you might get injured and you end up being seen by medical people. You might even be out of the race. In the grand scheme of things, that is not really terrible compared to what might happen during a SEAL operation. There you might have the enemy chasing you, or you might find yourself looking up the barrel of an AK-47 assault rifle, or worse. It can always get worse. For me, having been a SEAL before I got into adventure racing, it is easy for me to look at every little problem in a race like, "Oh yeah, it could be so much worse." So what if we are at seventeen thousand feet and we have a little altitude sickness. Good thing we're not at twenty-five thousand feet with frostbite and edema. It can always get worse. Really, we've only had a few deaths in the world of adventure racing, and just a few severe injuries. That is pretty remarkable when you consider what we adventure racers put ourselves through. And it is mainly because the sport attracts heads-up people who know what they are getting themselves into. And for the most part the organizations putting on the races know what they are doing and make safety the top priority. Sure we have had a couple of serious incidents. But for the most part, with the thousands and thousands of people who have raced in hundreds of races, it has not been a problem.

Adventure racing has changed my life. Being a SEAL has changed my life. And they go hand in hand. To tell you the truth, I have learned more about living in the outdoors through adventure racing than I did in the military. If you are going out on a mission in the military, you just load up a big pack with everything you might need. In fact, sometimes you take two of everything, just in case. SEALs have another old saying: One is none, two is one. We always carry two of everything—just in case one gets lost or fails. In adventure racing, however, you can't do that or you will be weighed down and too slow. You have to fine-tune everything. I learned how to pack better through racing. I learned to be more efficient getting from point A to point B. If I can save ten minutes in a race by taking a slightly harder path, I'll take it. In the military, what is ten more minutes? You're walking slowly anyway.

Adventure racing has definitely had a positive impact on my life. After a race, when I come back, I am exhausted. I look around and think, "You know, I'll never be able to explain what just happened." Each race is an experience of a lifetime. I will value each and every race I have done for the rest of my life. I will draw from those experiences. I will draw from what I have learned about myself. I will draw from what I have learned from my friends and teammates about how we can work with one another. Many of these lessons cannot even be put into words. It amazes me how many years of experience one can gain from a ten-day adventure race.

I definitely think adventure racing is one of the most exciting sports there is today. You have to be good at everything and you have to be a team player. You have to know how to navigate. You have to be able to push through pain and sleep deprivation. You have to know biking, running, climbing, paddling, gear selection, and nutrition. There is so much involved. You have to be strong, coordinated, fast, aerobically fit, anaerobically fit. A marathon runner or a mountain bike racer must master two or three athletic disciplines to excel in his or her sport. Adventure racing requires those disciplines plus fifteen or twenty more. I wish there was a better name than *adventure racing,* because it is so much more than just an adventure.

Another one of the things that I love most about adventure racing, being a SEAL, or just being an athlete in general is that at times, all of them require you to reach deep, deep, deep down inside and give it everything you have. You might not do a 2:10 marathon, you might not win a triathlon or an adventure race—but if you're able to dig deep, as deep as you can, and do your very best, that is a big victory in itself. I feel bad for the people who don't do it. I really do. I know that each person has the ability to reach deep down inside and pull it out, whatever it takes. I've seen this ability to dig deep save lives in combat—it has saved a lot of lives in SEAL missions—and it enables racers to go harder. Now when I'm training SEALs, or when I'm training athletes to do adventure races, I sometimes see people taking it easy. They might be talking, laughing, or joking around. I try my best to persuade them that if they are comfortably talking along on the trail, that's conversational pace. That is not race pace. I feel strongly that if you want to do your best, in competition, or in life, you sometimes have to do race pace. Sure, race pace hurts sometimes. But a little pain is okay.

One of the things that I tell athletes in training or at events is "welcome the pain." If you're going to go hard, giving it your all, and running at race pace, then there will be some pain. Welcome the pain. Learn from the pain. Gain strength from the pain. After all, if you don't push yourself physically hard enough, how do you know where your potential is? Welcome the pain. It will make you a stronger person, both on and off the racecourse.

Not a Cloud of Doubt in the Sky

NAME: KRISTEN DIEFFENBACH
AGE: 34
RESIDENCE: FROSTBURG, MD
YEARS ADVENTURE RACING: 4

I discovered running at the tender age of ten when I began accompanying my father on his daily jaunts around the neighborhood. While many people in our small Wisconsin community frowned upon such an activity for a growing young lady, both of my parents encouraged me to follow my passion. And follow it I did. I ran before school, after school, spring, summer, fall, and even during the subarctic Midwest winters. I ran for the middle school and high school teams and attended summer running camps. In fact, I am probably the only kid who has ever snuck out of the house late at night to go for a run!

In college and beyond I continued my career as an endurance athlete, running and cycling for Boston University and various club teams. It took me awhile after college to realize that I might be able to make a career following my passion, so back to school I went. Graduate school was much more demanding and forced me to seriously curtail my competitive activities. However, I never let academics stop me from training or playing in the woods. Retiring from competition freed me from team training and travel obligations. Suddenly I had license to try new things that had been frowned upon or forbidden by coaches and team managers. I discovered that mountain biking wasn't a lesser form of cycling. I spent time hiking, climbing, rafting, trying just about any new activity I came across.

As I neared the end of my doctoral work in exercise science and sport psychology, I realized that I was feeling the urge to compete again but I didn't know where to begin given that I had come to enjoy so many different things. Somewhere along the way I became aware of ultra-endurance events and adventure racing. I was intrigued, especially since most of the events I saw were off-road and involved some degree of orienteering. I was especially interested in the team nature of the adventure race. Even though I had been on cross-country, track, and road cycling teams, when it came right down to it, the training and racing were really individual events. With the mix of elements and the team component, adventure racing seemed to pose all kinds of new challenges, both physically and mentally.

I competed in my first adventure race in the fall of 2000 as the last-minute replacement on a recreational team. Although as a team we were not able to complete the race, I was immediately hooked on the sport itself and decided to pursue it further. Through one of the adventure racing internet lists, I found and joined a team named Tribal Fury with Jeff Durr and Brad Rogers. Despite living in different states, which made team training impossible, we did well together in several events. By the end of the year, Jeff and I decided that we were ready to do something longer than a twenty-four-hour event, but Brad was embarking on the adventure of fatherhood and had to take some time off. So Jeff and I again turned to the internet to gather résumés from potential teammates. We were fortunate to find Mark Lattanzi.

After several phone conversations early in 2002, Mark, Jeff, and I formed Team MaJeK and set our sights on Racing Ahead's 2002 Appalachian Extreme in Bethel, Maine. Due to logistics and work schedules, we only had one opportunity to train together prior to the event. We met up for an overnight training session in April about six weeks before the race. Mark and Jeff had a trekking, biking, paddling expedition planned for a full night of fun. The night was clear but freezing, we took a few wrong navigational turns, and I was battling a nasty cold/fever. However, in spite of all the bumps, the weekend helped us get to know each other and allowed us to set some realistic goals for our first long event.

Despite having realistic goals, I don't think any of us realized what we were undertaking by entering this race. Among the three of us, Mark, Jeff, and I had years and years of competitive experience, and we saw this as just another competitive venture to test our speed, strength, and skill. The only one on our team who expressed concern over lack of experience was Kelly, Jeff's wife. Kelly had signed on as our support crew and as it turned out she was to be our sole support for the majority of the race. She was worried about her ability to support us because even though she had been to a few of our previous events this was to be her first race as a support crew. As it would turn out, of the four of us, she probably handled the unexpected elements of the event the best.

The Thursday morning prior to the race, we met in Frederick, Maryland, and piled all of our gear into Jeff and Kelly's minivan for the long trek north. The drive was uneventful and we used the time to talk about recent race developments. We arrived at Sunday River midmorning on Friday, right on schedule (perhaps for the last time of the weekend!). It was a beautiful day with just a few clouds in the sky and the occasional sprinkle. As soon as the van door opened Mark, Jeff, and I were ready to go. We got there well before most of the teams so equipment check-in was a breeze as we took care of the release and medical forms, mandatory gear check-in, and the basic orienteering quiz. By 3:00 P.M. Team MaJeK was officially signed into the 2002 Appalachian Extreme. It was during this check-in period as I watched other teams drift in, saw the experienced racers greet each other, and heard folks telling tales of other adventures that I began to wonder what I had gotten myself into. "Am I in over my head? I don't belong here among these weathered outdoors folk." I had always played in the woods but now I began to wonder if I really had what it takes to survive in the woods. A cloud of doubt began to hover above me as I began imagining worst-case scenarios.

The pre-race meeting began at 5:00 P.M. with a very moving song about adventure racing composed by Liz, a member of the race support staff. I felt a surge of unity with the others in the group and I hoped that I was worthy enough to really become one of them. Looking around the room, Mark pointed out several of the high-powered teams present, including two Subaru teams and Team Montrail. We exchanged excited whispers, and the nervousness of being a novice who was definitely in over her head began to churn in my stomach.

The first major shock of the race came as the race directors announced that although the race start time was 8:00 A.M., the start location was about two hours away! Furthermore, camping was not allowed in that area and we were already at the closest hotel. Then came the handing out of passports, support crew materials, race instructions, and maps—all twenty-five of them! The gentle churning in my stomach was becoming a storm and the cloud of doubt was darkening.

It was almost 7:00 P.M. before we were able to scramble back to the room. The race start was just over twelve hours away and in the remaining time we had to wade through the twenty-five maps and accompanying instructions, organize our gear accordingly, eat dinner, catch a bit of sleep, load the vehicle, and drive the two hours to the race start. Mark and Jeff immediately got down to the business of plotting the orienteering points while I read and re-read the race passport, rules, and other materials, made new lists, reorganized gear, and prepped Kelly with more detailed support-related instructions. The adrenaline rush of our eleventh-hour preparation reminded me of how it feels in the last few seconds before the official fires the starting gun on the track. The tasks at hand, however, quieted the storm and kept me from dwelling on the fears and concerns that had hung over me all afternoon.

Midevening my brother David joined the crew. He was only available to help for the first few hours of the event, but we made good use of the extra hands while we had them. He was immediately put to work carrying gear to the car, tearing duct tape, stuffing food into little baggies, and so on. I was proud and excited to share my new endeavor with someone in my family. Apparently, he didn't see adventure racing in the same sparkling light as I did because after he returned home, he declared to the family that I was even more nuts than they previously believed.

The map work took almost seven hours, as there were thirty-six race checkpoints to plot. Further complicating the map work, we discovered that some points had to be plotted on several maps of different scale, which caused quite a bit of navigational anxiety. After a final gear check we settled down for a fitful three hours of sleep. It was a good thing that I was exhausted or I wouldn't have slept at all!

Four o'clock Saturday morning came quickly and we stumbled around with last-minute packing and loading. I'm not a morning person at all, and after a measly few hours of shuteye, I was feeling a bit cranky. Then I saw the parking lot full of bikes, canoes, gear, and people, and excitement and nervousness overcame my crankiness as I watched other teams preparing to leave. It wasn't long before our minivan—complete with a seventeen-foot canoe on top and three bikes on the back—joined the caravan for the two-hour drive to the start of the race. I tried to catch a bit more sleep on the way, but I felt like a little kid who was a part of a secret parade and the pre-race worry and excitement kept me wide awake the whole way.

The sun was up by 7:00 A.M., there wasn't a cloud in the sky, and there was just a hint of chill in the air—it was perfect. We hustled about checking gear, taking photos, and trying not to think about what was coming next. At 8:00 A.M., twenty-three teams of adventure racers set off on the 2002 Appalachian Extreme. Our first leg was a thirteen-mile trek consisting mostly of ATV and jeep roads. For a multiday race, the pace started much quicker than I had anticipated and I was in awe of the teams who seemed to run so effortlessly, without any apparent concern for what lay ahead. We jogged a bit, but we were all nervous about doing too much too early in this long race. I had always considered myself to be a capable athlete but at the start of this race, among these teams, I began to wonder if I really was an athlete after all. The potential shame of not being able to go the distance and finding out that I was just a wannabe added to the heavy cloud over my head that would stay there until the end of the race.

It took us nearly four hours to jog/hike the first leg and find all the checkpoints. We reached the first transition area feeling fresh and excited and with relatively dry feet (a short-lived phenomenon, I assure you). Our ace support staff, Kelly and David, had our canoe and gear set out and ready for a quick change from our hiking stuff into wet suits, dry tops, and life jackets. Apparently David was a bit taken aback at the sight of his sister bouncing around trying to get into a wetsuit, getting annoyed and cutting the lower legs off the darn thing so it was easier to get on—all the while trying to scarf down a peanut butter sandwich, most of which ended up on her face. Despite my battle with the wetsuit, the transition went relatively quickly and uneventfully and in no time at all we were on the water for about eighteen miles of large-lake paddling.

Jeff was our stern man, I sat in the middle, and Mark was up front. We tried to take advantage of the wind, thinking we were smart enough to rig a sail. But it was pretty apparent that either we weren't good engineers or the wind really wasn't that strong, so we gave up. Instead we focused on paddling at a steady pace and finding the lake checkpoints as quickly and efficiently as possible. We reached the paddle takeout in just four and a half hours. We were proud of ourselves, and that cloud over my head felt like it was drifting away as we reached the shore. I felt my old race confidence beginning to return when we found out that one of the top teams had to head back out on the lake to find a checkpoint they had missed in their haste.

At the transition area Kelly, once again solo help, did a great job of setting up our gear and putting out yummy snacks. In less than fifteen minutes we were out of the wet suits, into biking gear, and with full bellies we were soon off on two wheels. The first bike leg was a breeze! Nicely paved country roads with a few little climbs and some nice winding descents—what more could you ask for? I was finally feeling like I knew what I was doing. Despite our knobby tires, we set up a pace line and maintained a good pace for the thirty-five miles of road riding. We rode with a few other teams, played leapfrog with a few, and even dropped a few, so everyone was feeling really good when we reached the next transition area about two hours later.

"Mama" Kelly greeted us with some amazingly warm homemade chicken soup, Pringles potato chips, and other yummy stuff. While we ate, we reviewed the routes we had mapped for the upcoming trekking leg and it appeared that we would be going through some rural towns, across a few streams, through an old logging forest, and over some moderate hills. We estimated that the next leg would take fourteen to sixteen hours (a gross underestimation, as it turned out) so we took a bit longer at this checkpoint. We carefully went over our gear and food selections based on our calculations and the weather reports.

With full bellies and dry feet, we left on foot around 7:00 P.M. on Saturday. Within an hour and a half we were off the country roads and into the woods. Although we occasionally came across a paved road over the next twenty-four hours, pavement was definitely the exception rather than the rule. The early part of the night was spent navigating unmarked logging roads, finding and crossing dry and not-so-dry creekbeds, and locating the various manned and unmanned checkpoints. I was content to just follow along, like the kid sister who tags along on her big brothers' adventures.

I had my first bout of the stumbling umbles (stumbles, mumbles, fumbles, and grumbles) Sunday at about 1:00 A.M. I'd experienced the umbles before, so they didn't worry me in and of themselves. But before, they always occurred when I knew I was only a few hours from the finish—now they were upon me with days to go. These darkened the cloud of doubt—how was I going to make it through the next several days if I was already tired!? Several times I startled myself alert by seeing what I thought were predator eyes glowing from the underbrush, but the umbles always returned as soon as the adrenaline rush slowed. I found myself being both envious of and frustrated with Jeff, as he seemed impervious to the sleepies as he had in so many other races.

We made a few navigational mishaps in the darkness that night and did a good bit of bushwhacking over old clear-cut land where the forest was trying to take over again. It seemed reasonable to assume that a clear-cut area would be easy to cross but since the big trees were gone there were a lot of fallen logs left behind and tons of debris and new growth scattered across the floor. Thus the clear-cut crossing wasn't very clear at all.

Daybreak found us in an open field with a chilly wind, a bit of fog, and a decided dampness in the air. I imagined that this was what it would feel like to cross the Scottish moors and wondered how people lived in such damp, cold, barren conditions in the centuries before Gore-Tex, polypropylene, and SmartWool. While I pondered such things, Mark and Jeff decided to stop for a navigational check. The damp had crept into my bones so I huddled under a small tree to warm up, and ended up taking an unintentional ten-minute nap. The guys didn't even realize that I was asleep until they stood up to put their packs on. I woke feeling tremendously refreshed and significantly warmer. I also felt a twinge of guilt for having gotten ten more minutes of sleep than they did, and the feeling of weakness for needing the nap added a layer to the dark cloud above my head.

Moments later we came across a mandatory gear checkpoint. As we unloaded and showed the race staff our gear we learned that we were among the top half of the field. This energized us for our next major obstacle, a big hill with no apparent trail over or around. According to the map, the trail we needed was directly on the other side. It seemed simple enough and it was a relatively small hill so up we went, bushwhacking all the way. At first the going was very easy—that should have given us some warning as to what we were in for. Toward the top we encountered snow—kneedeep in some places. The trees that had been nicely spaced when we started grew denser. Soon going in a straight line was difficult, and by the time we crested the hill it was all but impossible. We caught our breath at the top, figuring it was all downhill from there. Ha! As we started making our way down the other side, the snow and the trees made seeing and moving difficult. The snow was now at least waist-deep on the guys in some places and that meant I was in it up to my armpits. We quickly and easily lost sight of each other as we moved. "Marco, Polo" became our rally call to ensure that we were all together. Then it started to rain. I was beginning to wish I found more joy in simple indoor sports like Ping-Pong! Fortunately, the trees kept the rain from getting us too wet, but what the raindrops missed, the snow made up for.

We found an icy stream running down the hill and tried to follow it for a while. I was terrified of slippery ice-covered rocks, the risk of hypothermia if we fell in, and, worse yet, the possibility of serious injury out here in the middle of nowhere. I didn't want to sound like a wimp, but when I finally did voice my concerns I found out that the others were worried too, so we returned to the slower-but-safer travel through the trees. Even away from the icy water and rocks I was very scared. At this point the race no longer felt like a test of endurance and will—I felt that my health was actually at risk and survival was now the game. With startling clarity I really understood the dangers of the elements and how even strong, fit people can be besieged by nature. I felt a new sense of personal power and control as the reality sank in that this was about my personal strength and fortitude, not about a comparison with others.

It took us over four hours to get up and over this mountain. By the time we reached the other side we were soaked through and covered with bruises from repeated slips and slides into trees and rocks. Although it was cold and windy when we emerged, the sun soon came out and the winds died down, which kept us from running into more trouble. Later teams weren't so lucky, with at least one team getting lost and having to be rescued due to hypothermia.

Frustration over our slow progress muddled our decision making and we wasted time trying to find a trail that was so obvious on the map yet elusive in reality. Opting for a slightly longer but more easily navigated logging road, we finally got under way again. I was trotting along after the guys admiring the landscape when I started seeing beautiful houses back among the trees. After admiring a few gorgeous places I began to wonder why anyone would live in such a place way out here. Then I realized that there were no mailboxes, cars, or driveways for any of these houses. I was thrilled when I realized I was experiencing the hallucinations I had read so much about in other athletes' race reports. For the duration of the race I was prone to seeing writings and drawings on rocks and stones, gorgeous structures, and even the occasional talking creature. The part of my brain that wasn't so affected by the lack of sleep and fatigue was absolutely fascinated with the breakdown and malfunctions of the other half of my brain, and I found the scientist in me watching everything and wishing I had packed my digital recorder.

Mark began having trouble with a bruised heel, I was trying to ward off plantar fasciitis pain in both feet, and Jeff was still moving forward like a machine. By 7:00 P.M. Sunday, after twenty-four hours (ten hours longer than our anticipated time!) and more than fifty miles of hiking and bushwhacking, we finally hobbled into the next transition area. Kelly met us with smiles, warm pasta, dry clothes, and assurances that every other team had experienced the same setback we had. At this point I was so tired and so glad to be safe that I didn't care where the other teams were. The race really didn't feel like it was about beating anyone else anymore. It felt more like a struggle to persevere. The cloud was still there but it now seemed focused on whether or not I was tough enough to make it through to the end. While we ate, the medical staff came over and treated and duct-taped our blisters. We were thrilled to have our feet taken care of by professionals.

In keeping with our race plan, we lay down to try to catch an hour of sleep, our first in the thirty-six hours since the race started. Kelly woke us just as darkness was setting. Awake and ready to go, I shouldered all our gear so that Mark and Jeff could portage the canoe three-quarters of a mile to the put-in. The lake was beautifully glassy and smooth under the moonlight. It was amazing. We slid out on the water quietly with Jeff in the rear, Mark up front, and me in the middle again. We reached the first portage easily except for a short detour when I tried to have a conversation with a woman and a man loading a boat. Mark and Jeff humored me for a few minutes and let me discover on my own that the people I was talking to were just figments of my exhausted imagination.

At the portage we got off the water and made our way one mile down the road to the next lake. It was a paved road portage and pretty easy going. I took most of the gear and the guys took the canoe. Except for one lone car that passed us, we didn't see a single person or animal along the way. I kept imagining what one of the town residents might think if they were to wake up, peer out the window, and see us walking stiffly down the middle of the road in wet suits carrying tons of gear. Would we be a part of someone's strange dream? Would an old man tell his wife about the strange parade of figures that passed through town last night while he couldn't sleep? It was such a calm night and the town was so perfect, I almost felt like I was a part of a strange dream myself.

The second lake was much larger than the first. We had a bit of navigation trouble early on trying to make our way around both real and imaginary islands. As we neared the far side, both of the guys started getting the sleepies. At first I couldn't figure out why we weren't moving. Then I realized that they were both almost asleep. Falling asleep in the boat didn't seem like a great option, so I decided it was song time! I spent the next six hours belting out show tunes, camp songs, Beatles songs, nursery rhymes, the happy birthday song, pop, rock, country, and anything else I could think of. I believe I even did the ABC song and the Itsy Bitsy Spider once or twice as well. I can't carry a tune, but at 2:00 A.M. in the middle of nowhere, who cares? Mark and Jeff joined in and it quickly became a game to sing out a song line or phrase and to see if, among the three of us, we could remember the whole thing. For some reason Mark and I got hooked on Terry Jack's song "Seasons in the Sun," which we repeated at least a dozen times.

We were still singing when the sun came up on Monday and when, midmorning, we left the water and climbed up onto a soft sandy beach. Kelly, an amazing cheery sight for sore eyes, greeted us with hot scrambled eggs, oatmeal, and dry gear. The sun was out, the day was warm, and our spirits were rising high. We were giddy from the singing and the sunshine and I was thrilled that we were still moving. While we rested, reports were coming in that the top team had spent four to five hours trying to find the next checkpoint. We weren't concerned, we were strong, we were confident, we were Team MaJeK. Bikes and packs loaded, we headed out again at 10:00 A.M., over two hours ahead of the mandatory cutoff. I would like to say that we quickly located the next checkpoint, but in our attempts not to repeat the mistakes of others we made plenty of our own and still spent almost four hours looking!

Our lost time was spent pushing the bikes through the underbrush and through bogs. The baby blackflies were out in force and for the first time during the weekend the temperature soared to the 70s. Our jolly mood at the last transition had apparently only been on the surface of our fatigue and exhaustion, and it didn't last long. Tempers and emotions quickly ran high and hot. We weren't listening to each other well or paying attention to how fatigue was interfering with rational ideas. Mark and I actually staged a coup against Jeff's navigation, and rather than work together, we all pulled in different directions. Under my breath (but probably not quietly enough) I cursed out everyone and anything having to do with the race and my being there. Of course, I had been angry before but I never experienced the feeling of irrational and helpless rage that I felt that day when we found ourselves trying to navigate through the most disgusting swamp full of those damn little flies! I have no idea what kept me from lashing out at my teammates but I am so glad I didn't.

Somehow we found the elusive checkpoint and began riding on a series of unmarked and often inaccurately mapped Maine forest roads. We did fine for the first part of the afternoon but at some point we made a series of wrong turns that lead us in a big circle. Jeff had always been flawless as our navigator in shorter races. However, we had never considered how the mental stress of the job coupled with a longer race would add to his fatigue, and how this in turn would impact his ability to navigate and lead. Once Mark and I realized what was going on we quickly took action to provide Jeff with a much-needed mental break while we kept moving. Mark took over the maps and I took most of Jeff's gear so he could concentrate on riding safely. I felt very useless and frustrated at my own inability to navigate and tried to focus on what I could do to help the team. Once again I found myself face-to-face with another weakness.

This section became even tougher (and the blunders we made became more serious) when we ran out of water and couldn't find a clean source to refill our water bladders. We had water filtration systems but all we could find was shallow muddy puddles. We knew that searching for water would seriously slow us down, but, worse yet, lack of water and dehydration could end our race altogether. Around dusk on Monday (just over sixty hours since we started on Saturday morning) the next checkpoint finally came into view—what a wonderful sight. And it was atop a dam. Water— filterable, drinkable water was easily within our reach! Timmy, the young race volunteer manning this checkpoint, made this oasis more refreshing by fixing us the most wonderful peanut butter sandwiches! The fresh soft bread and smooth creamy peanut butter made me feel like a schoolkid getting Mom's special afternoon snack before rushing back out to play. I tried to savor rather than inhale it. We were the last team still in the race to make it through this checkpoint. We were feeling a bit discouraged by the previous section, but we knew we were still in the game and the peanut butter sandwiches went a long way toward lifting our spirits.

On our way again, darkness was upon us before we had gone more than a mile. Our original calculations had us off this bike leg well before dawn and thus we hadn't brought along any spare bike light batteries. So we rode side by side using one light at a time in an attempt to save batteries. Luckily, the trails were smooth and the moon peeked out occasionally helping to light our way. I marveled at how the fear and anger of the day vanished as we worked together and enjoyed the beauty of the night.

All three of us had a nasty bout of sleepies around midnight, having had at most four hours of sleep since we woke up the day before the race started. The seriousness of the situation first appeared when I was lost in stargazing and rode away from the guys, thinking they were right behind me. They had stopped to check the map and thought I had just gone ahead to pee. When they realized I wasn't coming back and I didn't answer their calls, they were terrified that I had ridden off the trail and was down the hill in a ditch. When they caught up to me they were pretty upset until they realized that I was just as confused about what had happened as they were.

Shortly after midnight in the wee hours of Tuesday we came to a small bridge that had been washed out. It looked very unsafe and I was convinced it would be dangerous to cross. I was so sure of this because the small cats sitting on the other side grooming themselves told me so. I couldn't imagine why they would lie to me and I was terrified that the cats were right—even though the rational part of me knew that there was no danger and in a "normal" state I usually scoff at such warnings. Even now the memory of those cats and their message is as clear as the memories of the race meeting and the instructions the directors gave. Given my conviction that danger awaited us and the extreme fatigue we were all exhibiting we put down the tarp, got out the sleeping bag, and set the alarm for a two-hour trail nap. Getting up and going again in the cold was terrible! Cold and shivery but finally lucid again we made it across the creek as easily as crossing a sidewalk. In fact, the footbridge was only two or three feet off the ground and the crossing was perhaps five or six feet across—at most. I guess the cats were wrong after all.

At the next checkpoint, despite feeling fine physically, I had a surprise meltdown. I wasn't feeling muscle-tired and the recent nap had left me clearheaded, but apparently I just needed a good sob. I shocked my teammates and myself because we didn't have any idea what was going on. I always hated crying. I felt it was weak and stupid, and was completely unproductive. But this completely baffled me—I wasn't upset, sad, or even angry yet I sobbed like a child for several minutes. As I calmed down I realized I felt refreshed and had a renewed excitement for the adventure. The detached scientific part of me was amazed at the power of such an emotional release and I realized that tears have nothing to do with weakness—a realization that has since helped me both professionally and personally.

Soon we were on our way again and finally back on paved roads. The roadie in me was ecstatic! We got back into our well-practiced pace line and cruised along. I was feeling on top of the world: smooth and powerful. As we made our way toward the next checkpoint, we wove back and forth across the New Hampshire-Maine border. At one point we saw the bikes of a team we had traveled with propped up against the guardrail with a space blanket wrapped around the frames as if to keep them warm. We found out later that the team had dropped out of the race late in the evening on Monday and joined the party with a group of locals barbecuing at the house across the road. While a part of me was envious of their spontaneity and alternate adventure, a larger part of me wondered how they could give up when they had come so far!

The next few checkpoints were straightforward and the traveling was easy. As we pedaled into a manned checkpoint around 8:00 A.M. on Tuesday, after spending seventy-two hours on the course, we got the devastating (but not unexpected) news that we weren't far enough along to continue on the pro course and that we were being rerouted to an alternate ending. Due to our location, the local terrain, and the seventy-five-hour cutoff time for all categories, our race came to a very sudden end. We cycled up the road about five miles to a pick up location where we waited about twenty minutes for a mandatory shuttle ride that dropped us off just a few miles short of the finish line. We cycled in the remaining two miles from the relocated point and finished the modified course in just under seventy-three hours—good enough for eighth place. Of the twenty-three teams to start the race, only eleven finished, and only a few of those completed the full pro course.

Despite our awesome accomplishment for such a blundering novice team, I was frustrated and upset that we didn't do the full course. I found that I was both proud of myself and disappointed in myself at the same time. Such conflicting feelings are confusing enough in the real world but in my exhausted state I couldn't make heads or tails of them at all. I guess the intensity of the emotions I experienced was in line with the intensity of the experience itself. I went into my first long race without much thought to the mental and emotional impact it would have. I think what surprised me the most was the way that psychological exhaustion impacted all of us. Even having read about it and having heard about it from other athletes, I was really amazed at the things your body and mind do to keep you going and the things they do to get in your way.

Whenever someone asks me why I do this, or even when I ponder this myself, I find that it is impossible to describe this intensity and the addictive power of feeling anything—fear, pride, joy, frustration, disappointment, camaraderie, or fatigue. It is not something you experience in any other kind of event. Even now memories of the 2002 Appalachian Extreme teach me new things about myself.

Winning Isn't Necessarily Finishing First

NAME: OWEN WEST
AGE: 35
RESIDENCE: NEW YORK, NY
YEARS ADVENTURE RACING: 10

In September 1994, I was invited to try out for an extreme endurance race team captained by Robyn Benincasa. She was searching for three men to join her in some crazy race called the Eco-Challenge. This race was supposed to last for a few days and be pretty miserable—with lots of hiking, little food and no sleep. A lot like the Marine Corps. I was an active duty Marine at the time so Robyn's theory was that I'd be used to such rigors and I'd be able to navigate.

Robyn had already completed several Ironman Triathlons but eventually found the grueling race to be too short. "It's a sprint," she said of the 140-mile race. "Besides, I'm sick of racing against those skinny chicks." Robyn isn't a big woman herself—she's probably about five-foot-six, and her powerful, ripped physique is modest and easily hidden on those rare occasions when she's wearing more than sleek, woefully patterned workout clothes (she's even been known to race naked). What I didn't realize at the time was that I was dealing with the world's top female adventure racer and probably the toughest person I know. And I certainly didn't realize I'd be diving headlong into a lifestyle that centered on misery.

Robyn's tryout was three continuous days and two nights without sleep. Initially, I was well behind the professional triathletes and mountaineers, and was clearly the inferior athlete of the fifteen fanatics willing to be crushed by this woman, whose verbal fireworks were rivaled only by my most creative Marines. However, by the third day many of the kayakers and mountaineers had given up; the triathletes were whining about lack of food and sleep, and the others were lagging behind, unable to cut through their personal cobwebs. I wound up making the team because the

Marine Corps had taught me how to navigate and how to suffer. Thus, Team Nike/Benincasa—four men and a Robyn—began its training for the 1995 Eco-Challenge, which would be held in Utah.

The suffering began immediately and for the next six months we trained like demons. A typical workout consisted of a fifty-mile speed march from Oceanside to Mexico and a bike ride back, followed by some climbing and a fifty-mile canoe outing. We ran four marathons with twenty-five pound packs and completed an Ironman triathlon as the opening to a particularly gruesome workout, one in which I finished over an hour behind the others. Ultimately, we wound up finishing the 1995 Eco-Challenge in second place—after eight days of continuous racing, we lost to a professional French team by forty-five minutes. It was the best finish ever by an American team in these so-called adventure races, but frankly the competition wasn't extreme and we could have won. I made several navigational errors and our team dynamics were awful. Plus, Eco-Internet had not yet gelled . . . or recruited Robyn.

But what an adventure! We ascended a twelve-hundred-foot vertical wall along the Colorado River on single ropes. We marched across the Utah desert for ninety miles, stopping for water just once at our only source: a cesspool near an old well with a dead cow nearby. We mountain biked to the edge of a four-hundred-foot rappel and later destroyed our feet canyoneering in the Black Box. We rafted down the Colorado River and canoed across Lake Powell. And we cursed, fought, and yelled at each other from start to finish.

After the race, Robyn replaced everyone on the team except for me, perhaps afraid her next navigator would be even more screwed up than I was. One of the problems with putting together an expedition racing team is that you can't possibly hold an eight-day tryout—it's just too painful. Consequently, the best teams in the world build their teams over years, adding teammates they observe closely in actual races. So in our second race together, Robyn had added two men she raced with in a similar race—the Raid Gauloises in Patagonia—and I added a friend of mine from the Marine Corps who was an experienced adventure racer. With new sponsorship, Team Mountain Dew/Benincasa was seeded eighth in the 1996 British Columbia Eco-Challenge, the top U.S. seed.

The British Columbia Eco-Challenge was labeled the "world's toughest race," and it attracted the best teams from around the globe. Competitors ascended a grand total of over sixty-four thousand feet, in sum more than twice the distance from sea level up Everest. There were seventy-five teams entered, and we assumed at least sixty-five would finish because of the high quality of the racers. By race end, only thirteen teams successfully completed the race and for those thirteen, except perhaps for the first place team who departed the glacier before the storm hit, the question was not one of finishing, but one of survival.

Day 1

The race started at 6:00 A.M. with a twenty-five-mile ride and run—two people on horseback with our gear and three running. A hundred and fifty horses and 225 runners surged forward in the early-morning fog of a British Columbia valley and our team grabbed the early lead. After an hour we switched riders and I was the odd man out, left on my feet to forge ahead of the riders in search of a suitable route. When my time came to ride fifteen miles into the race, my teammates drove ahead as part of the plan not to wait for my coordination to catch up with my desire to mount the stupid equine. Horses and I simply do not get along and within ten minutes the horse refused to move. Short of a horse's death, race rules make the horses part of the team; you can't leave the animals behind. I checked the horse's feet and found that he had developed a huge sore on his right rear hoof—it simply could not or would not move.

Fifteen teams had passed us and our frustrations had turned to desperation by the time a rancher escorting the horse rush ambled by. But by this time Robyn had arrived, fuming at the 45-minute delay, and she was immediately all over the rancher. "Either take this animal off of our hands or we'll drag it over the next fifteen miles," she screamed.

The rancher was too shocked to deny the request and we were again on our way, albeit minus one horse for the team. Two hours later we reached the first checkpoint, a mandatory river crossing without ropes. The glacial river was flowing at well over ten knots and was well under forty degrees. We watched as the Japanese team ahead of us was swept a half-mile downstream into a safety net. We could see that many of the teams ahead of us had met a similar demise and were now sloshing their way back upstream, freezing, to the first transition area, which was fifty yards across the river from the checkpoint.

We entered the chest-deep water as a team, arm in arm, and I took the upstream position and formed the eddy while the others dragged me forward. We entered the transition area in third place, and quickly changed clothes to prepare for the next leg—glacier trekking. We planned for a thirty-hour leg and packed accordingly. Ice axes, crampons, Gore-Tex, a tent, lard, a stove, food, pills, a first-aid kit, lighters, headlamps, a rope, and all our necessary athletic gear were stuffed into packs.

We then dove into the bush and humped with urgency in an attempt to get to altitude and the glacier before nightfall, since navigation in the forest at night is brutally slow. The temperature was approaching ninety degrees by midafternoon and we had to take several ten-minute breaks to cool down. We reached the edge of a mountain by 6:00 P.M. and quickly decided that we (I) had taken a wrong turn somewhere—it simply looked too difficult to ascend. For Team Mountain Dew this was, in retrospect, where our inexperience showed. Where the best five teams simply continued up the mountain, we argued and searched for easier routes for over five hours. After all, in Utah much of the route had been marked. By the time we decided to ascend, the race was lost. We were forced to bed down in the dark, roped up, on the steep alpine face, most of us getting rest by lying back and straddling trees to prevent a fall down the ridgeline. When we reached the glacier the next morning, we found ourselves in ninth place, twelve hours behind the leaders.

Day 2

Two hours sleep. Sixty-eight teams left. Now on the snow in crampons, there was silence as reality set in. We had come to win and before the first quarter had ended in what was truly a brutal race, we had no chance of winning. But therein lay our motivation. As we charged continuously for twelve hours across the glacier in sneakers (for speed), then descended to do several miles of ankle-twisting sloshing down a glacial stream and a rope-bridge crossing, only to ascend again up a brutal hill that took a sleepless night to climb, there seemed to be a moment when we all came to the same conclusion—we would be proud just to finish the race as a team. Determination replaced bitterness.

Day 3

Two hours total sleep. Forty teams left. Dawn found us back up on the glacier, and our feet were nearing frostbite. The refreezing that had occurred at night made it hard to break through the ice layer on the snow. We began to slowly make up some ground on the others, following their tracks clearly in the snow. Eventually, we got word that about half of the teams had activated their radios and dropped out, shoring up our belief that to cross the finish line would be an accomplishment of which we could be proud. We marched out of the glacier and were nearly injured in a rockslide on the descent that night. We slept for two hours.

Day 4

Four hours total sleep. Thirty teams left. We marched through thick forest on a compass azimuth in what was, for me, the most strenuous part of the race. All of us were fading quickly, dehydrated and literally without calories to burn. With my face in the compass for seven straight hours, stung over thirty times when a yellow jacket nest erupted, and simply out of energy, it became a struggle to put my left foot in front of my right. Fortunately, my teammates helped me through it—one took over the navigation duties and Robyn gave me some of her precious Gatorade mix. Two hours later, I was back in the world, hydrated, and spewing my usual mix of b.s. in an attempt to keep the humor up. When we finally arrived at that second checkpoint, the only water in our bodies resided in the blisters on our feet.

Day 5

Six hours sleep. Twenty teams left. Required to carry our kayak paddles with us on the bikes, we taped them to the beams and began a hellish fifty-mile route across a ridgeline. Weighed down by our packs, we literally pedaled all day looking for the bike river crossing. I'm told we went through some beautiful country, but it's hard to appreciate the terrain when it's kicking your ass. Oh yeah, we saw a big bear too, but he didn't even have the decency to put us out of our misery.

Day 6

Eight hours sleep. Twenty teams left. We arrived at the checkpoint at 3:00 A.M. with one of our team members vomiting from exertion and all of us at our limit. To make matters worse, we found out the next leg was to take us back to the glacier for ice climbing and a longer trek than the first. Loaded for bear—literally in my case—we began the long ascent from the river basin, through the swamp, up through the forest, across the scree and boulders, to the glacier. Our packs weighed over thirty pounds. In the forest, six hours into the trek—we had been averaging five kilometers an hour—we hit a thousand meters of slide alder and wait-a-minute vines that required a machete and slowed us down to a snail's pace. We finally reached the glacier at nightfall, after only taking two thirty-minute breaks all day. Shortly thereafter, the thermometer and barometer began to indicate real trouble and we stepped up the pace in an attempt to reach a safety checkpoint at altitude before the weather hit. Roped up and weary from sleep deprivation, we stopped at the edge of the crevasse field, and it began to rain.

"We can't go any farther tonight. Someone will fall in," one teammate said. I agreed. Robyn wove up to us, mumbling. "What the hell is going on? Let's go!"

"It's too dangerous," I said. "We need to build our tent here. Someone's going to fall in a crevasse. Our best move is to wait out the weather."

"No. We keep moving. That's what I want to do." She was our captain and so we drove on in the rain, leaping haphazardly across crevasses. The cracks in the glacier were five feet at their widest, but with a heavy pack, even Carl Lewis would have been nervous.

Day 7

Eight hours sleep. Thirteen teams left. At 7:00 A.M., we arrived at the checkpoint soaked and shivering, and debated movement in the weather. Within an hour the temperature plummeted to the high thirties and the wind was gusting to fifty knots. Rain quickly turned to icy sleet and a teammate said, "I'm putting up the tent. This is about survival now, not the stupid race."

We built the tiny tent in the gusts behind the largest boulder we could find and lost the fly cover in the wind, which meant that we were certain to be very wet. The five of us crammed into the three-person tent and stripped down in our sleeping bags. The rain had soaked us though, and we were forced to go into the survival mode most feared by my Marines—getting naked with someone else in a bag to raise body temperature. With four men and one woman, it raised a brief dilemma, but to be honest when you're really cold you simply want *anyone* next to you. I won't disclose my partner, or partners, but suffice it to say that I'm now a big fan of three-somes. Snuggled up, we slept for twenty hours until the storm passed.

Day 8

Twenty-eight hours of sleep. Thirteen teams left. Happy to be alive, the temperature rose and we put on our wet gear with grimaces and curses, and were helicoptered to the icefalls where we met the others. Everyone had remained immobile for twenty-four hours except the top team, who had already crossed the finish line. After some long rappels down icefalls and another crevasse field, we boarded rafts and negotiated Class IV whitewater where we lost Robyn. She popped up about ten seconds later, an eternity when under glacial water. We eventually completed what seemed to be an eternal thirty-mile paddle to our final leg, a thirty-five-mile mountain bike ride.

We pedaled through the night and it was simply one of the best times of my life—we would finish. Along the way, we yelled congratulations back and forth and victorious screams into the night. I have been in team organizations and have played sports most of my life, but I had never witnessed the level of absolute teamwork required by that race. I've always hated losing and if someone was to have told the team before the race that eighth was an accurate ranking, I doubt very seriously that we would have entered. So it's difficult to describe the transformation that occurred. Suffice it to say that when we crossed that finish line, I have never felt so humbled to be associated with a group of people. We finished over a day behind the leaders, but still immensely proud of each other and our performance as a team. At 4:00 A.M., on Day 9, we crossed the finish line, victorious in eighth place!

Racing Solo—The Heart of Darkness

NAME: BRYAN GOBLE
AGE: 29
RESIDENCE: ATLANTA, GA
YEARS ADVENTURE RACING: 4

I began adventure racing four years ago and had a less-than-stellar start. In my first race, my team finished dead last. My second race didn't go a whole heck of a lot better—we wound up finishing second to last! However, we stuck with the sport and slowly but surely improved our skills and our finish places. That's not to say we didn't have setbacks. For example, two years ago at Odyssey's Endorphin Fix (E-Fix), I was part of a team of four that "DNF'ed" a little over halfway through the course. Mechanical troubles, mounting dissension among the team and the physical stress of the New River Gorge terrain all played an equal part in our failure to finish. But two years and over fifteen races of experience later, I returned to West Virginia, seeking vengeance. This time I would race alone, but little did I know I would be seeking revenge on a new course that would prove to be the most daunting I'd ever attempted.

A few days prior to the race, I carpooled up to Camp Washington Carver with another soloist, fifty-something Vernon Winter (The Vern). We picked up topographical maps from a local gear shop and drove through many areas that previous E-Fixes had taken racers through. We also took time to hike through the trails near the Endless Wall and located the climbing access points (ladders) so that we knew where we could get up or down the wall if need be. Additionally, prior to departing for West Virginia, I read every E-Fix race report I could get my hands on. In addition to being as well prepared as possible, my race strategy boiled down to keeping a conservative and steady pace, navigating as well as I could, and taking care of my nutritional needs. I knew that physically I was in good shape, but I wasn't nearly as strong an athlete as many out there and I'd have to race smarter, rather than harder, to have any hope for success.

Race day finally arrived. During his initial briefing, race director Don Mann advised that we would be starting with a five-kilometer run down Mann's Creek Trail and back to camp by road. The positive aspect was that all we needed to bring was our headlamps, one of the very few times we wouldn't have to carry all of our mandatory gear, which was pretty much everything we had, including our paddling and climbing equipment. I'd been expecting that our paddling gear would be transported to the put-in for us, which was the case in 2002, but no such luck. I was hoping to use my small one-day pack to carry everything, but this easily put things beyond its limits. Lugging my throwbag, PFD, and climbing gear easily added five pounds and a lot more volume than I had anticipated. Due to this news, I decided to install my bike rack to give my back a break on the bike legs. This turned out to be a good decision, except for the fact that it made bike-whacking all the more difficult.

Here's a tip for those of you who have never done an Odyssey race before: If you didn't have time to make a pre-race bathroom pit stop, the starting cannon is enough to make you pay for it, especially if you're not expecting it. And with that (and soiled shorts), I began the prelude run. While I'm not much for sprinting the first half hour of a forty-hour race, I do see the value in not getting stuck in a queue on single-track trail, so I went out faster than I would have liked and wound up finishing this leg in third place.

Next up was mountain biking and I quickly found myself enjoying the mostly downhill ride out of the camp and was amazed at how spread out the field already was. I shouted words of encouragement to teams as I passed, knowing that I'd see many of them later on the course. We had a nice road ride for a few miles before turning on our first of many dirt roads. During this time I joined a pace line with Teams Litespeed and Godspeed and we chatted a little bit. However, eventually those guys decided to turn around, thinking that we had passed our first turn. I had been keeping track of our position and mileage and was pretty confident that we were going the right way, so I resisted the brief temptation to follow suit. I kept moving down the highway and before I knew it, there was an Odyssey volunteer stationed to direct competitors to the appropriate turn. *Woo-hoo!* I'm in first place. "Relish it while you can," I told myself. Within a few, very short minutes, Litespeed appeared on their anti-gravity bikes and quickly passed me on our first climb . . . like I was standing still. "Slow and steady," I reminded myself, fighting the urge to give chase. A few turns and a hill later, Godspeed appeared and followed suit. I remember praying to the navigation gods that they grant me the vision and wisdom to see things that others would not. Unfortunately, they did not immediately return my call and instead, I had my first navigation snafu when I decided to back-track to an unimproved road that had the correct bearing, but wound up costing me about twenty minutes by the time I found checkpoint (CP) 1.

From there, we rode on hilly country roads and eventually zipped down paved roads into and past the town of Winona. I had read stories about the pool hall in town and how locals used to gather to make fun of the crazy adventure racers who would pass though. But on this Saturday at 2:00 A.M., Winona was eerily deserted. I continued on down the paved road paralleling Keeny's Creek, knowing that at some point I'd pass under some power lines and would have to hike-a-bike up to the top of the Endless Wall. As I was descending the paved road, I noticed an abandoned railroad bed that intersected the road, but it was a good four hundred feet above the target elevation of the power lines. Well, I should have listened to instincts, which were shouting, "If you can stay at a higher elevation early, then do it and hope it kicks out at the correct location." Instead, I continued down the road until I reached the power lines only to find myself looking up at a hellacious bike-whack. I started my hike-a-bike in an open field below the lines, which lasted a whole fifty feet before it became a dense mix of tall grasses, prickers, and bushes. "If only I had brought a machete," I thought to myself. Figuring that the areas parallel to the lines, under foliage, would be more passable, I moved in that direction. My hunch turned out to be valid but instead of dense vegetation, I found an equally dense boulder field. I did my best to throw my bike on my shoulder and make my way up, but with the weight of all my equipment strapped to me and the bike, I found myself only being able to take a few steps at a time before exhaustion set it. Worse still, my body was giving hints that I had not done an adequate job staying hydrated and on top of my electrolytes. I wasn't cramping yet, but I knew that they were on the way. During my "bouldering" experience, I crossed a cascading streambed and actually found it to be the easiest route up. After a good forty-five-minute effort, I finally came out at the top, near a substation marked on our maps. From here, it was just a matter of a few simple turns down country roads to CP2, the bike drop. The only catch was that the instant I tried mounting my bike, the vast majority of muscles in my legs seized up. Over the course of this race, I must have composed at least half a dozen symphonies of groans and moans any sadomasochist audiophile would have appreciated! I quickly dismounted the bike in virtual paralysis and allowed nature to take her course. After a good fifteen minutes of fueling, twisting, and stretching I headed up the road in my smallest gears—not really making progress, but at least moving in the right direction.

I finally reached CP2, and was very happy to be loading my bike on the U-Haul for transport to the end of the river swim. I was surprised that there were only six to eight bikes loaded and figured that I was still in the hunt, especially since we had scouted the Endless Wall trails a day earlier. The terrain above the gorge is pretty level and the trails made for a nice brisk jog. Before I knew it, I was passing Diamond Point and knew that my next move, down the climber's access ladder to the bottom of the wall, was just ahead. Not too long after, I heard a truck in the distance and knew I was at CP3. It was 5:57 A.M. and dawn was breaking.

The checkpoint attendant informed me that I was the second team through, and that Litespeed had been down at the river for nearly an hour waiting for the dark zone restriction to be lifted for the river swim. I didn't know exactly when that was, but figured I could make up some time and maybe even catch them. So I ran down the road to CP4, and arrived approximately a half hour later. Unfortunately, I missed the Litespeed guys by about forty minutes. The checkpoint captain advised that I had the option of putting in right at the checkpoint location, which granted us access to an immediate and intimidating set of rapids, or portage three hundred meters downstream and put in there. If I'd have had company on the river, I probably would have jumped at the chance to swim an extra set of rapids, but on this day, it didn't seem like the "responsible" thing to do. Okay, the truth is I'm just a big chickenshit, but hey, I'm still here aren't I? The three hundred-meter portage was miserable. My shoeless feet were taking a serious beating on the small gravel. So I put my swim fins on and walked like an idiot in the name of comfort. I entered the river and was pleasantly surprised at the fact that it wasn't nearly as cold as I was anticipating. We had been told to get river right (from the left bank), which required ferrying across the current as best as we could. Unfortunately, *ferrying* is not a term that applies to the discipline of river swimming. Pretty much when you enter a current, you're going to go wherever it takes you.

I was looking for a nice long easy float down the river like in the 2002 race. Not today. Approaching the second set of rapids I tried to position myself through a little chute between two exposed boulders. I managed to get through them, but the spillover formed a circulating hole that managed to get its claws into me. I took a *big* breath of air and clutched my boogie board as I went below the surface, not knowing how, where or even if I'd get spit out. A few seconds later, I emerged facing upstream behind the boulder with the current rushing past me to the right. I stuck my board out to catch the current and off I went in a splash and flash. Only one smaller rapid and a small stretch of dead water were all that remained before the takeout. In total, I was in the water a brief thirty or forty minutes, which was a big bummer since this is my favorite discipline in adventure racing. At the takeout, I took a less than graceful spill that resulted in a nice bloody wound to the elbow and a crumpled boogie board. I blame the fins.

As a relatively weak mountain biker, there's not much to look forward to when you're at the base of the New River Gorge (or any other gorge for that matter) with the knowledge that there's only one way to go . . . and it's not downhill! In fact, there was a thousand-foot climb in two miles before any hope of relief. On a bright note, at the top of the gorge, I passed a white-water rafting outfitter and decided it would make a good pit stop. Several odd looks from the patrons and a couple of vending machines later, I was good to go. The remainder of the leg took us on some ATV trails that ran parallel to more power lines (argh!) and down some rather rocky technical grade to the next checkpoint at Hawk's Nest State Park. Once there, the reality of the situation hit me. I had to climb back out of the gorge (again) and over a mountain pass another twelve hundred feet of elevation above. The good news was that once over the pass, I'd be able to enjoy a scream-ing downhill to the banks of the Gauley River. Slow and steady and up, up, and away. I finally crested the hill and began the long descent to the next checkpoint, which almost made the climb worth it. This section was amaz-ing and easily one of my favorite places on the course.

I arrived at CP8 and had a gear check before putting in on the water, but first we had to get the canoes from the boat racks to the water. As best I could, I lugged that damn thing down to the river. We were to transport all of our gear, bikes included, down the Gauley until we reached the

Kanawha River. Don Mann and his race crew kept me company and asked me how I was feeling and gave me a quick race recap. It turned out I had maintained second place, but Litespeed had continued to put some distance on me on the bike leg—which neither surprised nor disappointed me too much. Just before putting in, I realized that I needed a paddle and the staff pointed me toward the vans. I was dumbfounded at what I saw. Canoe paddles. Big ugly red canoe paddles. I had made an extremely bad assumption that we'd have kayak paddles to use. Instead, I instantly knew that I was going to lose a lot of ground on any teams behind me.

I put in and peeled out into the current and began zigzagging through the water. Stroke left, stroke left, stroke right, stroke right.

The majority of the paddle was a test of mental dexterity. It consisted of brief periods of intermittent moving water separated by miles of flatwater. The midday sun did its part to make me into a value meal for KFC. I thought I had left my sunblock out of my pack to reduce weight and so I sat there and fried. Eventually I stopped paddling to the fastest moving water on the river and began paddling for the shaded areas instead.

Then the wind came and I had to adjust my technique. Stroke left, stroke left, stroke left, stroke left, stroke right. Stroke left, stroke left, stroke left, stroke left, stroke right. Woo-hoo! I love to paddle, but this sucks!

My paranoia of getting caught by a pursuing team grew and grew and it wasn't long before I started hearing voices. Two hours later, Team Godspeed passed me. It was a pretty deflating moment. I began to wonder just how close the next team was while battling thoughts of just taking a nap while floating to the takeout. Finally, I reminded myself that this was a race, so paddle you slug!

The highlight of the paddle section was my pit stop on river right at the Save-Mor in Gauley Bridge, West Virginia. I went in with the hopes of stocking up on some grocery goodies, energy bars, and cold beverages. There were no energy foods other than Combos and the only thing cold they had was beer (very tempting) and milk. When I came out, I witnessed team Adventure Pocono passing me on the water.

Stroke left, stroke left, stroke right, stroke right.

The last portage was around a set of damn dams and damn waterfalls. We had to take out on river left on a steep embankment. I had to unstrap and take all of my gear out, set it aside, and manhandle the canoe up and out of the water, over the damn dam barrier, down the other side, and over some very slick shale, all the while wearing bike shoes. One of the guys from Godspeed was kind enough to offer to help me get the canoe down from the first big drop. I think it was out of pity, but I don't care . . . it was definitely appreciated.

Stroke left, stroke left, stroke right, stroke right and finally there was the takeout.

I unloaded the gear again and hauled it another fifty feet up the boat ramp. @#$!ing thing. Both teams who had passed me were in the transition area, but Godspeed was first out. I had to reshuffle my gear a bit and in the process found my sunblock. I lathered it on and immediately knew that I was going to be in a world of hurt for the rest of the race. In the distance I could see another team working through their final portage, so I decided to get out of the transition area quicker and take time to fuel up a bit later.

Next up was yet another "gorge-to-mountain" biking leg. We were provided with a barely legible, black-and-white topo map to navigate up and over Cotton Hill Mountain. The map was so faded that I couldn't really make out too much. The only thing I gathered was that the main Forest Service road didn't look like it passed over the top. Well, I was wrong because after catching me on the climb, Adventure Pocono definitely found a better way than I. I chose to deviate from the road and head up an old mapped ATV road just past a small cemetery. For me, there wasn't much of it that was ridable and it was clearly not traveled by other teams before me. However, I had a plan and I was sticking to it, regardless of the number of horseflies that bit me. After miles of hiking my bike up the mountain, my trail finally merged with a much better jeep trail. I still had a bit of climbing to do, but it was much easier going.

The last few miles to the checkpoint were on paved highway, which was a nice respite. A mile up the road, I stumbled into yet another convenience store to stock up on items for the rest of the race. This one had a much better selection than the first and I took advantage of it. I bought a few items, but before I stepped out the door, I had consumed them all. So I decided to do a little more shopping and picked up my favorite item of the race, a King Cone ice cream. Thank goodness for emergency money. Five minutes later I was at the CP9, ice cream in hand. I was definitely more than ready to get rid of my bike again. Little did I know.

I've been on a few really good death marches in races before and this leg ranked right up there with the worst of them. I left the transition area at dusk and knew that this section was going to be a significant challenge in the dark. We were given a series of unmarked waypoints to guide us along the way. The Odyssey staff had flagged the route "intermittently," so we had that going for us. Things started innocent enough and I was able to successfully bushwhack my way through laurel to the first flagging, located along the base of a rock wall. It somewhat resembled hiking at the base of the Endless Wall, just without any well-traveled trails. Whack, whack, whack I went along the wall, encountering a number of random seemingly deadends, but more whacking through laurel revealed more intermittent trail.

Eventually, the path kicked out at the switchback of a gravel road and I had to decide—up to the right or down to the left. A quick map check gave me a boost of confidence and I headed down to the left. By this point, darkness had set in and stripped the course of any help or pity. As I walked, I noticed an artificial retaining wall on my right. My map indicated that there should be some sort of trail that broke off to the right, so I began paying a little extra attention to the retaining wall. At that instant, I would have sworn that I was looking at four cemetery headstones lining the wall. I put my headlamp's high beam on to get a better look, only to be startled by a voice. The voice belonged to Derek Lawrence of Team Adventure Pocono, who had decided to take a bit of a reprieve. I listened attentively as they depicted their search for our next trail only to spend two hours in stinging nettles, a very slick cascading stream, and mountain laurel too thick to go through.

They had come back out to consider their options and honestly looked pretty unmotivated. This was the same team who'd won the Beast of the East in 2002, so I knew there had to be some pretty serious terrain up there. But I remembered that the cardinal sin in adventure racing is to follow other teams, whether in direction, advice, or experience, without your own set of parameters to make a judgment. So I climbed up on the wall, bid them adieu, and headed into the heart of darkness. The first stretch wasn't too bad seeing that at least a few teams had cleared some of the overgrowth and trampled down some of the nettles. Eventually, the road ended at the cascading creek, whose bed lay about forty feet below. I decided to try and find a safe point to cross, which turned out to be a collecting pool a bit downstream, but as I lumbered down the hill, I lost my footing and slid about fifteen feet on the incline, then a five-foot drop into the pool. I counted my lucky stars that I had only superficial wounds from the fall and after a good thirty seconds of making sure I hadn't broken, separated, or lost anything, I lifted myself out of the pool. To be honest, I was a bit shaky for the next fifteen minutes, but it didn't matter because I wasn't making any progress anyway. I crossed the creek and began climbing the opposite side, which was simply a laurel farm. I began to bushwhack, picking what appeared to be the clearest route. Wrong, try again . . . and again . . . and again.

Eventually, I got back out to the retaining wall and went up the road past the split where I originally kicked out and reconsidered my options. I decided that I would head up the road and, when the road turned to parallel the creekbed, I'd break down and into the creek and just hope that the ghost of Suunto, the navigation god, would appear and point me down the correct path. While coming off the road from above was physically easier than climbing the creek, it was still slow going. Suunto didn't show himself to me, but I believe his spirit was with me as I was fortunate in finding the old nettle-laden mining route that would take me farther into the madness. I employed a lot of strategies to make it through the nettles—I moved slowly, tried to follow where others had trampled before me and followed their steps to avoid them.

I was still getting stung. Rub, rub. *It wasn't helping.* ARGH! Ok, take a break and calm down. I told myself, "You just need to get through this. You're going to get stung and the sooner you accept it, the sooner you can get past it. Okay, so we'll move as quickly as possible Ouch, errrrrr, ARGH! #@$! JUST GO! NO STOP! There's no way that Odyssey could have intended us to go through this. This is brutal beyond brutal." And as I stood on the verge of insanity, I had a brief moment of clarity come to me . . .

"No, this is exactly what Odyssey intended for us to do. They've designed a course that will push every single competitor to their limits, whether physical, mental, or emotional. This will definitely serve its purpose in separating the strong teams from the weak and live up to the moniker as the toughest two-day race in the country. It's a masterpiece. If I can push through this and finish this thing, I know I'll have a new benchmark."

Honest to God that's what I told myself. Of course in reality, Odyssey had no idea that there'd be nettles on the course because when they'd flagged it a few weeks earlier, they weren't there. But hey, those thoughts really worked to get me going again and get me through. I still wasn't much of a happy camper, but it worked and I was moving.

I guess time flies when you're going mad and are sleep deprived, because eventually the trek kicked me out on a paved road at CP10. Ahhhhhhhh!

I looked at the passport to gather instructions and checked the map to see where I'd be going next, but things weren't making too much sense, so I made an executive decision to make this a full-service pit stop by fueling up and resting before carrying on. I prepared a gourmet meal that consisted of the following items:

1 No-Doze Tablet

3 E-Caps

12 oz of Water with Energy Drink

1/2 Energy Bar

10 slices of Pepperoni

1 Extra Strength Aspirin

8 oz Cola

1 Indigestion Tablet

I removed all of my fleece and rain gear and bundled up as best I could to bed down for a twenty minute nap—long enough to let my concoction take effect. The checkpoint captain set his watch to wake me and I set mine as well as a backup. However, shivering with folded arms tends to muffle watch alarms.

An hour and ten minutes later, the next team(s) stumbled into the checkpoint. As I awakened, I immediately realized that I'd overslept but had no idea how long. However, I did know that I was feeling like a new man in a new race. I didn't expect to feel that well, but I swear I was just as fresh as I was at the start.

I checked out of the checkpoint and headed down the paved road to the trailhead and along the side of the gorge to the Kaymoor Miner's Trail. I was in overdrive (the by-product of my rest and feast), and reached the Kaymoor Stairs in a flash and headed up the nine-hundred-plus stairs to the road above. The passport indicated that all we had to do was follow the road to the rappel site, so that's exactly what I did. Unfortunately, I wound up having to backtrack a bit, since I didn't notice a small climber's trail the first time through. Once at the rappel site, I quickly geared up for the hundred-foot rappel. After the rappel, I made my way down the Cunard-Kaymoor Trail. This was definitely one of the more enjoyable legs of the race, since the trail is a very mild and mostly flat set of double-track that follows a contour high above the New River below. I knew that this was likely the last time I'd be on my feet, so I pushed pretty hard through this section, jogging just about all of it. At the tail end, I passed a team of three guys who looked pretty beat down by the course. I almost felt bad for jogging by, but I had lots more work to do if I was going to have a chance of finishing before the cutoff. I knew things were getting tight, but was still a little too far out to get an accurate measure. After a small creek crossing, I popped out at a parking lot where our bikes lay waiting.

The CP staff told me that Team Litespeed had made it to CP13 in a little over six hours, but that they had forgotten to take their maps with them. I was familiar with (or at least I thought I was familiar with) most of the terrain between 12 and 13, so I had a good idea of what was ahead. The first section took us down next to the river on an old abandoned railroad line to Thurmond. This section made for some great early-morning cruising under the canopy of trees. At Thurmond, I crossed the river and headed up a long, steep, and continuous climb up and over Beury Mountain . . . and then up just a little more. I kept moving forward and up . . . not always riding the bike, but moving nonetheless. The remaining five hundred feet of climbing turned into an exercise in self-negotiation, deal making, and interval monitoring. I'd tell myself that I'd take a water break when I made it to the top of the next rise . . . and the next.

Well, another slight navigation snafu had me riding right past the turnoff to CP13, despite seeing the road and saying, "Hmmmm, that's probably the turn as it's heading the right way and going downhill like it should be, but let's go up a little farther to be sure." Several miles later, I decided to backtrack to that road, which kicked out at the checkpoint. The staff were camped out and roasting hot dogs, which they were gracious to offer. "Let me think . . . okay I'll take twenty-seven of them." They told me the cutoff had been extended an hour from 4:00 P.M. to 5:00 P.M. It was one thirty at that time so they cut my stay short and got me back out on the course. I was still going to be very tight on time . . . and I definitely kept one eye on my watch through the entire leg.

This leg was vaguely familiar because in the 2002 race, my team had taken the same road. Actually, we screwed up in '02 and had taken the wrong road, but on this day I would reap the benefits of yesteryear's navigational error. The road is not maintained and as a result, it is actually a creekbed in some parts. The road led to a waypoint flag, which indicated the trail down to Sewell Road, another less-than-stellar washed-out road. From there it was a ride back up toward Babcock State Park, along the Narrow Gauge and Mann's Creek Gorge Trails. Although scenic, these two trails were an absolutely miserable way to finish up the race. Think technical single-track on mild hills littered with roots, rocks, and ruts everywhere. I was on and off my saddle continuously. Sprinkle in a few more nettles (just for good measure) and add a touch of dehydration. Fatigue and a case of jelly legs put me a little closer to the trail's edge on more than a couple of occasions, but I managed to keep my wheels on level dirt. After enough pushing and pulling of the bike, I kicked out onto the most wonderful road of all . . . the road to Camp Washington Carver and the finish line!

At 4:52 P.M. . . . forty hours and fifty-two minutes after we started, I finished the race with eight minutes to spare. I later learned that of the thirty teams who had set out two days earlier, four completed the pro course and only four more completed the adventure class. I was definitely happy to have survived the whole thing, but to finish as the first place soloist/third overall was a great feeling. For me it kick-started a 2004 dream season that would go on to include racing at the AR World Championships, the Subaru Primal Quest, and a victory at the Beast of the East.

Competing vs Participating

NAME: LOUISE COOPER
AGE: 51
RESIDENCE: WEST HILLS, CA
YEARS ADVENTURE RACING: 9

Photo by Tony Di Zinno

Racing has changed quite dramatically over the past few years. I fondly remember competing in this "new" type of event which involved experiencing "adventure" in a unique way, with a group of friends, requiring you to learn new skills and, above all, enjoy the journey through some exotic land. Yes, there was prize money to be awarded to the first team who completed "such journey," but it was usually so minimal when divided among five team members and crew that it was more of a bonus than an award. The prestige of crossing the line first was more appealing. The introduction of media and prize money changed the sport forevermore. The media was a necessity to get the sport acknowledged and accepted, and the prize money changed the dynamics of the teams and the perspective and motivation of racing. The courses had to be designed to look dramatic on TV, and racers were now dancing through hoops to humor the masses watching this new insane sport.

I feel fortunate that I was able to compete at a high level at the inception of adventure racing, and that I got to experience the true adventure in the sport before it became contrived and urbanized. I'm sure there is a place for all the new disciplines being added to this sport, but I like to remember the purity with which it started. I was sidelined with breast cancer for a year, and, being on the older end when AR started, I couldn't afford to miss a year, which is probably the reason I fought back so vehemently to try and reestablish myself. I know I will always be able to compete, not necessarily at the same level as a young pup, but with age comes a certain comfort and acceptance that further endorse my appreciation for what was, and the maturity to accept change and progress, even if I disapprove.

1996 Eco-Challenge, British Columbia

With emotions ranging among wild excitement, trepidation, and anxiety, Bob, Kasy, and myself left for British Columbia. Feeling pretty good about my efforts, this would be my first experience with a new team. In the previous races, I had had the luxury of just having to show up as my now ex-husband organized the logistics. Here we were three strapping Kiwi boys, one nervous American, and I, a South African expat, ready for the race of our lives. The course suited my Kiwi boys: mountains, snow, and rough terrain including hideous slide alder, seemingly placed to hinder any forward progression.

The race started with horse riding, two team members on horseback, and three runners, perfect for us, with backgrounds in running. As we noticed one teammate struggle at a horse-to-run transition, we immediately put him back on the horse while the rest of us traded off with the other horse. No words were spoken, as the eye contact we all made said it all . . . red flag! It was too early in the race to be concerned (so we thought), as we knew him to be a strong athlete with good skills.

The next bit of excitement came as we had to launch ourselves in a freezing fast-moving river that had unexpectedly swelled its banks and was now impassable by horse. Okay, so now I was the one in panic mode, the fear of being swept away gripping my heart. Not to worry as my team grabbed me and supported me across. I know I said many a prayer, along with several expletives that I'm sure managed to escape.

After a short jog over to the transition, we hurriedly packed what was needed for two solid days of trekking. Starting up a ridiculously steep hill in what seemed like Death Valley heat, we had only traveled twenty minutes when our same poor fellow keeled over, muttering curses about the heat, the weight of his pack, the stupidity of the race, the sun, the moon, the stars, and anyone (or anything) else he could think of. We immediately opened his pack to distribute his weight, and to our amazement, found an assortment of unnecessary luxuries added to his pack, including four cans of Red Bull!

We were trying a new race technique where I was to carry less weight, more proportionate to my body size. Well, that didn't last long, as I inherited an assortment of mountaineering gear, food, and mandatory gear. For two days and nights, we literally dragged this poor man up and down hills, through snow, and across rivers. He appeared to enjoy the pampering, and it wasn't hindering our progress as we forged ahead in good standing, before the welcome relief of TA2.

At this point, in spite of our laborious trek, we were in fourth place, and were feeling pretty chuffed with ourselves that we had exercised such good teamwork. We laid the poor fellow down to rest and packed his gear in ready for the next section, which was canoeing, followed by mountain biking. Mark Burnett came over to our campsite to strongly suggest that we not rest too long as it would behoove us to hit the water before dark, as there was some whitewater at the start of the paddle: two rather large rapids, to be exact. This was not exactly music to my ears.

We knew we still had several hours of daylight, but also knew that the poor fellow needed some rest. What we were not aware of was that he was mentally shutting down, showing all the classic signs of withdrawal: complaining about the conditions, questioning whether it would be wise for him to continue, doubting his abilities. Perhaps we were in denial of these signs or perhaps we were not sensitive enough to give him the permission he seemed to be desperately seeking to drop out. Quitting was an idea as foreign as icebergs in Hawaii and we never considered it to be an option at the time. Due to his fatigue, it was suggested that he get an IV. He was keen, and we all agreed, as we sat down to wait for the life-giving fluids to enter his system and work their magic. Finally, after what seemed to be days, with darkness already set in, he was given the go-ahead. We donned our life jackets and helmets, and set off for the river. A welcome relief to our competitive nature was that in all the time we were at the transition, no other teams had come in.

With strict instructions on how to navigate the first rapid (in pitch black I might add), we set off. I was sitting in the middle of the boat, Bob was in the front, and the poor fellow was in the back, after insisting he guide. Not three minutes later, we were tumbling through a rapid the size of Niagara Falls (it was probably only a Class III, but I'm telling the story!) and my heart was nowhere to be found in my body. When we emerged, we all somehow managed to grab hold of the boat. Now there we were, floating down the river in glacier meltwater, in complete darkness. Trying to hide the intense fear and anxiety I felt, I sheepishly asked Bob what he thought we should do. His answer was delivered in the same deadpan tone and with the same humor as Bob Newhart, "Louise, I'm buggered if I know!" Well, there's a practical answer that filled me with confidence!

At that point I knew we were screwed! Not thirty seconds later we hit the next rapid, and once again were swallowed by that icy water, and mercilessly tossed around and sucked under over and over before finally being spewed out in a fast-flowing current. All my whitewater safety training became very clear, as I threw my feet out in front of me and gripped my paddle like my life depended on it. I lost track of time but it seemed like three days I was floating down that frigid river before I finally felt the current slowing so my feet could touch solid ground. Slowly I was able to stand and, using my paddle, ease myself over to the embankment. A little farther down I saw a light, which turned out to be the headlamp of the poor fellow. As I crawled over toward him, still somewhat panic-stricken; it soon became very apparent that he was becoming hypothermic.

I yelled for Bob, and heard his voice coming from across the river. He had washed up on the other side. Great. We continued yelling until we established that the best thing to do was to stay put until someone came to help. I turned back to my teammate and devoted myself to keeping him warm, by rubbing his arms, making him move around, and wrapping myself around him to shelter him from the wind. This was working to keep myself warm too, so it can't be construed as any heroic act of kindness. As I sat there trying to think of something more constructive to do, I became aware that somehow I had ended up with Bob's paddle. I started to laugh as I visualized my frenzied and desperate movements under water as I must have grappled to hang on to something, anything, perhaps even Bob!

A significant amount of time later, we heard a boat coming down the river, calling our names. Neil and Scott had made it to the dam, and after we didn't arrive, they realized what must have happened and Neil pulled over, climbed up the embankment, and found a trail to run back to the TA, where he alerted the organization to our plight. There was no rescue boat (I reiterate that this was in the early days of racing!), so they commandeered a totally inadequate media boat for the rescue and came to find us. The rescue is a story of its own. Suffice it to say we made it back to the TA, where the poor fellow was put back on an IV, and we went to our tents to have a sleep. No more teams were allowed to enter the water after we left that night. They were transported down to the dam where they were then put in boats. We proved to be good guinea pigs for the race.

The next morning Neil went up in the helicopter with Mark to try and spot our boat. It had sunk along with all our gear. We were given another boat, and, after scrounging up extra mandatory gear from other support crews, we repacked new backpacks and set to continue. Twenty-three hours had passed since we had first come into the TA, and we were now in thirty-fifth place, pumped to attack the course. However, the poor fellow was giving up. He had banged up his knee, which was now developing an infection, and he was out. Could anything else go wrong? We went back to our tent for a team talk, where we looked at one another and determined the fire was still there. We were going on, ranked or not! The race was still on! We had a job to complete!

Like four possessed individuals, we hit the boats, and continued to fly through the course, laughing and joking as we picked off team after team. This was racing. We had come to do the best race we could, and were doing just that. We survived; after more overflowing icy rivers, a hellacious snowstorm (that shut the race down for twenty-four hours), a helicopter ride over the ropes that had iced up, lack of food and sleep, we crossed the finish line in eighth place, albeit unranked. There were four very satisfied racers standing with their bikes at that finish line. We came to race and we accomplished our mission. We knew what was important, and we have a wonderful finish photo that says it all.

Looking back on my adventure racing career, the difference between competing in a race and merely participating is most apparent. *Success* is a relative word with many definitions that resonate differently to different folk. Success in a race is not a guarantee. There are so many factors that determine the outcome, many of them out of our control. Every race we've entered has been affected at some stage, some with a positive outcome and some with a less favorable one.

To our team, that race epitomized competition regardless of ranking. We were thrilled beyond means with our race. Especially when compared to a race where we finished in good standing.

1997 Eco-Challenge Australia

This was going to be our race! We had unfinished business and a fire in our bellies that was going to be hard to extinguish. We had come off two races where we had finished as bridesmaids. The Raid Gauloises had robbed us of our victory with a penalty that cost us the race by an hour. We followed this with another second-place finish at the X-Venture race in Baja where we watched Eco-Internet blow by us in the last kayak to the finish. The competition would be fierce, but so was our desire.

Our five-person team had been reduced to four, a new format for Eco-Challenge, and three very determined and motivated racers showed up in Cairns, a few days earlier than required. The passion was intense, and by the time our fourth teammate showed up, we were hot to trot. I remember dismissing the comments he made, about being unprepared for this race due to work constraints. Sure. He was a Kiwi. How "unprepared" could he be? The team all lived in different parts of the country (or world for that matter) so training was a trusted given. His words came back to haunt all of us on Day 1, when it became very apparent immediately that this usually fine-tuned racer was in no condition to compete at the level required to win or at least attempt to or even stay with the big dogs.

The disbelief was intense. How could one let the team down? But, in typical Kiwi fashion, the boys pulled together to salvage what we had. Neil slung the extra pack over his shoulder like an extra fleece jacket, and off he went. One has to understand that Neil also hunts in New Zealand, and it is not uncommon for him to go tramping with a huge deer slung across his shoulders as he heads for home. He probably didn't even know he was carrying the extra pack!

The mood of the team during the race was continued optimism, but the passion and zest were missing, as we moved through the course just fast enough to stay ahead of the teams in front of us, but not fast enough to catch any teams. We weren't competing. This is not what we came to do. The frustration was building beneath the cool temperaments of the individual team members, and little was said. After all, the team is the most important aspect of the race, and it is key to support one another. But there was no getting away from the feeling we all shared.

We crossed the finish line in seventh place, a respectable finish, and all went on to enjoy the post-race festivities and camaraderie with our friends and family. It took a few days before our true emotions were able to emerge, and we were finally able to verbalize the frustration that was festering deep within. The "flat" feeling we all felt was not a post-race depression, something that is frequently felt after an event is over, but rather the disappointment of not feeling like we had accomplished our goal of competing!

We certainly did participate, and one might even say we did well, but the element of competition had been removed as we trudged along just

fast enough to maintain our position. We never really had the type of clo-
sure one needs at the culmination of an event! We didn't try, we just, well,
we just moved along. That final acknowledgment was the cathartic element that allowed us to finally let go of the feeling, and start planning for
the next event we would be competing in.

The comparison was very real to us. Winning or losing was not the key
element that drove us, but feeling like we had done the best we could rang
high. BC certainly did it for us; Cairns fell very short.

Professionalism

NAME: ADAM W. CHASE
AGE: 39
RESIDENCE: BOULDER, CO
YEARS ADVENTURE RACING: 5

Although I have raced as a "professional" adventure racer for the last five years I am only a professional in that: (a) I am able to deduct any adventure race-related expenses on my tax return without worrying that the IRS will audit me; and (b) I am a tax attorney when I'm not racing or training. Needless to say, I am also a bit nerdy.

Quickly approaching the age of forty, I am excited to have a way of giving back to a sport that has given so much to me, including allowing me to race in New Zealand, Sweden, Norway, Morocco, Argentina, Chile, and about twenty of the United States, be the captain of a USARA National Championship team, Raid World Championship, winner of the AdventureXstream Expedition, and to compete in the Raid Series and Eco Challenge.

I came to AR from ultra-distance trail running and am the co-author of The Ultimate Guide to Trail Running *and president of the All American Trail Running Association. In this essay, I share my somewhat divergent thoughts about how I got involved in the sport, the impact it has had on my life, where it has taken me, and what drives me to do it.*

Early in my adventure racing "career" I was asked to join a fully sponsored team, Team Hi-Tec. Our prospective team flew to Hi-Tec's headquarters in central California, where we were interviewed by Hi-Tec's upper management. I had come to adventure racing from an ultradistance running background that was preceded by some Ironman-distance triathlons but was new to adventure racing and, as I should have predicted, the question was soon posed, "So Adam, what qualifies you to be on Team Hi-Tec?"

I fed them the only answer that came to mind: "I grew up in Boulder, Colorado." I guess it did trick because I got to race for the team and, thus, my adventure racing went from newbie to sponsored adventure racer with almost no AR experience. I was honored to race with more weathered teammates and that such a reputable race program deemed me worthy, especially when I didn't know enough at the time to realize I probably wasn't.

Now that I've had a good crack at the sport, I've learned a lot, changed a lot, grown a lot—albeit not measured in inches—and seen some awesome places. The following is my attempt to share some of the greatest impressions and lessons I have been lucky enough to experience through the sport.

Motive for Change

My desire to pursue adventure racing had several origins. I had grown a bit complacent as an ultrarunner and although it was admittedly due to fortunate timing, I had probably done most of what I could do in the sport. Although it sounds boastful, I had won more than twenty-five ultras while setting a handful of course records in the five or six years I had been in the sport. Like Jerry Seinfeld, it is better to leave before you really begin faltering. Had I begun ultras now, I wouldn't have had a chance at such success, given the higher level of competition that currently exists. That was a good reason to turn to a new athletic pursuit.

Adventure racing was very alluring. Starting out with Hi-Tec and then Team ARgear.com, Team Oxydol, Team adidas/Salomon and, eventually, Team Salomon USA, which has allowed me to captain a team, select my own race mates, and travel throughout the world, was more than I could have ever asked for and it continues to be incredibly rewarding. I have been able to race with some of the best in the sport and win or place well in some awesome races and I feel very fortunate for that opportunity.

In comparison with other endurance athletics, like triathlon, marathon running, Nordic skiing, and mountain biking, adventure racing remains new and exciting enough that sponsorship and prize money, not to mention publicity and general media attention, are quite generous. I certainly did not get the same kind of magazine interviews, television coverage, invitations for public speaking engagements, or general attention in my triathlon or ultra days and I would be a liar if I didn't admit that the recognition is nice, even if a bit undeserved.

It seems almost unfair to me that I can be racing at the "pro" level, making money at such a fun sport while traveling on a sponsored budget to exotic venues and playing with the best of equipment, when athletes in other disciplines, athletes much younger and more talented than I, are barely eking out an existence. But I'll take it . . . and be very grateful. I'm sure a new generation of uber adventure racers will soon populate the sport, but there is a steep enough learning curve to create a buffer of a couple of years to allow those of us who are a bit more established in the sport to ride the wave a tad longer before we are dethroned in Freudian, totemic fashion.

New Identity

The funniest thing about making the change from ultra trail runner to adventure racer was the effect it had on my beloved fellow Boulderites. In Boulder a person is not defined by his or her profession but, rather, by his or her sport of choice. I had long been known as an ultra trail runner and the switch to adventure racing really threw folks, especially because few knew what an adventure racer really was.

I have found it amusing to watch friends squirm at social gatherings when they have had to introduce me to someone new. "Adam is a . . . is a . . . what is it exactly that you are doing now that you aren't running those ridiculously long distances?" Or some would just revert to calling me a tax attorney, which is an accurate moniker, being that it is what I do when I'm not training or racing and would be how I'd be introduced almost anywhere else in the world.

A Team Sport

Regardless of the fun of identity confusion, it wasn't the glitz factor that really drew me to adventure racing. It was the team aspect that provided a renewed fervor and passion for athletic pursuits that I found so addictive. I had lost some drive in my running and snowshoeing and although I still loved both endeavors, I just didn't care that much about pushing my limits or "hurting" anymore because I felt I had proved what I had wanted to and now it was just for fun.

That doesn't work very well in adventure racing because you have a whole team to care about, especially from the captain's perspective. I am not sure if the motivation comes from the fear of slowing my team down or whether it emanates from the desire to be strong enough to tow or carry extra weight, but adventure racing infused a whole new vitality into my training and race psyche.

It didn't hurt that I was lucky enough to be on teams that frequently won or were at least in the chase, but it counts so much more to impress your teammates than it does to raise the eyebrows of others. Only your teammates know the real truth, and to earn their respect is priceless.

You share so much with the members of your team and the bonds that you create are strong enough that it is difficult to explain to those outside the sport except, perhaps, soldiers who served together in combat situations. I only know this because I've raced with teammates who have fought in some tough battles in Afghanistan and Iraq and they have confirmed that theory. Sharing such heightened sensations and trusting your life in the hands of a teammate is not something you typically do with co-workers or social buddies and the depth of understanding you develop is unsurpassed, assuming the race experiences are mutually positive.

When one of my teammates fell during a rappel in a race in Utah, jerking to a halt after sixty feet of free fall and then slamming into a rock face with only thirty feet of rope separating her from what would have been imminent death, it was overwhelming to see how well our team pulled together in helping to get her out of the backcountry to a trailhead where a waiting ambulance took us all to the hospital. We kept her calm and helped to carry her and light the way down the dark trail. My other teammate managed to recall our fallen teammate's exact address and birth date as we checked her into the hospital and then, after some stitches and X-rays, she rallied to joke and laugh, despite her obvious pain and post-trauma emotions. We were a team, regardless of the outcome. We had raced together in countless situations and continued to race for a whole season after that. Our fondness for one another remains just as strong, and even though we haven't raced together in almost two years, we still keep in close touch and try to get together for a run or a ride just because we like each other so much and have so much deep history.

The team dynamics of adventure racing have always been fascinating to me and I have come to learn that the choice of race mates is one of the most important aspects of the sport. To build a team that has the requisite skills, with an ace navigator, a badass woman, and a workhorse who could tow or carry extra loads, is important, but more crucial than that is to recruit people who can keep it all in perspective and race for the joy of the sport.

All too often I have seen teams who have failed to align the individuals' goals so that one racer is in it to win, another to just participate, and yet another to go until it gets difficult and then come up with an excuse to stop. Those teams invariably fall apart, even when each member is an excellent athlete in his or her own right.

To me, a sense of humor is probably the most important quality in a teammate and I have learned from experience that a team that is laughing together will almost always race better and faster than one that is bickering. Adventure racing plays an important role in my life, but it is not important enough that I would do it if it weren't fun, and for me it is only fun if I enjoy my teammates.

Athletic Diversity

The new athletic disciplines were also tremendously alluring to me as I began adventure racing and it was exciting to observe my body's adaptations to sports that I had only dabbled in prior to adventure racing, disciplines like mountain biking, ropes activities, and kayaking and canoeing. The diversity in my training regimen was a treat and I found I could add more hours of play without suffering an injury as long as I rotated different muscle groups.

Almost any type of training counts toward making you a better adventure racer, even going out late and dancing until the wee hours the night before a long day of training so you can get more used to the challenge of sleep deprivation and the toll it exacts on your body. One time my teammate for my Eco-Challenge team and I rode our mountain bikes a hundred miles over a couple of mountain passes, leaving our hometown in the early evening and arriving at a resort town at around five in the morning. From there we had volunteered to assist in a mountain marathon and trekked to an aid station at twelve thousand feet above sea level. After fulfilling that duty we swept half the course and removed the route markings as we made our way wearily back to the race finish. It was a perfect arduous training day.

Given the fact that adventure racers need to be competent at so many disciplines, including trail running, mountain biking, paddling, in-line skating, and ropes activities, building and maintaining core strength is probably the most important aspect of a training regimen. Fortunately, just doing a lot of those sports will help serve that end, but daily abdominal exercises, like crunches and leg lifts, helps supplement the cause.

I have gotten in a bit of trouble when I give racing clinics and tell relative newbies that the most effective training program for adventure racing is to intentionally "overtrain" to the point where you teeter on the brink of injury . . . or total physical and emotional exhaustion. I call it "stress management," and if the goal of most athletic training is to prepare the body for a race by simulating race situations, then heavy workloads—at least at your relative, individual level—will help you adjust to the rigors of racing, especially if you are gearing up for a race that is twenty-four hours or longer.

Marathoners do long runs to train for their event, so why wouldn't you try to thrust your body into heavy fatigue mode and then push yourself even more during long training sessions as a way to mimic the burden you will bear during a race? You don't, of course, want to break yourself down to the point of injury or where you are doing pure junk miles, but such stress management allows your body to recruit its recovery systems while on the fly, rather than when you are immobile. I try to do this and then, about two months before a bigger race or more important part of my season, I'll ease back a bit on the volume and get a bit more rest while increasing the intensity of shorter sessions that tweak some speed and increased fitness into my aching body. Rest is not my forte, but I've been told it would greatly enhance my performance. I usually tell people that I'll rest when I'm dead and that I'll be dead a long time.

Life Skills

Unlike sports like bowling, golf, and cricket, adventure racing offers its participants some real skills that apply to regular life. These are, in fact, the skills they teach at summer camp and in corporate training sessions. Honing one's orienteering and navigational abilities is life enhancing. Improving your ability to function in a team environment so that you are better at teamwork is priceless. Through adventure racing people improve their communication skills, force themselves to be more realistic, learn to better deal with failure, and, perhaps most importantly, find that their limits were beyond the limits they had previously believed were "it."

I have enjoyed the fact that the sport has also pushed me to focus on my organizational and planning abilities while forcing me to be more selective in picking teammates. Where I used to be somewhat laissez-faire and trusting that all people were disciplined, fun, and honest with themselves, I've had to become more discerning and caring when it comes to matching team personalities in attempting to orchestrate the right dynamics for performance and enjoyment. I have learned the hard way that some people will lie to themselves about their own abilities in order to get on a team and it has always shocked me that anyone would purposefully get on a team where they were sure to be the anchor, regardless of the discipline. I still don't understand that one.

Sponsorship

One thing that is crucial to succeeding in adventure racing, at least at an elite and national or international level, is securing sponsorship. Given the extremely high cost of entry fees, travel, support, equipment, and the amount of time away from work, it is almost impossible for an unfunded team to make it for more than a season before any normal savings accounts would be depleted or credit cards maxed. Granted, there is some good prize money in the sport, but I can't recall a time when an unsponsored team actually won prize money.

Getting sponsored or finding a spot on a sponsored team is just as difficult as racing well and my only advice on this front is to approach the challenge from the perspective that you are selling something and you need your potential customer to understand that they want to buy what you have to offer. Rather than coming at it with the "will you sponsor me" attitude, if you can be impressive enough that you can say "here is what I can do for you," you will be much more likely to hook a sponsor or two. Then, of course, once you have something on the line and can afford to enter some races, the best thing you can do is to rack up some impressive wins.

Dealing with sponsors should be a mixture of friendly relationship and job. I have always enjoyed interactions with sponsors and am amused by the fact that my teammates and I have tended to be more frustrated by sponsors that don't "use" us other than to send us to great races in beautiful places. Rewarding sponsorship relationships are those where the sponsors are enthusiastically following a team's performance, hiring photographers to document the races and then using the footage for advertisements and athlete slide shows at clinics.

There are some athletes who have come to adventure racing from other professional sports, but many of us have found adventure racing to be the first place where we are treated so well. I have raced with a few prima donnas who seemed ungrateful for all that their sponsor provided, but for the most part adventure athletes appreciate every pair of shoes, every jacket, every airplane ticket, every meal, and every hotel room they get, and that certainly goes far with sponsors. Giving back to your sponsors by providing race reports, copies of media coverage, team pictures in sponsor gear, and by spreading the good word through clinics or merely by telling your friends and family, means a lot, and the more you can do the better.

The Goal

I have yet to figure out what my real objective is in adventure racing or how and when I want to get off this merry-go-round that has taken me to so many wonderful race venues. There are some of the obvious things like the prize money, the trophies, the stories I've been able to tell my young sons, the television coverage that old friends from high school happen to watch, and the magazine articles that have brought me notoriety with my clients, but those don't get me up and running when I'm dead tired.

Nor am I really motivated by winning the national championship, qualifying for the world championships, being named a top team in AR rankings, or the like. No, I would have to say it boils down to the relationships I've forged while racing and the lessons I've learned. I have thoroughly enjoyed being out there in some of the most impressive of places, hammering it out to my body's limits with the finest of company. From that I've been taught that there is a thin line between the fear of failure and the yearning for approval.

I've struggled internally over whether I'm doing this to prove something to myself. Are we just a bunch of insecure overachievers trying to justify our existence, striving to show something tangible for the years of "work," the thousands of hours of seemingly selfish pleasure seeking in our training and racing? Was this really worth spending so much time away from my sons as they went from infants to toddlers to little boys? Those are hard questions and the answers are all the more difficult when you are struggling on your third or fourth day into an expedition race on a different continent, hanging by a sleep-deprived thread as your addled body is on the verge of unconsciousness due to hypothermia.

There is, of course, the pure pleasure of racing and training, the basking in the glow of a mountain you've just run, ridden, or otherwise befriended. And then there is the question of *Why not?* I have always subscribed to the *live without regrets* philosophy and thus far I feel confident I have chosen the right path, but adventure racing has taught me to question everything and so, like any good student, I have to turn that inquisitiveness against my teacher too.

Tapering
by Robert Nagle

Adventure races come with their own built-in taper schedule.

A week of crazed packing,

last-minute calls to obtain obscure pieces of mandatory gear,

saying goodbye to your spouse,

explaining to your kids why you'll be away for a month,

paying gazillions of bills,

painting the house (hey—you promised),

realizing your passport will expire while you're away and getting it
   renewed,

double time at your job to get everything you committed to completed,

last-minute shots (inoculations, that is, though you crave the others),

followed by

two days of sitting around airports,

arguing with the oh-so-friendly-people of the quite-unfriendly-skies,

desperately repacking at the ticket desk to meet weight restrictions with an
   increasingly hostile queue behind you,

grousing about all the excess baggage payments,

cramming your body into a narrow tube with 280 others for twelve hours
   or more,

begging for second or third meals at every serving,

watching Discovery reruns in Thai about how glorious these events are

missing your connection and spending an extra night sleeping on stone
   waiting for the next one,

finding the 50 percent of your baggage that didn't arrive with you,

nervously watching the gangs of teenagers with AK-47s who are patrolling
   the airport,

sleeping on the airport tarmac atop your bags awaiting someone to collect
   you,

trying to explain in Zairois what a fi-fi hook is and why you desperately
   need one,

returning to the airport for your missing baggage,

returning to the airport for the one or two of your teammates who missed their connections,

returning for *their* lost luggage,

more desperate trips around town describing the aforementioned fi-fi hook to bewildered locals and trying to buy one (ha!) then have one made (much easier), then trying to make it meet Mark Burnett's specs (nice try—buy one from the Swedes instead—they have two of everything),

wanting to eat the local food but being a conscientious team player and abstaining so you won't get ill

trying to live on PowerBars and AlpineAire,

sneaking a fried banana at the market,

visiting the porcelain throne (again and again and again . . .)

catching up with all those amazing people you haven't seen in twelve months,

two days of disapproving looks from the technical crews of the race organization ("You read that Eco-Internet once got away with baling twine instead of a climbing rope, go away and get a real rope")

buying a piece-of-shit rope that amazingly has a UIAA tag even though it looks like it wouldn't hold your dog (the tag, not surprisingly, looks even older than the rope :-) and paying a mere four hundred bucks for it,

another quick dash to the porcelain throne,

trying to build a packing case,

sleeping on top of your luggage again ('cause your bed is buried someplace beneath it),

nattering till 4:00 A.M. with that French guy with whom you shared a plastic bag in New Zealand last year,

trying to avoid the press (or desperately seeking them out, depending),

at last a chance to sleep—the opening ceremonies and race briefing :-)

what, what, I was dozing, we gotta do the maps now?

more crazed packing

six hours or more so crunched over the maps you can't stand up straight,

a sixteen-hour truck drive down dusty roads in 125-degree heat, thinking you can doze until you're projected a couple of feet into the air at every pothole (again and again and again)

clamoring for the truck to stop (damn that fried banana),

crawling into a bivy in the pouring rain to sleep for ninety minutes before the start.

Enjoy your taper—I know I've loved all of mine.

Testosterone-Crazed Young Males: One of Adventure Racing's Greatest Challenges

NAME: CATHY TIBBETTS
AGE: 50
RESIDENCE: FARMINGTON, NM
YEARS ADVENTURE RACING: 7

Photo by Marc Witkes

Like many adventure racers, I came into the sport in a rather round-about way. I had long been a runner and by the early 1990s, I had discovered trail running. I live in northern New Mexico, in an area I consider to be one of the most beautiful places in the country, and endless miles of high desert single-track start right out my back door. Every time I went out, I ran farther and farther—I just wanted to see more and more. In 1995, I ran my first ultramarathon, the Monument Valley fifty-miler, and finished as the first overall female. I was hooked on the sport.

Over the next few years, I ran marathons and ultramarathons all over the world. I ran the Antarctica Marathon and was the first female finisher. I also ran the Himalayan 100 Mile Stage Race, the Western States 100 Mile Endurance Run, and the Marathon des Sables multiday stage race across the Sahara Desert five different times. Unfortunately, all this mileage eventually took its toll and I developed a few injuries. I wanted to find other fun sports to do when I was unable to run and as a result, I started to mountain bike and kayak.

Adventure racing seemed to be the perfect way to combine my love for ultrarunning with my newfound interests in biking and paddling. Since I didn't know any adventure racers in the local area, I got online, found a team looking for a female racer, and competed in my first adventure race. I had a blast and, like ultrarunning, I got into adventure racing in a big way. Over the next few years, I successfully competed in a number of Hi-Tec and Balance Bar races, the Beast of the East, several of the Four Winds races, the Primal Quest, and the Eco-Challenge.

There are many things I love about adventure racing—the physical and mental challenges, the exotic and pristine locales, and the teamwork needed to be successful. For the most part, I have been extremely lucky to have great rapport with my teammates. As a matter of fact, some of the guys I've raced with are so much fun to be with that it seemed like we laughed our way through the entire race. Unfortunately, I have also been on a few teams where things just didn't "click." Talk about a miserable experience! Invariably, this negative team dynamic was caused by what I call "Testosterone-Crazed Young Males"—in my opinion, one of adventure racing's greatest challenges. As I think about some of my encounters with these hormonally overcharged athletes, I can't help but remember a few particular races that are forever etched in my mind.

"It's all your fault we're lost," Dick screamed at us. "I don't want to be here."

Even in the midnight blackness of the frigid canyon I could see veins bulging in his neck.

"I strive for excellence in everything I do," he raged. "You guys are nothing but adventure tourists."

Except for Dick, we were all seasoned adventure racers with countless top finishes to our credit. Dick had done two short races solo and had never finished a long one. (Not his fault, of course.) Still, he knew he'd be in the lead if it weren't for us.

"If I ever end up on a team like this again, I am quitting the first day." Dick was shouting at the top of his lungs, but by Night 4 of our event, those of us on Team KIVA were used to him. In his twenties and the youngest person on our team, he was the biggest obstacle we had in getting to the finish line.

"That team we passed is so slow it embarrasses me to even *look* at them," he sneered.

Dick had complained to other teams that we were too old for his excellence. He complained to me that teammate Zach was a fat know-it-all. Steve didn't know how to navigate and he wouldn't have blisters if he would just make his mind up to not have them. (His theory was true for poison oak as well.) I never knew what he said about me, the forty-nine-year-old 120-pound team female (mandatory gear), but I'm sure I got slammed the worst. Gender and age are factors that work against you in adventure racing. Except it's not my gender and age that are the problem—it's those of the testosterone-crazed young male. The fact that I was a nationally ranked distance runner with numerous wins and a course record made no difference. "We're not on the same page," Dick accused me with disgust. I had to agree with that one.

Now, I'm married to a much younger man and am testosterone's biggest fan. But somehow, in adventure racing, the sweetest men can morph into teammates from hell the minute the starting gun fires. Most of them are in their twenties and regard their male teammates as just as unworthy as the females.

Jeff Stewart, a thirty-seven-year-old policeman from Scottsdale, Arizona, did his first expedition-length adventure race on a team with me, Ray, and a testosterone-crazed young male named Peter. After the race, Jeff confided that he took the race preparation quite seriously. For months he got up at 4:00 A.M. so he could get workouts in before and after work. Jeff believed it was necessary because he'd be racing with a stud. After all, Peter kept telling him how incredibly strong he was.

However, by the second day of the race, Jeff realized that Peter was totally unprepared and didn't know what he was doing. Jeff went on to describe how "we had to help him on the ropes plus do all the bike repair and navigating. We even ran out of food for a day because he assured us there was some store along the way that didn't exist. Then he had the nerve to blame us for losing his sponsor. And he got a letter printed on the race website saying that next year he'd be back with a serious team. At that point I told my teammates, "You're gonna have to stop me or I'm going after him." "The good thing," Jeff reflected, "was that because of Peter, the rest of us bonded and have raced together ever since."

The testosterone-crazed young male is oblivious when his three teammates continue to race together and find somebody to replace him. He remains steadfast in his conviction that he will soon lead a team of *real* athletes on to victory, digging deep down to overcome the limits of human endurance and return home with a true understanding of all mankind. And maybe even fend off a mob of reporters at the airport. My friend, Maureen Moslow-Benway, a forty-two-year-old racer and mother of three, had the same experience with a teammate from her first Eco-Challenge.

Maureen told me how her team had put the word out that they were looking for somebody with strong water navigation and sailing skills. She added that "Johnson claimed to be ex-Special Forces and extremely strong in those areas. As a matter of fact, he told us he was an accomplished athlete in all areas—there was absolutely nothing he couldn't do. Unfortunately, by the time we figured out he wasn't what he said he was, it was too late—the Eco-Challenge was a month away and none of our alternates could go."

Maureen added that "It was one thing that he couldn't navigate or mountain bike well, but he wouldn't listen to anybody. For example, one time we needed to find a checkpoint on a nearby island. We were paddling toward an island that had several competitors' boats coming and going, plus the Eco-Challenge support helicopter was on the shore. We told Johnson that island was the checkpoint (which it was), yet he *still* insisted that it wasn't and screamed at us for not trusting his navigation skills. The tension he created was incredible and as a result, by the end of the race we all had negative feelings about the experience, despite the fact we performed well.

"Even after the race he wasn't done with us," Maureen continued. "The following year we were doing a radio talk show about our next Eco-Challenge on DC 101, the biggest rock station in the Washington, DC, metro area. Johnson heard the show and called in to say that he had raced with us before and we were nothing but a 'bunch of bozos.' He never really got it that the three of us were returning to do the next Eco-Challenge and he wasn't."

While lifelong bonding is the upside of racing with a teammate that everyone hates, it won't happen when you're outnumbered by testosterone crazed young males, which happened to me in a race in Page, Arizona, several years ago.

I had never met Randy and Bob, but they were always online offering enthusiastic advice on the AR forums. Bob even claimed to be an ex-Navy SEAL, expert in water navigation. Bob was so good, in fact, he didn't need to use the map. It remained in the bottom of his pack for the entire race and there was no wrestling it away from him. He was a strong enough paddler, which was a good thing because, 1) Randy held his paddle upside down with his pinkie fingers in the air, and 2) Bob couldn't find any of the checkpoints so we spent all day paddling up and down Lake Powell.

That afternoon I was relieved to see a woman waving at us from the shore. She had a clipboard. There was a boat nearby belonging to the race organization and some competitor boats were on the beach. I was flabbergasted when he paddled in the other direction.

"That's not the checkpoint," Bob announced.

Hours of paddling later we made it back to the lady with the clipboard. (She, too, had been flabbergasted to see us paddle away.) From there, we needed to head south to an eight-hundred-foot rappel. I noticed that for some time we had been heading into the sunset and suggested that contrary to what Bob's finely honed instincts were telling him, I didn't think we were heading south. Bob accused me of being grouchy. But we did change direction.

We were in second-to-last place when we hit a bottleneck at the ropes with all of the teams waiting. The ropes course wasn't going to happen and race organizers were frantically trying to find another way for the event to continue. I was kind of hoping the whole world wouldn't notice how long it took us to get there. But they all looked our way when Randy screamed, "We are *kicking ass!* We're positioning ourselves to win!"

That was it for me. We didn't finish the race. We never spoke again. And I totaled my SUV on the way home.

At least it was only for a weekend. Elise Harrington, a forty-seven-year-old U.S. Rogaine Champion and one of the strongest women I have ever met, ended up spending a week at an Eco-Challenge with three testosterone-crazed young males.

"It was the highest place I have ever finished in a race," Elise said. "But it was on the most dysfunctional team I have ever been on and it was the least fun I have ever had."

Elise went on to describe how everyone had a problem with everyone. Nobody would share food. Nobody would share water. Woody took a swing at John when he bought five bags of chips and refused to share them. "During the first few days of the race I spent all of my money buying them food," she said. "Their cash was always buried in their packs. In the middle of the race, I was out of money and asked Woody to buy me some food. He refused, saying he might need his money later. I had to borrow money from a race photographer," Harrington said. "That could have gotten us disqualified.

"But the worst time for me was in the middle of a hot afternoon and they wanted to pass Team Malaysia," she continued. "They wouldn't let up and I was on the verge of a bonk. I knew from my bike racing days when to back off. If I rested for ten or fifteen minutes I'd be okay. If I didn't stop, I'd hit the point of no return. They wouldn't listen. Finally I couldn't put my foot in front of me and stopped to rest for ten minutes. Well, here they are former Navy SEALs and they left me!" Elise exclaimed. "They aren't supposed to leave anybody behind.

"I got some water from another team. Then I passed the Malaysian team who had stopped from heat exhaustion. An hour later I caught up with my team. They were resting in the shade.

" 'Elise, we're stopping here for several hours because Woody has heat exhaustion,' John said. 'He has it and it could be serious.'

"I was so angry. They had only done one short adventure race and had no idea what they were doing. Their idea of helping somebody was to yell 'Come on.' The one time they carried my stuff, they ate my food. Instead of stepping up to help the person who was struggling, they would all take a step back. It was the most miserable seven days I have ever taken vacation time for."

After the race Harrington checked into a different hotel.

"None of us has spoken since. Two of them were best friends before the race and they still aren't talking to each other."

The testosterone-crazed young male is not to be deterred by the lack of verbal communication. After Jeff Stewart, Ray, and I rid ourselves of Peter, he sent us hate letters. Mine was three pages single-spaced; Ray's was six. He itemized every single thing that we all did to ruin his brilliant adventure racing career. Except I wondered what race he was even talking about—it sounded nothing like the one that I had just been at.

Ray got his hate letter the same day and it wasn't long before the phone rang.

"Did this stuff actually happen?" Ray asked. "It is so full of half-truths, exaggerations, and lies. I am beginning to wonder if I am the crazy one."

Ray, Jeff, and I have been racing together ever since. With jobs and family commitments, sometimes we just can't get together and we end up racing with strangers. Sometimes they work out, sometimes they don't. But we were strangers when we first landed on a team together and it was a winning combination. The wonderful friendships that evolve from adventure racing are well worth weeding through the testosterone-crazed young males.

Besides, there is hope for them. They grow up.

Several years after Elise Harrington's ordeal at the Eco-Challenge, she ran into Woody at another race.

"He was a few years older," Harrington said. "And now he had done a few races.

"I wasn't even sure he was going to speak to me," she continued. "But he came up to me and said, 'I never gave you credit for how good you were at that race. I had nothing to compare you to at the time. I apologize for that and wanted to let you know.'

"That really made me feel good," Elise said, "despite everything that had happened."

I had the same experience with Dick the year after we raced together.

"That's too bad things ended the way they did," he said. "I was really an asshole."

I'd still never race with him again. But it's nice to know that the light eventually comes on with these guys. And then they'll get to race with testosterone-crazed young males themselves.

The Family that Plays Together, Stays Together: An Interview with America's Most Renowned Adventure Racing Couple

NAME: TRACYN THAYER
AGE: 35
RESIDENCE: BETHEL, ME
YEARS ADVENTURE RACING: 9

NAME: NORM GREENBERG
AGE: 38
RESIDENCE: BETHEL, ME
YEARS ADVENTURE RACING: 8

L to R: Norm Greenberg, Jon Wilkinson, Tracyn Thayer

What is your athletic background?

Tracyn: I was born and raised in Maine and grew up hiking and canoeing all over New England, particularly in the White Mountains of New Hampshire. These outings instilled in me a lifelong love of the outdoors and a fascination with mountains. This ultimately led me to attend college at the Colorado School of the Mines and in 1991, I earned a degree in geophysical engineering. After a three-year stint working for an oil well service company, I quit my high-paying job to take a much less lucrative, but far more rewarding position at the Nantahala Outdoor Center (NOC) in North Carolina. From that point forward, my focus has been on quality of life.

Norm: I was born and raised in Baltimore, Maryland, and grew up canoeing and hiking as a Boy Scout. I attended college at Cornell, where I became heavily involved in rock climbing. After earning a degree in anthropology, I went to work for the Hurricane Island Outward Bound School in Newry, Maine, where I led backpacking, winter camping, and canoeing trips throughout the Northeast. After five years at Outward Bound, I joined the Peace Corps and served in Togo, West Africa, before joining Tracyn at the NOC in 1995.

How did you meet and become a couple?

Tracyn: In 1993, I was working in Louisiana as a geophysical engineer
and happened to be visiting my grandmother near Bethel, Maine, for the
holidays. On Christmas Eve, my best friend from high school and I ven-
tured to the local pub, the Sunday River Brewing Company, for some
microbrews. We caught up on each other's lives and chatted about high
school days skiing at Sunday River Ski Resort. After a couple of beers, we
were about to call it a night, when our waitress informed us that she was
going home, and "Norm" (we didn't actually know his name at this point)
would now be waiting on us. Well, once we saw our new waiter, we decided to order a pitcher of beer! My friend and I joked about how we hoped
he was old enough to drink the beer he was serving (in Maine you only
need to be seventeen to serve, twenty-one to drink), and we were the first
to admit that we were totally checking him out. We nearly finished the
pitcher before calling it a night, making sure to leave a fat tip, so he'd
remember us for one reason or another.

Fast-forward to the next day . . . my friend and I were skiing, and it was
frigid. The wind was blowing with gusts up to sixty miles an hour, and the
wind chill hovered around twenty to forty below. Needless to say, we'd take
one run, go inside, drink hot chocolate, go out for another run, and then
repeat. Soon, we started drinking beer instead of hot chocolate (and bad
beer at that!). Eventually, we decided to head back to the brewery for some
food and better beer. As we were about to leave, Norm appeared, apparently arriving for his shift. The couple of beers in my system had given me
enough guts to approach him—although, by Norm's account, he
approached me. Norm said something to the effect of "you're here again,"
to which I replied something witty like "yes." Then we introduced ourselves to each other. I said, "I'm Tracyn, like the paper" (tracing paper),
and he said "my name is Norm, the standard by which all other things are
measured." We then each independently kicked ourselves for saying such
goofy things. Thankfully, we discovered (a significant time later) that we
were each in such "la-la, goo-goo land" about each other that neither of us
remembered those dorky analogies for our names.

We made plans to meet after he got off work, around 11:00 *p.m.* or so.
I went to my grandmother's house and waited until I could return to meet
Norm. I wondered if I'd made a big mistake, or if he would just blow me

off. When I arrived back at the brewpub, Norm was nowhere to be seen. After a brief bit of feeling like a fool, I asked another waitress if she knew if Norm was there. He was back in the kitchen doing side work—thank God! He finally came out and we sat in a booth and began talking. Norm was working part time at the brewpub, and at a ski shop since it wasn't very busy during the winter at the Hurricane Island Outward Bound School. I instantly fell head over heels, and wondered how I'd ever get back on a plane in a few days and continue my life in Louisiana. We talked late into the night, and I called my dad at my grandmother's to let them know I wasn't coming home. I knew Norm was the one when we "slept" together that first night, but agreed to wait on the sex, so as not to confuse the youthful rush of hormones with any real, more mature, significant feelings.

How did you become involved in adventure racing?

Tracyn: In 1996, we were both working for the NOC, in western North Carolina. A friend and co-worker of ours, Julie Dauphine, was on a military team for the British Columbia Eco-Challenge. While up in Vermont doing a mountain training session with her team, Julie met another team that was in search of a female member. She suggested me, and after taking a complicated event, and making it sound amazingly simple (in less than two minutes), I agreed to let her pass my name on to the team captain. Several weeks later, I traveled to Whitefish, Montana, for two weeks to tryout for the team. I passed their inspection and before I knew it found myself at the starting line that following August watching Mark Burnett ascend to the top of a yellow Land Rover, and give us the countdown to the start over a megaphone. Norm joined the team as a member of the support crew, and we experienced the Eco-Challenge from different angles, but together.

Norm: In 1998, with a lot of passion and a desire to make the sport of adventure racing more accessible than the Eco-Challenge, we brought the idea of a thirty-hour race for teams of three to our employer. In March 1999, we directed our first adventure race at the NOC. By 2001, the program had grown to an Endurance Series, an eight-hour AR, the thirty-hour AR, as well as clinics and a four-day Adventure Racing School.

Then, in early 2001, we were asked by Geoff Hunt and Pascale Lorre of Southern Traverse in New Zealand to direct a qualifier for the newly established Discovery Channel World Championship. We brought the idea of hosting the qualifier to the NOC, and after much back and forth about it, the NOC decided not to host the event. So in March 2001, we established Racing Ahead, Inc., and began directing adventure races for ourselves. Our first project was the Appalachian Extreme, a seventy-eight-hour race in western North Carolina, and to some extent, the rest is history.

Tracyn: Three years later, we are now based out of Bethel, Maine, and put on six events—the six-hour Discover Portland (Maine) Urban Adventure Race, the twelve-to-twenty-four-hour New England AR Series, and the three-plus-day AR World Championship Qualifier, the Appalachian Extreme. Having our own company has definitely tested our relationship in many new ways, since we spend literally every hour with each other on most days. And although we have our moments at times, overall we have a good division of responsibilities. Plus, the luxury of having our son, Dylan, with us every day in the office is something we'll never be able to put a price tag on!

What was the first race you did together?

Tracyn: The first race we actually competed in together was the Eco-Challenge in Cairns, Australia, in 1997. We raced with two of our former teammates from the British Columbia Eco-Challenge. That year, the team format went from five to four and I had convinced the guys that Norm would surely be an asset to the team.

As we approached the starting line, we decided as a team that we would *not* run from the start, but would pace ourselves instead, knowing we had many days of racing ahead of us. The gun went off, and lo and behold Norm took off, definitely the victim of adrenaline, nerves, and a lack of experience, although I must admit that the rest of us only had one race under our belts. Night fell, and Norm sort of hit the wall. I pulled him down a poor-quality dirt road in the middle of the Australian Outback by his trekking pole, wondering if I'd overestimated his ability. But as night turned to day, Norm rallied, and we realized that was the first time he'd actually stayed awake all night and once he knew he could do it, he was fine. He raced well from then on, and after that first night, the entire team was on an equal playing field.

How long and how many races have you done together?

Norm: 1997 marked the start of our racing together and since then, we've completed over twenty races together.

Have you ever raced separately? If so, do you prefer to race together?

Tracyn: When we first started racing, it was readily apparent that there are many more opportunities (and demands) for female adventure racers, and I definitely used this to my advantage to get more races under my belt. But in 1998, we made the conscious decision to compete together, even if it compromised the number of races I was able to do. We thought it was more important to have adventure racing experiences together than to tell each other about our experiences.

What is it like racing with your spouse?

Norm: It's a great experience. Each of us can share and simultaneously undergo the same intense experiences with someone we care deeply about. I don't have to try to explain it to her afterward. We know each other so well and we can push each other harder when we are racing and training. We easily see through each other's excuses, but also know when the other is really hurting or needs help, and how to best provide assistance. I know Tracyn's strengths and weaknesses, and she knows mine. We can rely on each other for picking up on little signs and we cover each other's back at a level that only comes from being a couple away from the racecourse.

Tracyn: I agree that it's been a great experience. I've grown to love and respect Norm even more from racing with him. I continue to be amazed at his ingenuity and resourcefulness in times of problem solving. I am often thankful I don't have to say a word, and Norm knows how I'm feeling—good or bad. He will grab my pack without saying a word, or let me take his without any sort of macho *I'm the man* attitude about it. Frankly, I can't imagine being an adventure racer and not having Norm involved. I think it would cause a huge rift in our relationship. Instead, it's an activity and a part of our lives that is uniquely ours, and it didn't exist for either of us before we were a couple.

How has being a couple helped you in races?

Norm: In adventure racing, it's all about efficiency, and the fact that we don't have to guess how each other is doing helps the team as a whole. It's rare that both of us are down at once, and the one who's up can help the one who's down with limited energy spent on analyzing the other's status. Some of our teammates have had some reservations about racing with us, until they have done so. We believe that we do a good job of not making any of the less positive issues of our relationship issues for the team as a whole. We have worked really hard to keep them separate.

Tracyn: I remember a time during the Australian Eco-Challenge when we were nearing the coast, on the approach to the final sea kayak leg. It was dark, and a river section of paddling had been canceled due to an abundance of crocodile sightings, so we were mainly following the course of the river by trekking across fields and roads. At one point, we had to cross a railroad bridge with ties that were about one foot apart, leaving plenty of view (even in the dark) into the supposedly crocodile-infested river below. The bridge freaked me out, so I asked Norm to hold my hand and walk with me across it. He dutifully accepted, and I was very thankful that I didn't have to admit being afraid to my other teammates. I don't think I ever would have asked a typical teammate to do that, and was relieved I had Norm.

Norm: Tracyn always knows when I'm sucking wind. The first night of the Primal Quest we were fastpacking through Telluride on our way back to the top of the ski resort, and I kept falling behind. Tracyn came back and simply said, "Hold on to my trekking pole, I'll pull you." And with no hesitation, I took it.

Tracyn: Norm is also instrumental in helping me get through bike-whacking, by far one of my least favorite elements in an adventure race. As soon as my bike ends up on my shoulder and I'm trekking with my bike shoes, I begin to exploit my four-letter-word vocabulary (which I don't use much in nonrace situations). Norm knows instantly that I'm about to chuck my bike down a slope, over a tree, through the bushes, or do something else, that in the long run, does me no good. He will remind me that (a) we can't afford a new bike for me, and (b) cussing isn't really doing any good, and another team may hear us. Usually, I calm down and just look at the section as another obstacle to get through. Then I apologize to my bike and dream about riding on unobstructed, huge-shouldered pavement. Additionally, in adventure races, the longer the race, the less inhibited racers become, and being a couple has certainly helped us in this department. For example, we raced together in the Endorphin Fix one year as a two-person team and made the mistake of not carrying an extra pair of shorts to hike in. After twenty-four hours in our hot, wet, sweaty bike shorts, we were hiking in the heat of the New River Gorge. To put it bluntly, I needed some crotch relief, so I pulled my bike shorts down around my thighs and let things "air out." Norm turned around to see me and asked, "What the heck are you doing?" I replied, "It feels good, you should try it," and before I knew it, I heard a long "aahhhh." We hiked like that for quite some time.

Norm: And let's not forget the 2001 Beast of the East when we were hiking to the final paddling leg and came to a big river crossing. Tracyn and I were determined not to get completely soaked, so despite the chilly temperatures, we took our clothes off, put them in dry bags, and made our way to the edge of the river. First, however, we had to check into the checkpoint, and we did so, nonchalantly, with our pack straps as our only "cover" (PFDs were not required). The CP staff pretended (or maybe they were also too sleep deprived) not to notice, and signed us in and out.

What have been some of your most positive experiences?

Norm: We have been able to travel to so many amazing places, share awesome cultural experiences, learn new skills, and conquer seemingly insurmountable challenges—all of them together! Plus having won the Beast of the East in the two-, three-, and four-person category and having competed in all of the AR world's "'big races" (Raid Gauloises, Elf Authentic Adventure, world championship in Switzerland, Southern Traverse, several Eco-Challenges, Primal Quest, and Expedition BVI) are pretty cool accomplishments that we have experienced together.

Conversely, how has being a couple presented problems?

Tracyn: The only problems we ever have seem to occur just before and just after the event. Before an event, we tend to lose patience with each other and take the race preparation stress out on each other. Frankly, there have been a few times when we questioned if the way we treated each other was worth doing the event. But thankfully, the stress would pass, and we would return to focusing on the goal of performing our best for the race. Similarly, because racing is so much about being efficient, oftentimes when a race is completed, it takes some time to get back to what I call our polite "talk"—the pleases and thank yous. It may sound a little silly, but we are so focused during an adventure race on the goal at hand, whether that be a paddling leg, a navigational decision, deciding when to sleep, etc.... that our conversation technique becomes really basic and to the point. As a result, I get pretty frustrated with Norm when he forgets to snap out of that mode once we cross the finish line. Generally, however, AR has presented far fewer problems than it has rewards. I will be forever thankful for all of our adventure racing experiences as part of the same team.

Norm: I confess that I'm not the best at coming back to the please and thank you stage, but it's a pretty small deal in the big picture. Occasionally, as for most couples, when we disagree on something, it can become more emotionally charged than if we were just teammates. This doesn't happen all that often, but occasionally, it does occur. We do our best to keep it our issue and not let it affect our other teammate(s).

Any lessons learned that you could share about racing with your significant other?

Tracyn: I think the biggest lesson that we have learned from racing as a couple is that we couldn't have done it (and not driven our teammates crazy) if the foundation of our relationship was at all unstable. We raced once with another couple where it became clear very early on in the event that their relationship was a mess. I don't recall a single time when they said an encouraging thing to each other, or if they did, the memory is totally overshadowed by the completely disrespectful way they treated each other. It was a great lesson for Norm and I, and helped remind us how *not* treat each other. I actually felt really bad for the couple, and our analysis of their dysfunctional relationship was confirmed when they got divorced not long after the event. It was sad, but perhaps for the best.

I would encourage a couple thinking of racing together to take some time to reflect on their relationship, and to make sure that they feel pretty confident in its stability. Healthy competition between the two is good, but all-out, nonsupportive competition can really bring you down as a couple, and surely as a team. It's important to remember that a couple's issues are totally magnified in stressful situations, and it's not fair to expect one or two teammates to offer counseling and/or understanding.

Norm: It's really important for a couple to be honest with themselves on whether or not their relationship is capable of withstanding the intensity of adventure racing. Don't avoid being honest with each other in the same way that you would with your other teammates and don't go overboard just because you feel more comfortable with your significant other. Generally speaking, if a situation tips toward potentially negative, treat your partner as you would your other teammates. If a situation could really use a boost, and you recognize this before your teammates do, go overboard to accommodate. That's what's really cool about racing as a couple—being able to recognize the early signs of discomfort, frustration, hunger, and fatigue.

How do you enjoy directing races, rather than competing in them?

Tracyn and Norm: When we first got into race directing in 1999, there were very few races at the time. Our goal was to share with others and make a sport we had a great passion for more accessible. Nowadays there are many races all over the country, and our goal has changed slightly. Due to our experience with expedition-length races, we continue to concentrate on creating an authentic race, true to the roots of the sport—races where physical skills are balanced by the need for mental and navigational skills. We continue to find it rewarding, but frankly it's the racers who surprise themselves through the course of the race and cross the finish line who are most satisfying to watch, not necessarily the front-runners. For example, there was an all-female team who did one of our twelve-hour events this year. One of the team members had done support a bunch before, but had never raced. She just wanted to cross the finish line. From what we were told post-race, her teammates really helped her out a lot, and she had to dig deep to finish. However, when she did cross the line and the uncontrollable tears of joy filled her eyes and cheeks, it was truly moving for everyone watching them finish. However, to be honest, racing is much simpler in many ways. It's tough to be responsible for the safety and enjoyment of so many people. But when the race is complete, and the racers are happy and proud of their accomplishments, it all seems worth it.

What are your future plans?

Tracyn: Ever since we got pregnant and had our son, Dylan (born June 1, 2003), family, friends, and other racers have been asking us if or when we plan to compete again. I can only speak for myself in saying that I'm extremely happy with the level of success we had as racers pre-baby, and I know I now do not have the time to train to my potential. I think if I were to race again, it'd be years from now, so that my training time would not interfere with watching and helping Dylan develop into a beautiful, unique little person. In my opinion, adventure racing is a pretty selfish sport and is all-consuming. I think I'd be fooling myself if I expected to simultaneously be able to compete well, maintain my relationship with Norm, run our business, and have quality time to be with Dylan. I'm still too competitively spirited (at this point anyway) to want to race just for fun. I also prefer the longer, expedition-style events, which are a bit more difficult to do off the couch. So for me, at least in the short term, I would be content with not racing again. With that said, I do look forward to being able to make more time to train and to stay fit. As Dylan has grown (and it all happens way too quickly) he becomes more and more mobile, and we are able to safely take him on more and more adventures. He loves the backpack, the Burley bike trailer, and traveling all over the country in our little twenty-one-foot RV.

Norm: At the moment we are fully occupied with the double duty of producing six races per year, teaching multiple AR instructional programs, and raising our contribution to the next generation of adventure racers, our fifteen-month-old son, Dylan. Being business partners has created a whole new set of challenges for the skills we developed as teammates. Each day tests these faculties, and demands that we rise to new heights. The addition of a new "teammate" in the office requires us to be even more efficient with our time, and to prioritize. But once he is a little more independent we hope to get back into racing, albeit at a more part-time level. I can foresee that one day, in the not-so-distant future, we will once again compete in one or two of our favorite expedition-style races in some beautiful places around the world.

A Winning Team Has One Heart

NAME: ROBYN BENINCASA
AGE: 38
RESIDENCE: SAN DIEGO, CA
YEARS ADVENTURE RACING: 11

Photo courtesy of Tommy Baynard

I was born in Long Island, New York but grew up in Tempe, Arizona, where I competed at the state and national levels in gymnastics, diving, and cross-country. After graduating from Arizona State University with a B.S. degree in marketing, I went to work for a pharmaceutical company as a field sales rep for the San Diego territory. At that time, San Diego was *the* mecca for triathletes and I couldn't help but be bitten by the "bug." I began to compete in triathlons and eventually went on to successfully complete six Ironman races, including two podium finishes for my age group in Kona, Hawaii. However, by 1995, I was beginning to get totally bored with triathlons and very tired of wearing panty hose to work every day. So I decided to embark on a mission to live my dreams of becoming an adventure racer and a professional firefighter.

I first became interested in adventure racing the preceding year when I competed on an all-woman team in the 1994 Raid Gauloises in Borneo. Although we finished in dead last place, finish we did, and I had the time of my life! After spending days trekking through the jungle covered in leeches and climbing through bat-infested caves, triathlons seemed pretty tame by comparison. My interest in adventure racing really grew in 1995, when my team and I finished in second place overall in the inaugural Eco-Challenge, which was held in Utah. After that, there was no turning back—I was totally hooked on the sport.

Over the course of the next few years, I competed in dozens of adventure races around the globe. I raced in all of the major races and teamed with many of the most renowned competitors in the sport. I learned firsthand what worked and what didn't and I discovered that team dynamics made all the difference in the world. I had been on successful teams filled with conflict and strained relationships, which always left me feeling drained and, in my opinion, made our success bittersweet. I had also been on losing teams with terrific team dynamics, which if nothing else at least made for positive, memorable experiences. And best of all, I had been on winning teams with wonderful team dynamics, an incredibly powerful combination.

In 2002, I decided to start my own company to teach others the lessons I had learned about the importance of teamwork and how best to achieve it. I named my company World Class Teams and by using the lessons I had learned from adventure racing, I developed a program based around what I call the Eight Essential Elements of Human Synergy. These elements, Total Commitment, Empathy and Awareness, Adversity Management, Mutual Respect, We Thinking, Ownership of the Project, Relinquishment of Ego and Kinetic Leadership, are what I consider to be the key components of successful teams. If mastered, these elements can create a world-class team, whether it be in the corporate boardroom or in the mountains of Tibet, the jungles of Borneo, or the deserts of Utah. I love to share the lessons I have learned from my experiences as a world champion adventure racer and successful businesswoman.

Total Commitment: The 2000 Eco-Challenge in Borneo was a magical race experience for our team. I had never been on a team where everyone was totally committed not only to moving forward, but also 100 percent committed to each other. As a result of the team's synergy, we were able to perform far greater than four individuals possibly could. For example, toward the latter stages of the race, we thought we had won. However, Team Spie, an extremely strong French team, caught up with us at the bat caves. In order to regain the lead, we had to dig deeper than any of us had ever dug before, but because of our total commitment, we found strength we never knew we possessed. We went on to win the race and there is no doubt in my mind that although the French were the physically stronger team, we were more committed. As a result of that experience, I learned two great truths. First, a solid and unwavering strength of purpose is the main foundation for racing success and second, a great team is committed not only to finishing the race, but to one another.

Empathy: During the 2000 Raid Gauloises in Tibet, I learned firsthand the importance of empathy. My team was doing well and I was feeling relatively strong until we hit a canyon section that had a series of fourteen rappels into drops and pools. I began to fall behind as my teammates pushed on ahead. I was exhausted, but the fact that my teammates were out of sight really had me feeling discouraged. All of a sudden, I looked up and saw John Howard holding out his hand to give me a boost. John had awareness of how I must have been feeling and stayed behind to help me out. I will never forget that for as long as I live. The fact that John cared meant a great deal to me and gave me the emotional lift I needed. Shortly thereafter, I began to feel better and we went on to finish as one of the top teams. I learned that day that sometimes the little things you do for your teammates can have a tremendous impact on their performance. Everyone on the team should make a practice of noticing the physical, mental, and emotional changes in the people around them, and do whatever is necessary to make them happier, more comfortable, and especially faster. Sometimes this may mean carrying a teammate's pack or sharing some of your food; more often, it may just mean lending a hand or words of encouragement. In short, be the teammate that you would want to race with.

Adversity Management: As most of you have probably figured out by now, the sh** is *always* going to hit the fan in an adventure race. Your ultimate success therefore, is a matter of how well you and your teammates control the resultant "splatter." This lesson became abundantly clear to me during the 2000 Raid in Tibet when we were the lead team in the final stages of the race, and we arrived at the mountain bike transition checkpoint only to discover our support crew (and bikes) were still hours away. A couple of us, myself included, were crushed and basically did little more than moan about our dilemma. Thankfully, we had several people on our team who totally rose to the occasion. John Howard was somehow able to scrounge up some dilapidated, yet ridable bikes from local villagers. Keith Murray put forth a tremendous effort to rally the team and bring our morale back up, and Robert Nagle negotiated with the race director. Unfortunately, as a result of a time penalty we incurred for using borrowed bikes, we wound up not winning the race. Nonetheless, we certainly demonstrated how champions overcome adversity and I learned an invaluable lesson. When adversity presents itself, make sure you view it as a challenge rather than a roadblock. Relax. Take a few deep breaths and then fully assess the situation and all of your resources before acting. It's amazing what obstacles can be overcome when people work together.

Mutual Respect: Ralph Waldo Emerson once said, "Trust men and they will be true to you. Treat them greatly and they will show themselves great." Over the years, I have discovered this saying to be true. Acting like a good teammate is far more important than feeling like one. During the 1998 Raid Gauloises in Ecuador, our team became divided when on a trekking section, we came upon a fork in the road that had two trails leading off. Our two navigators, John and Ian, each wanted to take a different path and couldn't agree which way to go. They each went their own way, leaving the rest of the team to decide whom to follow. It was an awkward moment for everyone. Thankfully, a quarter mile later, the two trails converged. As luck would have it, there was a camera crew nearby and when the camera turned on, everyone acted appropriately, despite the fact things were pretty tense. Our team had a code of ethics to never allow anyone outside the team to know that we had any problems or weaknesses. To outsiders, we were always one strong and united group. Fortunately, a half hour later, everyone felt like a team again and we ultimately wound up winning the race. However, we all learned an invaluable lesson that day—that acting like a team can sometimes be more important than feeling like a team when it comes to performance. Through the years, I have also discovered that when a teammate shares ideas, be curious first and critical second. Treat each other with respect. And by all means, before you "go off" on a teammate, first ask yourself this question—"Is what I'm about to say going to make this team better, faster, more productive, or more successful in the long run?" If not, then don't say it.

We Thinking: It has often been said that there is no *I* in *team* and nowhere is that more true than in adventure racing. Great teams think in terms of "we" and "us" at all times. They view all gear and equipment as *ours,* all problems are *ours,* all mistakes are *ours,* and all successes are *ours,* no matter who played the hero or who was lagging on that leg. Unfortunately, in addition to being on some terrific teams, I have also been on teams that were somehow able to find the *I* in *team.* For example, I was a member of a well-known team, but, although it was composed of a good group of people, for whatever reason, we were never able to come together when the going got tough. When the chips were down, we always wound up spending a lot more time blaming rather than fixing, and as a result I always felt like I was competing with my teammates as much as or even more than I was competing against our competitors. Things really came to a head for the team during the 2003 Balance Bar 24-Hour Race in Vail, Colorado. During the race, one of the legs entailed whitewater swimming and it was mandatory to wear wetsuits. Unfortunately, when we got to the transition area, one of my teammate's wetsuits wasn't there. He, and ultimately the rest of the team, spent the next two and a half hours yelling and blaming everyone, instead of just trying to fix the problem. The team just couldn't rally and find a solution. Mercifully, the race director finally broke down and gave us a wetsuit. Ironically, after we finished the race, we found the missing wetsuit—right in his hotel room, where he had left it!

Ownership of the Project: In order to create "buy-in" among team members, everyone needs to be emotionally tied to its outcome. The first step is to gain consensus on team goals and expectations for the race. The entire team must agree on subjects such as, Are we going for a top-ten finish, or will just crossing the finish line be enough? How much sleep is enough? And what's more important, finishing well or remaining friends? Unfortunately, I learned this lesson the hard way during the 1997 Eco-Challenge in Australia. I competed on a mixed nationality team with two Australians and two Americans. Unfortunately, the Americans came Down Under with the sole goal of winning while the Aussies came for a holiday. Everyone on the team had different goals and expectations and not, surprisingly, when the going got tough, the team fell apart. That team was doomed from the start. I discovered that it's critical for everyone on the team to have the same goals and objectives. And once the race has started, do whatever you can to make each team member feel important and needed. Everyone should have jobs to do that will directly affect the outcome of the race. That way, they will feel instrumental to the team's success. After all, why continue racing if you're not contributing to the team's success?

Relinquishment of Ego: This is the most important aspect of good teamwork, although it's often the most difficult. After all, we're adventure racers who want our teammates, crew, and spectators to know how strong we are. However, in order to achieve your team goals, it is imperative that you leave your ego at the starting line. After all, as the old adage goes, in adventure racing, you're only as fast as your slowest teammate. Thus, in the end, it's not about you—it's about doing whatever it takes to make your team move forward a little bit faster. One of the best examples I have ever seen of someone who was able to let go of his ego in order to help the team was Keith Murray during the Raid in Tibet. Keith is a phenomenal racer and, more importantly, a wonderful human being. One day during the race we were at altitude, and I was having a very tough time. Keith carried my pack for the entire day—which was a tremendous help. Despite the fact he clearly put forth a Herculean effort, just before we arrived at the transition area where there were dozens of people and media teams, Keith stopped and gave my pack back to me to carry. I was amazed. Most guys I know would have wanted to carry the pack into the transition area so everyone could see firsthand just how strong they were. But not Keith. By allowing me to carry my own pack for those final few minutes, I was able to enter the checkpoint with my head held high—and more importantly, we were able to portray to our competitors that we were still a strong and viable team. One thing I have definitely learned over the years that is a certainty—at some point in time, everyone on the team will be the strongest link and at some point, they will be the weakest link. The world's greatest adventure racing teams recognize that and constantly help each other out. If you must bring your ego on the course with you, try to wrap it around the success of the team rather than your personal performance.

Kinetic Leadership: It has been my experience that teams with a military "chain of command" style of leadership (i.e., the team captain is the team's sole leader) are destined to fail. After all, nobody can be the smartest, most talented, or most experienced person in every event. Adventure racing's best teams allow leadership to rotate around. For example, during the mid- to late-1990s, I was a member of Team Eco-Internet, arguably one of the sport's greatest teams of all time. Even though we had a team captain, we allowed leadership to change seamlessly from person to person, depending upon the skills they brought to the table and, just as importantly, who was the strongest at the time. For example, in many of our races, John Howard led our trekking sections, Robert Nagle led the horseback riding sections, Ian Adamson was in charge of the paddling sections, Steve Gurney spearheaded the mountain bike legs, and I was the team's emotional cheerleader. Needless to say, although each of us filled very different roles, all of them were critical to the success of the team.

When all eight of these elements come together in perfect harmony, human synergy is the result. It's an incredibly powerful and rewarding experience. As a racer, you feel as if you are part of something much greater than just the sum of the individual parts. And it's a feeling you want to capture over and over again.

For the past decade, I have traveled the globe, competing in some of the world's most difficult races with three or four of my closest friends. During this time, I have been in a nonstop search to understand the keys to successful teamwork. I have seen the good, the bad, and the not-so-pretty in both my teammates and myself. I've learned countless lessons, but among the most important things I've learned is that by helping one another, we help ourselves; that success comes from mentoring one another unselfishly; and that in the long run, we will all be the weakest link and the strongest one at some point in time. I also have discovered that the greatest adventure racing teams operate on four brains, eight arms, eight legs, and *one* heart.

Conquering the Beast, One Bite at a Time

NAME: CHRISTINE (AKA KIWI) COULDREY
AGE: 31
RESIDENCE: SILVER SPRING, MD
YEARS ADVENTURE RACING: 3

Photo by Will Ramos — www.0bounds.com

There comes a point in time where you have to stop talking about what you want to do, and actually go do it. In 2001 I volunteered at Odyssey Adventure Racing's Beast of the East. The race, and some of the people I met there, left such an impression on me that I dreamed about it every night for the next week. That really started me thinking about getting into this adventure racing business, but there was much I had to learn.

Up until that point, I was really an on-road racer. I had competed in a lot of triathlons, and had recently accomplished a long-term goal of completing my first Ironman. To make the transition to off-road racing was going to take some time. I had triathlon plans through September 2002 when I was going to do a double iron-distance triathlon. In the meantime, I started working on mountain biking, whitewater paddling, and hiking. I also volunteered at every adventure race that I possibly could. I learned that many people fail due to a lack of planning and knowledge of the sport. So I set about learning from the mistakes of others. Spending time at these races also allowed me to meet a lot of people involved in the sport. Through the people I met, I realized that you don't need to be a superhero at every sport to succeed at adventure racing. So a little bit at a time I assimilated the knowledge and skills needed to race. I hate to fail, so I try to make sure that I have the necessary level of understanding and skill for what I am about to undertake. I got to know Mark, Patrick, and John, a few guys I met at the races. I liked them, and trusted their navigational ability (I was still completely lacking in that department). We did a few short races together and got along well. One thing I learned along the way was that good teammates are *very* important.

After having a great time in both the E-Fix and the Wild Onion Adventure Race earlier in the year it was time to take the next big step and do a long adventure race! Patrick, Mark, and I were all set for the 2003 Beast of the East although without John (personal commitments prevented him from joining us), we couldn't make a four-person team. We decided to race as a two-person team and a solo, and for some unknown reason I volunteered to be the solo. This meant that I would be carrying the team mandatory gear as well as my own. However, that scared me a lot less that the knowledge that I would be racing for three and a half days with only minimal sleep! What sort of a beast would that level of sleep deprivation turn me into? Would it break me down mentally, physically, or both? Well, I would never find out unless I gave it a go.

After an eleven-hour sleep in the hotel (the last time I would be in a bed for five days), we headed over to HQ to start the check-in process. For those of you that haven't been to an adventure race, the first obstacle is to get all of your worldly possessions to gear check-in, keep them all with you, pull out the appropriate pieces of equipment at the correct tables, and not lose anything. It really is quite a challenging feat. But I made it through that with only a few minor issues. At this time I realized how difficult it is to keep track of the most precious of all documents: the passport. I developed a sort of paranoia, never before having been in charge of such an important piece of paper. If I lost this I would not know where I was headed and there would be no proof of where I had been. It would be the end of my race. Needless to say, that passport would stay with me at all times, no matter how tired I got. At the end of gear check, maps were issued. But before the map study could begin, I had promised the Odyssey medical team that I would take part in a sleep-deprivation study. So I spent the next twenty minutes in front of the computer watching playing cards flip over. As cards flipped over, we had to push one button if the playing card was red, or a different one if it was black, one button if the two cards showing were the same, the other if they were different, and a whole variety of modifications on this seemingly simple theme. These were designed to test reflex speed as a measure of cognitive function. This was going to be really challenging after three and a half days of not sleeping. It was tough enough having slept plenty!

The map study was a long and arduous task. Mark, Patrick, and I took turns in plotting our course, and with so many different maps it seemed to take forever. Certain maps quickly became more popular than others. Little did we know that the "little colored map that we didn't like" would guide us through some wonderful pieces of the countryside. Something that caught my attention during the race briefing was that Team Litespeed (one of the teams that was expected to do well) was also a local team. I'm not sure why this struck me or even why I would remember it two days later, but quite fortunately it did. Somehow time flew past, and we barely had time to load our packs and bikes and get ready for the start. There was very little time to be nervous; just getting everything ready for the start made us look forward to the mental rest we would get once we got going.

The Beast of the East started at 7:00 P.M. on a Thursday. One lap around the start area and we were off up the first climb (of many) of the race. That first hill that we had to climb had us all wondering how on earth we were going to make it up the many mountains that separated us from the finish. At that point I couldn't help but recall the words that someone once said to me: "How do you eat an elephant? One bite at a time." Little did I know that those words would become my mantra during this long race. To start a race knowing that I was going to be moving for eighty-five hours was too much to think about. So all I tried to concern myself with was the next pedal stroke. There was one point going up that first hill that I felt like I was going to faint. So I stopped to lie down on the road for a few minutes. Not a great way to start a race, but losing those few minutes wasn't going to make or break it. Finally we reached the top! Down the hill a bit and it was time to get off our bikes to start trekking. Although I love to ride my bike, at this point I was happy to be back on my feet.

The first trek started out great. There were plenty of teams to talk to, we made some new friends, and everyone was in good spirits. As we walked through the night, I had no idea where we were headed except that we were going toward the Blue Ridge Parkway, which more or less meant that we were going up! And we continued to go up for three hours or so. With Patrick navigating and only a few minutes lost to an incorrect turn, we made CP2 at about 2:00 A.M. and did a quick transition for the orienteering section. While Mark checked his feet and Patrick changed pants, I took the map and came up with a plan: Minimize the bushwhacking and only get the one orienteering point that was more or less on our way to CP3. It is always a tough call to decide not to go to all the orienteering points. But given the distance that needed to be traveled and the bushwhacking involved, we decided that we didn't have enough time to do that and make the paddle cutoff time. Stories that we heard later and the difficulties encountered by other teams confirmed that we made the right decision.

I think it was at this point that Mark and Patrick decided that I needed to learn how to use that compass thing that I had hanging around my neck (I was actually going to pack it in the bottom of my pack so I wasn't tempted to try and use it and get us all lost). All I knew about the compass was that the red arrow pointed north as long as there wasn't any metal around. But with some pointers from the boys I actually started to participate in the navigation too. As so often seems to be the case in the middle of the night, the trails that we were on didn't seem to quite match our maps. Thankfully Patrick and Mark were able to work out where we could possibly be (exactly on track), and before long we came out at the intersection that we had been aiming for! Then all we had was a short bushwhack up the hill to the OP. I would like to lodge an official complaint to Odyssey here for discrimination against vertically challenged individuals. The punch point was so high in the tree that I couldn't reach it. What's up with that! Fortunately Mark's long arms and legs allowed us to make the appropriate punches, and we headed back down that hill.

Now all we had to do was find the rappel site. Somehow I ended up with the maps at this point. The boys knew that I pretty much couldn't get us lost, so I think that they just made me carry the maps because they didn't want to carry them. But it did make me feel important. We got to the trail that we thought would lead us to the climb site and were just double checking the map when Team Litespeed came by saying, "That's the trail that we come out at." We said that we were going up that trail to the climb site. They replied, "No, it's too hard to get around to the back." So we sat down to look at our maps again and realized that in plotting our course we had forgotten that we were coming down rather than going up. This meant another five miles of walking to get to the climb site. That seemed like an awful long way and it was tempting to try to take what appeared to be a shortcut. But then I remembered: "Team Litespeed is a local team. Aha! They probably know what they are talking about." And they did.

Rappelling 450 feet at around 8:00 A.M. was incredible. The view on the way down was awesome with mist-covered mountains as far as the eye could see. I felt so lucky to be out there doing this race, not to mention how good it felt to have some of the weight taken off my aching feet. They were really starting to hurt! After the rappel there were many more miles to walk on the road to get to the next CP, where we could get off our feet and onto our bikes. These were some of the longest miles that I have walked. It was hot, our minds were wandering, and there was way too much time to think about how we were not there yet. For a while during that section I wasn't even sure how I was going to get there. Then I remembered my mantra: Just like eating an elephant: one bite at a time, or more precisely in this case, one step at a time.

Thankfully we were back on our bikes, and I had forgiven mine for the hard time it gave me on that first climb. My feet still hurt, even on the bike, but oh how I love my bike! We had plenty of time to get to the paddle to make the 2:00 P.M. cutoff, but you never know what might be just around the corner. So we had to keep pushing the pace. Before too long we arrived at the river where our support crew helped us get our paddling gear ready. We selected our canoes and took off down to the river.

None of us is a great paddler. We all paddle some, but don't come from paddling backgrounds, so there were sure to be a few tough moments during a thirty-five-mile paddle! We were keen to get to the end of the paddle before dark and so tried to keep pushing. I had been rather afraid of the white water, but seeing the river erased all of those fears. There were no rapids in sight. Actually by the end of the long paddle, I found myself hoping for some significant rapids to get over the boredom. It was a long way for all of us, but it hit home to me during that long paddle that it's easier to deal with your own pain than see people you are racing with struggling. We each had our down moments; some of them were longer and deeper than others. We all had our good bright sparky periods too. And we made it to the shore, incredibly happy to be there before it got dark. There had been many trees down in the river, and crashing into one of them would have been bad.

Little did I know that Mark and Patrick had been talking between themselves during the paddle. Mark had not been feeling great since the start of the race and had decided that he was going to quit at the next CP. I had been worried about both of them for a while, but didn't realize just how bad it had gotten. I'm grateful that they didn't say anything until we were out on dry land. It was hard to accept the fact that Mark wasn't going on with us, but he was really dehydrated. Some days it's just not your day and looking back, I give him a lot of credit for realizing that, pushing through it for as long as he did, trying to get better, but then having the courage and strength to make the decision to quit. I know it was a hard decision for him to make. If only there had been time for him to sleep for a few hours and rehydrate, I'm sure he would have been able to continue. But now there was a 30-mile ride to be done and Patrick and I had to be on our way. We hated to leave Mark behind, but our reward for reaching the end of the long ride would be two glorious hours of sleep!

After twenty-four hours of racing, I would never think that I could get on a bike and kick some butt. But that is exactly what Patrick and I did. We killed that ride and had an absolute blast doing it . . . climbing, climbing, climbing, and then bombing down the hills! How there can be so many big climbs in thirty miles I don't know, but it was great! I had struggled a little at the start of the race, but now I felt myself coming into my element. Even better were the two hours of sleep that we got (although I felt like I was half awake much of that time). I was so paranoid about losing my passport that I tucked it into my shorts before going to sleep.

At 3:30 A.M. it was time to crawl out of our oh-so-cozy cargo van. We changed clothes and packed our bags for a twenty-hour trek. Now, that is a lot of food to carry! At 4:00 A.M. we were off. It was dark and we were really looking forward to the sun coming up and warming us. At the first stream crossing we met up with Shari and Mary (some Odyssey regulars). A few minutes later we came to an intersection that looked as though it could be the one we needed to take, but we weren't sure. Patrick and I decided that we were not quite there yet and needed to walk a little farther. We walked twenty more yards and stopped to take another look at the map. Suddenly there were two *huge* (seriously, they were at least two inches long!) insects buzzing around me. Patrick believed that maybe if we walked back down where the girls were the insects would stay put. Well, they didn't. They followed me all the way back down (I guess I smelled pretty ripe). We got down there, and I heard Patrick shouting, "Run, Chris, run! Keep running!" Well, I have learned in life that if someone tells you to run with such urgency in their voice, it's better to run first and ask questions later. So I ran! We eventually escaped the killer insects, but felt really bad because we left them down with the girls! Mary and Shari decided the only way to escape the insects was to run up to see us. They didn't hate us for bringing the insects down to them, so we decided to hang out with them for a while. And boy did we get a lot of laughs out of that incident. I guess you had to be there (in the same sleep-deprived state we were in).

From there we headed out on Hospital Rock Trail. It quickly became obvious why it was called that: One little slip and you would need the hospital. That was one of the hardest trails that I have hiked on in my life. Our trek took us down fifteen hundred feet, then back up fifteen hundred feet. That's a cycle we would repeat over and over. But it was such an awesomely beautiful state park there in South Carolina that it really didn't seem like much effort at all. That park is definitely somewhere I want to return to for a vacation some day. Yet another climb took us up to a river that we had to cross. On first glance there was a lot of water pouring over those rocks. Was it just flooded from the recent rain? How would we get across? Closer examination revealed two wires above the water: one for our feet, one for our hands. Those of you who know me know I don't like things like that, and will avoid them at all costs. Especially with wet slippery feet! I hoped for another way to cross, but that wasn't an option. After watching Mary and Shari cross, there was nothing I could do but hold on tight, put on my brave face, and do it. Off I went . . . no looking down . . . no thinking of slipping. I was nearly across the river when two trekking poles came whizzing past my ear. Patrick had thrown his poles over so he wouldn't need to carry them, and threw them a little too close for my comfort. That just added to the thrill of it all. Well, one of the biggest reasons that I race is to face my fears. And here was yet another point in which I was doing that. And I prevailed!

The next leg took us up a big mountain. Near the top were some of the most spectacular parts of the course: huge rock formations with water dripping off them. It made me dizzy to look up. There was a suspension bridge over one of the most beautiful waterfalls. That was the first time in a race where I thought that carrying a camera would have been worth the weight just to get that picture. But it probably wouldn't have shown how awesome it was anyway. I'll just have to go back there and visit again too. From there we headed on up to the Foot Hills Trail. Now, this is a trail I don't care to ever see again! The first half was on a jeep trail and by this time my feet hurt so badly. Fortunately the skin was still intact (unlike many other racers' feet). Anytime we stopped moving, however, the throbbing in my feet was incredible. Walking actually made them feel better! This trail bored me and I went through a couple of tough hours, one bite/step at a time. We put in a couple of bonus miles looking for the trail at one point. But then we found it and we were onto the endless single-track section of the Foot Hills Trail. Somewhere during that section I had a miraculous recovery and I was good to go again, just as the others were in a downswing. We stopped to rest a couple of times due to the fact that Shari's feet were literally falling apart.

We just desperately needed this trek to be over with, so I took it upon myself to try and keep people moving as much as possible. I was rather worried that the others were going to be angry with me for not letting them rest as much as they wanted to, but I just needed to get to the van to sleep! I figured this would be a good time to help by carrying some of the others' packs. I did this and there was some noticeable recovery in the weary soles of those around me. It was fortunate that earlier in the race I had gained some experience on the navigating front, as Patrick was feeling the effects of the race. I took the maps and, with some help from Mary, I was able to figure out how to get us to the next ACP.

The final descent seemed to take forever. Tensions were running high and voices were raised between Shari and me over where the CP was. It didn't really matter, as we would go past where I thought the CP was to get to where she thought it was. But neither of us wanted to give in. Fortunately we both had the sense to shut up after a couple of minutes of getting nowhere. About that time it started to rain in biblical proportions. Shari's feet were killing her and Patrick and I just needed to get back in the van and get some rest as quick as possible, so we parted ways with the girls. We felt a bit bad leaving our friends, but our desire for sleep and the need to be out of the rain was just so great that we figured they would understand. For the second time in the race we ran as fast as we could. That downhill went on for ages! Patrick would periodically ask, "Are you sure this crosses Route 178?" I was sure, but I didn't think it would be so far away. We finally arrived at the ACP, after twenty-six hours of walking. By far the longest I had ever walked in my life! I had one bad blister, but I considered myself incredibly lucky given the terrain that we had walked over.

Sleep! We once again rewarded ourselves with two wonderful hours of sleep (my passport tucked into my shorts of course), further comforted by knowing that the next section would be mostly biking. But at this point I felt like I could do anything that was thrown at me. The harder it got out there on the course, the stronger I began to feel! It was as though the Beast was seeing how much it could throw at me, and I was taking everything it had to give. I tell you, that was a pretty awesome feeling.

After our nap, we were transported to CP13 where we would start the biking. It took awhile for us to really wake up, but just being on our bikes (and off our feet) was great. On this last day, eating enough proved to be a struggle. I was finding that I could do only one thing at a time. That meant that eating while riding was out of the question for me. We biked back to an area that had been an ACP earlier in the race, and the familiarity was rather comforting. Then we rode down to the CP where we would trek to the ascending site.

We trekked up to the "Dirty Dozen," Odyssey's ropes experts known for their sense of humor. It is always great to see the Dirty Dozen. They always make me laugh. But it was time to get down to the business at hand. Patrick and I had experienced some problems during the ascending sections in a previous race, and I felt like I had something to prove this time. There was a rope assist that we went up before the climbing would really begin. At the top of that section, we had to stop and set up our ascending gear. I haven't spent much time climbing, so gear rigging doesn't come naturally to me. I can be dead tired and still do things like ride a bike or change a flat, but I was really struggling here. It was like I was brain dead, and we had a bit of a laugh about that. I got going a bit after Patrick and the guys at the bottom made a bet as to who would make it up first. It sounded like the money, or in this case the beer, was on me. Sorry, Patrick, that's the reason I wanted to get up there so fast (you see, beer is a big motivator in my life). What a great feeling it was to finally get to the top: I had fought the ascending demons and won!

Back onto the bikes and we were off again. Again we were riding down, down, down, and it was a blast! In fact, we were having so much fun that we missed the turn at the bottom. Back on course, we soon found ourselves climbing again for many miles. The thought of getting off my bike and walking was appealing, except for the fact that we had walked so much over the past couple of days. So I opted to gear down and stay on my bike.

We arrived at CP17 to find out that the course had been changed due to some dangerously high river crossings. That meant that some of the hike-a-bike section that I had been so worried about had been eliminated. Surely it wasn't going to be as easy as it looked! We still had some dreaded single-track trail to ride (for me, any trail on the bike is dreaded, especially in the dark after three exhausting days of racing), but before we took off we sat down for some PB & Js. Very tasty! It was about this time that Patrick and I both realized that we were going to make it. We were going to finish the Beast of the East in a very respectable position. Sure, we still had a number of hours ahead of us, but for the first time the end was finally "in sight." We laughed and joked a lot during that next section. I can't repeat some of the things that we laughed hardest about, but it felt really good to be able to laugh so hard that far into the race. Then the single-track started. I followed Patrick as he led the way. I managed to ride most of the first sections until we got to Black Mountain. The prescribed course said to take Trail 127 over the mountain. There was a very tempting unimproved road that, although longer, would surely have been faster (and probably easier). Black Mountain Trail was going to be a tough hike-a-bike over a forty-two-hundred-foot peak. We saw one team take the road, but for my own personal satisfaction I needed to go over that mountain. Bring it on, Beast! Well, I have to admit that getting my bike to the top of that mountain really pushed me to my limits. But I did it, one bite at a time. Nothing was going to stop me now!

The ride down was tough too. I hadn't eaten enough all day and I more or less had to walk all the way down. Patrick was kind to me and led the way. When there were sections (however short they would be) that he thought I could ride, he would ride ahead, stopping to wait where he thought that the trail had become too rocky for me. I was so tired that I didn't even realize that my headlamp had begun to fade close to the end of the ride. And I got rather upset, because I couldn't figure out why I couldn't see where I was going anymore. Er, that was a bit dumb, but it was all okay again once I worked out what the problem was. Then there we were, at the bottom. It had been a long way down, but we had made it. Just a short ride to the finish, and we were greeted by Don Mann and a few others who were awake and congratulating people even though it was 2:45 A.M. We had finished.

After the race Patrick and I had to go do our sleep deprivation tests. We both fell asleep at least once during the test, but they told me that I might have done better sleep deprived than fresh! Four hours of sleep and a shower later and the whole race seemed very surreal. The Dirty Dozen rewarded me with that beer that I'd won earlier in the race, and I headed off to the awards ceremony. It was great to be able to relive the experiences with everyone there. I enjoyed the race a great deal more than I thought I would and I was a lot less miserable than I thought that I would be. And now, once again, I had that feeling there was nothing I couldn't accomplish. The sleep deprivation that I had feared at the beginning of the race hadn't turned me into a beast after all. Instead I had conquered the Beast, one bite at a time.

I May be a Stray Dog, but I'm *Not* Lost

NAME: MARSHALL ULRICH
AGE: 53
RESIDENCE: IDAHO SPRINGS, CO
YEARS ADVENTURE RACING: 10

We'd been wandering around the desert for days. Three of our team-mates had chosen to withdraw from the race, but Mace and I were per-fectly content to make our way fifteen extra miles out of the wrong canyon and around to the correct one. As we made our way up the canyon, along came the remnants of another team, including Dr. Bob and Lisa. We decided to join forces, and finish the race together. "We were just wander-ing around, lost . . . like a bunch of stray dogs," Dr. Bob would comment later. Thus, the Stray Dogs Adventure Racing Team was born.

In the Beginning: Eco-Challenge Utah 1995

I had no idea what adventure racing was when Chuck Blish called me in November 1994. But after spending twenty minutes on the phone with him, I agreed to be a part of Team Mile High, one of fifty teams to com-pete in the first Eco-Challenge in Utah. Later, I learned that adventure racing was developed in New Zealand, then expanded with the first Raid Gauloises, a French-based race organized by Gerard Fusil. Some people already had a reputation as being the top athletes in the field: people like John Howard, Ian Adamson, Keith Murray, and Robert Nagle.

I was a world-class ultrarunner—having won two silver medals in the national 24-hour run; being the first person to complete "The Last Great Race" (completing all six 100-mile races in one year, finishing in the top ten in five of them); completing several over-200-mile runs (including the 310-mile, record 88-hour Run Across Colorado); and winning the Badwater Ultra 146, a race across Death Valley to the summit of Mount Whitney, three times (setting a record of under thirty-four hours to the summit, a record that still stands today; and I would go on to win

Badwater a record fourth time in 1996). But adventure racing was "all Greek to me."

Looking back, I'm grateful I had the opportunity to participate in the U.S. debut of adventure racing, organized by Mark Burnett (now of *Survivor* and *The Apprentice* fame). Mark had participated in the Raid Gauloises and used that as a pattern for his race. He reportedly collected numerous credit cards and, by design, forced himself into deep debt to pull together the first ever Eco-Challenge. Just a few months later, Mark took the top twelve teams to finish the Utah race (six American teams and six international teams) to New England to compete in the ESPN Extreme Games/Eco-Challenge. Discovery Channel bought the rights to cover Eco-Challenge, followed by USA Network . . . and the rest is history.

In "the Utah days," Eco-Challenge teams consisted of five members, one of whom had to be the opposite sex. So, typically, teams were four men and one woman. Team Mile High included captain Chuck Blish, me, Mark (Mace) Macy, Justin Bein, and Daphne Solone. We began training together because, at that time, there were no short courses or schools to teach us the skills we needed. We just muddled through it in our own (very special) ways. We spent a lot of time laughing at ourselves—perhaps the most important skill we learned.

Chuck put the team together. Mace and I, being ultrarunners, were "good on our feet" and brought knowledge about nutrition (feeding yourself over a hundred miles), sleep deprivation (over a period of 3 days, at least), taking care of our feet (although we had much to learn), traveling in the dark (an important skill in adventure racing), and dressing appropriately (over changing terrain and altitudes). Justin was to be our navigator, and Daphne, a very experienced triathlete, was, to quote Rebecca Rusch (a very experienced adventure racer I've had the honor of racing with), jokingly, "a mandatory piece of equipment: the girl."

Mace and I also had the reputation for persisting, no matter what—a reputation that was put to the test as we spent the first few days wading, swimming, and scrambling through rivers and cold slot canyons, often a bit confused and out of water. Our packs and equipment were too heavy, navigational skills inept, climbing not to be admired, and whitewater skills crude, to put it kindly. On Day 3 we approached Capital Reef and had to decide which canyon to go down. Trying to hone our navigation "skills," Mace stood on the edge of one canyon, and I on another, and yelled to each other, "Do you see anything?" Of course, we didn't . . . and we chose the wrong canyon. It was when we reached the bottom of Capital Reef hours later that Chuck, Justin, and Daphne chose to withdraw from the race. The cool thing was that Mace and I realized that we didn't much care that we were a bit lost, and continued around to the correct canyon, where we met the remaining members of Team Columbia Sport: Robert (Dr. Bob) Haugh, Lisa Smith, and Cory Shane. Making a full, if unofficial, group of five once again, we dubbed ourselves "Team Columbia High."

Lessons Learned

We finished the first Eco-Challenge as a fragmented, unofficial team, and I came away with true respect for the sport. I learned that having a good time was instrumental to finishing. The 370-mile race was a process, just like life, with inevitable ups and downs. Taking things in stride, and looking at every problem as something to be solved, rather than something to complain about, was the key. Not letting anything, or anyone, beat you down. I realized that living life to its fullest was the ticket to finding out more about myself. I had touched upon this within the solitude of ultra-running, but now I was not alone. I was part of a team. We could look to our teammates and draw strength from each other, growing stronger as individuals.

But, more importantly, racing afforded us a chance to take a good look at our weaknesses. It would allow us to identify those weaknesses—the ones that can cripple us in a race and in life—and try to grow beyond them. As I wrote about the 584-mile Quad Badwater (crossing Death Valley four times, and summiting Mount Whitney twice), "I have found that one thing all extreme events have in common is that they have very little to do with the event. So when people ask me why we take on such challenges, I suggest that it might have to do with compensating for something that is missing in our lives, proving to ourselves and others that we are, perhaps, worthy."

It was shortly after the event when Mace, Dr. Bob, Lisa, and I were joking about how we were from all over the country, wandering around the course "like a bunch of stray dogs." When people would ask what Team Stray Dogs was, we would (depending on the company) lovingly reply, "We're just four mutts and a bitch." We would race together again over the next decade, developing a profound bond and admiration that only adversity can solidify. I am honored to call them dear friends to this day.

ESPN Extreme Games/Eco-Challenge New England 1995

I was invited to be on the "Twin Team" for the Eco-Challenge in Maine and Rhode Island. In Utah, Angelica Castaneda had put together a team of four women and one man, Adrian Crane, and had finished in the top six. Angelica has an identical twin sister, and the two were famous for doing extreme endurance events, and finishing together. They are superb athletes and astounding individuals. Much of their sponsorship came under the auspices of racing as the "Twin Team," and thus this is the name Angelica chose to race under in New England. For the first time, I raced with Adrian, Whit Rambach, and Tommy Possert. With the exception of Whit, we were all ultrarunning "misfits" and had won (or had held records) at Badwater. We were "desert rats" competing in a race with huge amounts of paddling. But we were confident that with Adrian's navigational skills, combined with the strength and experience of the team on the ground, we would do well.

Canoeing across Moosehead Lake, we watched patiently as all of the teams rounded the corner and disappeared out of sight toward the first checkpoint . . . and we went the opposite way. Adrian and Tom had discovered an alternate route by which we would portage the canoes along an active set of railroad tracks, drop into a second lake, then arrive at the checkpoint. It was a calculated risk, saving time (if not energy—portaging the canoes was hard work!), but it paid off, as we arrived at the checkpoint hours ahead of the rest of the teams. We took other calculated risks during that race, including running much of the land portions and sleeping only twenty minutes each night.

When we finished the bike leg and were flown to Martha's Vineyard, we had increased our lead. But by this sixth and last day we were so sleep deprived that we couldn't even remember the names of our own teammates. We would imagine that we were in a different place and time, and paranoia set in. If one member would imagine that we were about to go over a spillway, the rest of us would adopt that thought, add our own unique frightening spin, and become fearful ourselves. Looking back, I estimate that we were functioning (if you can call it that!) on 20 percent of our brain power. Added to sleep deprivation, Tom had *never* been in a kayak, and we didn't know a tide chart from Adam! During that last leg of the race, a long sea kayaking paddle from Martha's Vineyard to the finish line at Newport Beach, we lost our lead to Team Thredbo, a team of world-class paddlers: Jane Hall, John Jacoby, Novak Thompson, and Andrew and Rod Hilsop.

We crossed the finish line in second place. We were pleased, but it was extremely painful to think straight, and the medical team worried that Tom had slipped over the edge and might not return to normal. After a night's rest we breathed a sigh of relief as Tom finally recognized us, and we all appeared to be almost as normal as when we started. "Normal" being relevant, I suppose, as some people may not think I'm normal. But I'm as normal as anyone else—I just have a few quirks here and there. Who doesn't?

Lessons Learned

If God made man go without sleep, this would be a screwed-up place to be! During ultraruns, adventure races, and mountain climbs before (and since) I have experienced many hallucinations. But this went beyond simple hallucinations. It was truly terrifying to be that far from reality. To be that fearful and paranoid. Since New England, the team and I sleep an average of two hours a night during any adventure race. Sleep pays dividends. The time spent sleeping can be made up easily during the course of the race.

By watching Angelica, an outstanding individual and the best woman athlete I have ever met and had the privilege to race with, I learned what a team captain should be. She led with grace, and let her actions speak for her more than her words. I gained even more respect for her during the race as I watched her set a good example with her athletic abilities and, even more, with her strength of character. She proved to be brave, honest, and humble, and taught me that it's entirely my responsibility to put those qualities of character in motion in my own life. She also taught me that we all have choices to make. If we make a bad choice we have no one to blame but ourselves.

Maine was the first time I had the pleasure of racing with Adrian Crane, who would race as a Stray Dog in four more adventure races. Adrian has accomplished amazing things in his life. In 1997, he was the U.S. National Long Distance Orienteering Champion. He holds numerous records, and has raised thousands of dollars for charity (a passion we both share, as we realize that the event, or the accomplishment, itself is really not the valuable thing). He is one of three people, along with me and Tony Molina, who have competed in all nine Eco-Challenges. Of my nine Eco-Challenges, I've competed in eight of them with Mace. Over the past ten years, Mace and I have seen teams change members due to personality conflicts or in an attempt to raise their finish rank. Of course, changes in the team are a natural thing, based upon people's schedules and commitments in their racing and *real* lives, injuries, desire to continue in the sport, changes in the rules, and (yes, it's a reality of this expensive sport) sponsorship dollars. But Mace and I have kept the core of Team Stray Dogs intact, building the team upon mutual respect and admiration.

Eco-Challenge British Columbia 1996

The original Stray Dogs—Mace, Dr. Bob, Lisa, and I—along with Jacques Boutet, got together for this race across the mountains and glaciers of British Columbia. And what a time we had! We started with two horses, switching off running and riding, until we came to a glacial river. Plunging into the less-than-forty-degree water, I was swept down a couple of hundred yards only to be plucked out like a fish on a string. I remember lying on the opposite bank, flopping around, trying to rid myself of multiple leg cramps. The beauty of it all! Adventure racing at its finest!

We climbed up the riverbank, and thought that the short (thirty mile) trek ahead of us should take about a day and a half. As we walked up the mountainside we were all wondering why Dr. Bob's backpack was so heavy, and discovered it was because he was carrying way too much food. We'd learned a valuable lesson about weight in Utah, hadn't we? Not wanting that lesson to go to waste, the obvious solution was to lighten his load by getting rid of the extra food. We spent fifteen minutes stripping the wrappers off the food and throwing it into the woods for the varmints to feast on. Great idea, huh?

For the next *three* days, we trekked up a long valley; which, by the way, seemed a perfectly logical way to go. Yes, we did get a bit hungry, since we ran out of food the first day. No, Dr. Bob didn't say a word about it. We had a great time swearing and laughing at ourselves, knowing how naive and goofy we all were (with the exception of Dr. Bob) to throw away Dr. Bob's food. We finally made it out of the woods, and were well on our way to a successful outing.

During a canoeing section, I thought it would be a good idea if we could all get a bit of rest. After all, we'd learned a valuable lesson about sleep deprivation in New England, hadn't we? Dr. Bob and I were in one canoe; Mace, Lisa, and Jacques, in the other. We set out with strict instructions from the race organization to avoid the left fork of the river just up a spell. So . . . as much as we tried not to, Dr. Bob and I went down the left fork because . . . well . . . sleep had seemed more important. Fortunately, the left fork was not as treacherous as was supposed. As Dr. Bob and I waited on shore below the point where the forks of the river reconnected, the other canoe was nowhere to be seen. After night fell, along came the rest of our team. In true Macy style, Mace went on to tell the story of how Jacques had assured him and Lisa that he was proficient at being "the boat captain" (the guy who steers the canoe from the backseat). As the canoe headed into and got overturned by a strainer, Mace and Lisa increased their vocabulary, teaching each other swear words that the other didn't know existed. Together again, we spent the rest of the night taking turns paddling and sleeping in the bottom of the canoes in what felt like freezing weather.

In the mountains the weather blew in. About Day 6, the conditions worsened, and the team decided to withdraw from the race. This would be the only Eco-Challenge where I would not complete the entire course (only fourteen of seventy teams *did* finish!). Funny thing, though. At the time, Mace and I realized yet again that we didn't much care.

Lessons Learned

Humility is one of the greatest lessons learned in this unique sport. As I have always said, "Some of my best learning experiences have taken place when I have had the pleasure of being humbled." In British Columbia, I was humbled by the enormity of the course; but, even more, I was humbled by Dr. Bob's ability to take things in stride and never complain. He rose above the human tendency to say "I told you so" about *our* choice to get rid of his food, and he suffered the ensuing hunger with more grace than the rest of us.

Learning to trust yourself, and your friends, is another lesson to be learned. We all tend to take odd turns in life—like Dr. Bob and me going down "the wrong fork" of the river. But somehow, someway, those odd turns always seem to work out for the best, often in spite of ourselves. Odd turns can turn out to be blessings, depending on how you look at it. When things seem out of control, we have to trust in ourselves. We also have to allow ourselves to trust the people who know and love us. More than that, we have to be individuals whom others can trust. As Joe Cocker sang, "I get by with a little help from my friends" and "have a little faith in me." I know that I can trust my friends, and I strive to be a person that others *can* have faith in.

Eco-Challenge Australia 1997

This year marked the change from five-person to four-person teams. Because Lisa was racing on a different team, Mace, Dr. Bob, and I had to find a woman for the team. We suspected that this Eco-Challenge would involve a lot of ocean kayaking, so we asked Sharon (Shaz) Davis, the two-time woman's Australian marathon kayak champion, to join the Stray Dogs.

This was also the year that support crews were eliminated. From now on, all of our gear would be contained within our bicycle boxes, plus fifty-gallon Rubbermaid totes. Race organizers would move these containers along the 337-mile course to two or three transition areas. The Eco-Challenge had thereby simplified logistics, cut the number of competitors, and reduced support personnel. It forced teams to be more self-sufficient. It also forced teams to think ahead about what would be needed. Ultimately, it meant that we would all carry more food and equipment.

What was truly unique about Australia was the diverse climate, foliage that contains all forms of barbs and thorns, and a wide and strange array of animals. The race started in the arid Outback where the kangaroos roam; traveled through the rain forest where crocodiles hide; continued up Bartle Frere, the highest point in Queensland; headed through enormous sugarcane fields, where seven of most deadly snakes in world could be hiding; and transitioned to the coast, where we would begin the final sea kayaking leg. Dr. Bob felt that this would potentially be his last Eco-Challenge, so the Stray Dogs were focused on just finishing the race. We had a great time because we allowed ourselves to move at a somewhat slower pace, enabling us to absorb the experiences along the way.

During a mountain biking leg I vividly recall Dr. Bob unintentionally standing his bike on its front tire, sliding down the frame, and doing a head spear in the middle of the trail. He just lay there for a few seconds as we rushed to his aid. Seconds later, all of us were laughing about the absurdity of biking on a trail, in the dark, covered with hidden rocks that would "jump out and grab ya."

During the long trek after we came off Bartle Frere our feet were getting shredded. Mace casually commented that he thought he "might have a blister or two." I was horrified when he took his shoes and socks off and saw that at least half of each foot was engulfed in two or three two- to three-inch diameter blisters. "No problem," he said, putting his shoes back on, mentioning how important it is not alter bio mechanics or it would probably make them worse. Typical Mace. His feet were often the worst, but he never complained.

Squalls producing ten-foot waves were rolling along the reef when we emerged from the sugarcane fields to the kayaks on the ocean shore. Mark Burnett greeted us, mentioning that he was glad that we were so experienced in sea kayaks. Not having done the New England Eco-Challenge, Mace replied, to Mark's horror, "I've *never been* in a sea kayak." Well, Mark just about pulled the plug on us, but we all swore we'd be careful, and off we went. As a safety precaution, all teams carry a radio, which is sealed and can't be used—if the seal is broken it means that the team is calling for help, and the team is disqualified. On this occasion, however, Mark advised us to keep our radios on as an extra safety precaution.

We paddled the whole day through. As night fell, the squalls increased in frequency and intensity. We heard over the radio that "the course had been cleared" because of the bad weather, and that "no one was left out on the ocean." Mace immediately got on the radio saying, "Hey guys, we're Team Stray Dogs and we're still out here!" We were advised to paddle to a small island just off the finish line and park it till morning. Once again, we didn't much care—no problem. Once we got the okay, we finished the race in twenty-sixth place; well down in the ranks, but satisfied with what we had accomplished.

Lessons Learned

Mace suffered a lot during that race, with his severely blistered feet, but I have never seen anyone suffer so much in a race as Dr. Bob. In an effort to stabilize himself as fatigue set in, Dr. Bob had grabbed just about every plant in Australia that had hide-ripping barbs and thorns. He lost about twenty pounds, and his hands, arms, and legs were cut and swollen. I remember him sitting on the plane on the way home, just barely able to move, looking straight ahead in a comatose-like trance. But he *never* complained.

Now, when I think that I am hurting, I think back to that race and Dr. Bob. Of his ability to suffer and pay the price. As I wrote after the Badwater Quad, "To answer the question, 'What does it take to do an extreme event?' It takes the support of family and friends. It takes making and sticking to an agreement with yourself that you are willing to suffer and pay the price. It has been said that anything worth doing is worth doing well. Sometimes that includes a bit of suffering. That is indeed what life is about. I believe that to appreciate the profoundness of life, we have to live it to its fullest, both the joy and the suffering."

Eco-Challenge Morocco 1998

Mace, Shaz, Isaac Wilson (new to the team, since Dr. Bob did in fact retire from adventure racing), and I headed to Morocco for the fifth Eco-Challenge. Mace and I had already been to Morocco to complete the Marathon des Sables, a 150-mile desert stage run, so we were familiar with the climate and the Atlas Mountains. I had been sick with some kind of dysentery during the Marathon des Sables so we safeguarded against that by bringing a full-spectrum antibiotic.

We started the race on camels, then jumped into kayaks to head out onto the North Atlantic. Isaac is a strong paddler, like Shaz, and their skills immediately became apparent. We spent two days on some of the roughest water that I have experienced, including fifteen-foot waves and over fifty-mile-per-hour winds. Some of the breaking surf near the checkpoints was so bad that we were required to have one team member swim in to shore, leaving the kayaks in the care of the other teammates, as it would have been almost impossible to get the kayaks back out to sea if we had paddled in. At the end of the kayaking leg we did have to paddle to shore, "surfing" the waves as best possible. Shaz and I capsized and had to swim in. As we did, we looked over and saw Mace and Isaac surfing the waves beautifully—right up until the nose of their kayak planted itself in the soft submerged sand near shore. The back end of the kayak rose straight up, giving them an unwanted bird's-eye view of the water they were about to drop into. Luckily, we were all fine, although Shaz had swallowed a huge amount of water, and inhaled the rest. Race officials immediately fished her out and put her on oxygen. When she arose, spitting out the "piss and vinegar" words that we became so fond of hearing, we moved on.

We trekked onward through the Sahara Desert and up into the Atlas Mountains. At one point we had been without water for nearly a half day with none in sight when, miraculously, there appeared a man headed over to a nearby . . . yes, you guessed it . . . well. As the man helped us fill our bottles, we all thought how it was as if an angel had appeared in the form of this man. After helping us, he filled his containers and vanished over the horizon, and the desert was empty.

The temperatures dropped that night, and continued to drop the next day as we approached the top of a thirteen-thousand-foot peak. I was hypothermic and had to stop. Over the next couple of hours we holed up behind a ridge out of the wickedly cold wind, and my teammates pitched together to help get me warmed up and functioning again. Later on Shaz would have her difficulties too, and it was like pulling teeth to get her to relinquish her backpack in an effort to allow her to conserve some energy. As before, we persevered—learning of our own weaknesses, and of the strength of the team.

We finished on a long (over hundred-mile) mountain bike leg, drafting behind Isaac (who had been on the U.S. junior bike team), pedaling to a tenth place finish. It was a great feeling—being escorted the last few miles into Marrakech by a race official on a motorcycle. As we shook hands at the finish we experienced the elation that is afforded only to those who have gone through a long, hard race together.

Lessons Learned

As we set out onto the rough North Atlantic, I learned not to think about what it was we had to do, but to just do it. It wasn't the first time that I was scared of the unknown, and let that thought cross my mind. But I just focused on the task at hand. You see, if you take too much time to process information, you can psych yourself out of even *starting* something you really want to do. The trick is to get started, and just keep going.

My experience on the mountain taught me yet again that I don't have to be alone in the world. Trying to be self-sufficient at that moment failed to make sense. I realized that the strength of the team lies not with the strength of us as individuals, but within supporting and complementing each other. Our strength came from sticking together no matter what the circumstances or how crappy things got.

Once again, I was taught to count my blessings and have faith that things will always work out—in a race and in life. For whatever reason, that man high up in the Atlas Mountains was there, leading us to the well when we needed it most. Maybe it was divine providence, or maybe we willed it to happen. Whatever the reason, curiously things worked out, as they always had before and I'm sure always will.

Eco-Challenge Argentina 1999

What a magnificent environment the Andes Mountains of the Patagonia region was to race in! The lakes were pristine and the mountains majestic. But Argentina meant more than just a drastic change of scenery—there was another change within the Eco-Challenge rules. Now all members of the team had to be from the same country, so we could no longer use Shaz, who was Australian, on the team. Lisa was no longer racing, so Mace, Isaac, and I—along with Louise Cooper, an experienced and capable ultrarunner and adventure racer—made up Team Stray Dogs.

As we paddled the lakes and portaged over the land our hopes were to finish well, drawing upon positive experiences in past races. With the exception of Isaac suffering a bout of hypothermia at the end of that first paddle, things were going well. After getting Isaac up and running again, we mounted our horses and continued uneventfully to the start of a long trek. But within hours we were heading up the wrong drainage. Through the second night, we continued along, finally reaching the top of a mountain. As we looked across to a distant valley we saw the Discovery Channel helicopter. "Damn!" we all thought to ourselves, "we're still lost." We had lost about twelve hours and had scrambled across and up and down a couple of extra valleys, but eventually made our way to the checkpoint.

Continuing on, a storm blew in and the ropes section at the top of the mountain was closed for safety reasons. Teams were given the option of resting and waiting until the ropes section opened again, or trekking around the mountain—a longer route, but it meant we would continue moving. None of us wanted to stop, so we chose the trek—and were the only team to do so. We trekked throughout the night and arrived at the next checkpoint a half dozen spots or so ahead of where we had been. A calculated risk, but one that paid off!

Unfortunately, we lost another twelve hours trying to find a passageway up into and over a heavily forested area to the start of the final paddle. Paddling those last long miles, we had time to reflect on the humbling and frustrating experience of being lost for a total of almost twenty-four hours; but we still finished in the top twenty. Team Stray Dogs may have "strayed" off course, but we stuck together in a "pack," and successfully completed the course . . . as friends.

Lessons Learned

Never give up! I knew this from other races but, being lost twice, for so many hours, was a difficult test. To be honest, I never thought of quitting. I just never let the thought cross my mind, and I doubt that it crossed the minds of my teammates. Out of frustration comes clarity. Sometimes that clarity just takes a while to present itself.

As in a race course there are many ways to go in life. Sometimes going the long, hard way may actually be the best path. Sometimes continuing on the path I've chosen, trusting that it's the right one, having patience to continue, and following through, is the best thing I can do. Sometimes I choose the wrong path, and get lost. If I come to realize that the path is clearly wrong, rather than being stubborn and continuing on, there is nothing wrong with admitting my mistake and going another way. The trick is knowing the difference: when to continue on, and when to admit your mistake.

Whichever path I choose, I have to take responsibility for my choice. If I blame others when the path I am on becomes obstructed and obscured, I am not taking responsibility for my own life, and I become a powerless victim. Instead of being a victim, I must choose to accept the responsibility, and the consequences.

Eco-Challenge Sabah 2000

In 2000, Louise decided to put together and captain her own team and Isaac decided to race on a different team, so for Eco-Challenge Sabah, Malaysian Borneo, Mace and I asked Adrian to race with us, along with Maureen (Mo) Monaghan. Adrian would be our navigator and we had great confidence in Mo, who was an excellent athlete and, while now a U.S. citizen, had been on the Irish National Mountain Biking Team. This race would challenge many teams, including ours, as it involved a lot of trekking through thick jungles; days of paddling crude native outrigger style boats; and climbing in hot humid caves, wading through ankle-deep bat guano.

Minutes into the race we went from the top twenty to dead last as a rogue wave in the South China Sea hit our outrigger from the side, immediately capsizing us. We were told that if the outrigger capsized, there was little or no hope of righting it. I remember looking at Mace and agreeing with him that we would be the first team ever to be finished in less than an hour of racing. After the initial shock, and a bit of laughing at ourselves and our predicament, we gathered our wits. We all stood on one side of the craft, pulled on ropes that we had attached to the opposite side, and, in a cooperative tug, heaved the craft upright. We were shocked and looked at each other in disbelief. On one level we joked about not wanting to continue, as it would have been all too simple to break open the radio and just call it quits. After a few more wisecracks and more laughing, we got over that and, in keeping with the sprit of Stray Dogs to persevere no matter what, paddled on.

On the first island, the team had to split up, with only two members doing the next land leg of the race. Since our mast had broken, Mace and I went on the island swim and trek while Mo and Adrian fixed the outrigger. It was during the island trek that we met up with Charlie Engle. We had lost our map when we capsized, so Charlie agreed to share his (whew!). We spent the rest of the day and that night swimming and slopping through mud, generally having a great time, poking fun at our predicament when we got slightly lost. Once again, Mace and I didn't much care, and loved the fact that Charlie didn't much care, either. Some of the inexperienced teams had heard that "the Stray Dogs are navigating," and, knowing that we were Eco-Challenge veterans, were eager to follow. Yep. They didn't know that it was truly a case of the blind leading the blind! We did manage to find our way (eventually), and met back up with Mo and Adrian.

With the mast fixed, we paddled from island to island. On one island, we climbed up the belly of a hollow mountain in what is referred to as "the bat caves." What a smelly place that was! We climbed up hills and over jagged knife-edged cliffs and, as morning broke, rappelled down a three-hundred-foot cliff into the thick jungle. I had inadvertently left a water bottle behind, so Mace shared his water with me until it was gone. A couple of hours later Mace was in the worst condition I had ever seen him. He had literally sacrificed his water, and his well-being, to help me continue. Reluctantly, he finally gave up his pack and we all staggered back to the outriggers, thoroughly exhausted. Here, we met up with John Howard and his team, who had decided to withdraw from the race. John knew that we had lost much of our equipment (not just the map) when we capsized, and his team graciously provided us with everything we needed to finish the race. Although the race was over for them, they were eager to help us finish in any way that they could.

After just one more day, we did finish. We had come back from capsizing the boat, a near race-ending event, to finish in twelfth place.

Lessons Learned

Humor is the antidote to misery. When we were floating out in the South China Sea, at first we thought there was no hope. We literally humored the boat into submission and, when it wasn't looking, we up-righted it. Then we laughed and joked ourselves through the rest of the course. I remember sitting out a storm on an island, watching as other teams sought refuge in lifeboats hanging on the sides of huge commercial shrimp boats that were also waiting out the storm, while others hopeless-ly clung to their overturned or waterlogged boats. After the race most of the teams who finished talked about laughing somewhere along the line, as we did. What else is there to do at times? There's truth in the old saying, "If I didn't laugh, I'd cry."

Empathy is required. At one time or another we have all been reduced to less than human. We must remember our own humility, and be there to help the person who is in the greatest need. While our own survival instincts are key to allowing us to prevail, occasionally we *all* need the help of our teammates and other teams. If someone is in the toilet (so to speak), but others are willing to help and encourage that person's will to survive, we can all succeed.

With the combination of humor and empathy, we get through it some-how . . . we always do.

Eco-Challenge New Zealand 2001

Mace, Adrian, Mo, and I were excited to race together again in New Zealand. This course—with the vertical-gain equivalent to climbing Mount Everest . . . twice—would seemingly agree with the team as Adrian, Mace, and I were all very familiar with mountain venues. Mace and I live in the Colorado Rockies, running fourteen-thousand-foot peaks for training; I had summited Mount Whitney nine times, all after finish-ing the Badwater race across Death Valley; and Adrian lives near the Sierra Nevada in California, and holds the record for the fastest climb of the highest peaks in all fifty states. The sheer beauty of the course was appre-ciated by all of us, especially by Mo, who had never seen the majestic beauty of mountains like those of the "Southern Alps" in New Zealand.

Most of the elevation gain was covered during the trekking/moun-taineering and mountain biking legs of the race. During the second night of one of the steep, long, and rocky bike legs, my lighting system began to dim. To further complicate the situation, a rock kicked up and nicked my rear hydraulic brake line, rendering it useless. Mo rode close to my side, just behind me, to provide lighting and coach me on how to effectively brake on very steep downhills with no rear brake. I still went over the handlebars more than once. But my skills sharpened and the whole experience made me a much better mountain biker.

The mountaineering sections proved fairly easy, as we were all accustomed to working together as a team. There *were* differences of opinion about safety—in particular, whether or not it was necessary to clip into the ropes on some of the steeper sections. In a very democratic process that was respectful of everyone's opinion, we agreed not to force any member on the team to do something they did not feel comfortable with. So it was an individual's choice to clip in, or not.

The rest of the course was essentially business as usual, and we finished in eighteenth place. It seemed that the team was continuing to gel, and we all looked forward to racing together once more.

Lessons Learned

Learning to adapt to a situation and improvise is key in adventure racing, and in life. "Rolling with the punches"—instead of being paralyzed, ineffective, and helpless—enables us to deal with challenges in our lives. Losing my bike light and brake line could have been a negative thing but, with the help of Mo, we turned a negative into a positive: My skills evolved and we learned the importance of teamwork once again.

Everyone's voice counts. If your interactions with others are diplomatic, any difference of opinion can be resolved. We may have to change the way we think about something and compromise, but there is always a solution. By looking at things from all angles, we reach a better understanding of each other, and obtain a more profound and empathetic view of life.

Eco-Challenge Fiji 2002

Some teams, mainly the French, had been bragging that it was easy to finish Eco-Challenge. In Fiji, Mark Burnett apparently wanted to send a message to everyone that his race was not easy. At the pre-race meeting, Mark said that this would be the toughest Eco-Challenge ever, and even offered money back, "no questions asked," to any team that didn't want to start the race. He explained that, because of the difficulty of the course, the last ocean kayaking section would be divided into three categories: a long, an intermediate, and a short course. He predicted that only a few teams would be able to finish. He was right.

Sponsorship dollars were hard to obtain (after the September 11, 2001, terrorist attacks and downturn in the economy), forcing Mace and I to change the team. While we were disappointed to not be able to have Adrian and Mo on the team, we were pleased to race with Charlie Engle (whose map we had shared in Borneo) and Dianette Strange, a small but capable woman who had finished several adventure races.

Around midnight we were loaded on a bus and driven to the start in the middle of a field. Our backpacks were packed and, as with every Eco-Challenge, there were those who bolted out from the start. For two cold, overcast days we swam canyons and trekked up streams because the jungle was too dense to travel through. And, as with every Eco-Challenge, after a couple of days the difficulty of the race reduces egos. In this race, by the end of the second day, half the teams had missed the first cutoff.

The second night we decided that it was too dangerous to travel through giant boulders in the dark, so we stopped and huddled beside a stream. Dianette, who has *no* body fat, became hypothermic. As she shivered uncontrollably, we took turns huddling and trying to keep her warm. At times she would slip into an almost unconscious state and speak incoherently. It was a long, fearful night, and we were thankful when dawn broke enabling us to move and generate the precious energy that is a key to staying warm.

The next four days continued to be cold and overcast as we paddled up streams, trekked up even more steams, and mountain biked up and down obscure trails and muddy dirt roads—and we watched more teams drop out. Finally, we crossed over to the opposite side of the island and were bathed in sunshine. On the seventh day, we finally saw our gear boxes and could change our clothes and get more food. On our tenth and last day, we rappelled down a cliff near a steam. As I hopped onto a boulder eight feet above the streambed, my feet immediately went out from under me, and I found myself falling headfirst downward. Next thing I knew, I was laying in the streambed, reaching into my mouth to see if I had lost any teeth or broken my jaw. Luckily, my water bottle, which was on my backpack shoulder strap next to my chin, had absorbed the impact, saving my jaw. Although I had landed on my right shoulder and it ached, I was mostly intact. Mace came running up and asked if I was okay. When I said, yes, in true Macy style he joked that, as he watched me fall, his first thought was that it would be a bitch to get me out of there; and his second thought was that it was a bummer that we would be out of the race so close to the finish.

We carried on and arrived at the ocean shore, where we hopped in the kayaks and paddled the short course to the finish. Burnett was right. Out of eighty-one teams who started the race, only twenty-three finished (we were happy to be seventeenth). Many of the top teams, including the French, did not finish; and for good reason—it was a hard race.

Lessons Learned

Never assume anything. At the start, we had assumed that we would be able to get into our gear boxes every few days. We got caught—just when you think you have things down, the unknown reaches up and grabs you in the ass! It also taught us to accept our fate and make do with, and be grateful for, what we had; especially our food, no matter how meager.

I was reminded to always have hope. When Dianette was cold and shivering and there was no end in sight, it seemed hopeless. Although we had to wait for days before the sun came out, it did come out, warming our souls and giving us new life. During those tough times, we never lost our sense of humor—one of the first skills we had learned in Utah. Hope and humor, more than anything, gave us the will to continue. Life is much the same. Taking the good with the bad, and deciding to see the brighter side, makes life truly a joy worth living.

So . . . I'm Really *Not* Lost

Although the fate of the Eco-Challenge is unknown, adventure racing will continue to take its competitors to exotic places on a physical and mental level. For me the journey of running, adventure racing, and mountaineering (my new goal is to climb the Seven Summits—so far I've completed five, including Everest) has given me a profound sense of gratitude for what I have, who I am, and where I am going. Adventure racing presents the opportunity to learn new technical skills but, more importantly, it provides the opportunity to learn more about yourself and the importance of positive interactions with others. Each of the nine Eco-Challenges that I participated in provided valuable life lessons, including the following:

Learn to laugh, especially at yourself—never take yourself too seriously

Work as a team, and draw strength from each other

Have fun

Take everything in stride; don't complain about your "problems"—find solutions

Learn from your own weaknesses

Humility is important—allow yourself the pleasure of being humbled and you *will* learn from it

Keep a positive attitude, no matter what

True friendships are those built on respect and admiration, solidified by facing adversity together

Strength of character includes being brave, honest, and humble

Being humble must include the ability to *not* say "I told you so"

Count your blessings, especially your friends

Things always work out if we trust ourselves, allow ourselves to trust our friends, and can be a person whom *others* can trust

Have the invaluable ability to suffer, with grace

To appreciate the profoundness of life, live it to its fullest, both the joy and the suffering

Don't think too much, just do, or you might psych yourself out

You're not alone, so you don't have to be self-sufficient; it's okay to draw strength from others

Never give up

Be responsible for your own choices, good and bad, and accept the consequences

Turn a negative into a positive—it will empower you

Humor is the antidote to misery

Empathy is required

Adapt to any situation and improvise; "rolling with the punches" is one key to success

Every voice counts—with diplomatic interactions, any difference of opinion can be resolved

Never assume you know everything—there's always more to learn

Be grateful for the gifts you're given

Always have hope

For me, I hope the next few decades will be as fulfilling and enlightening as the past five.

Chasing Big Dreams at Beaver Creek: Balance Bar 24-Hour Adventure Race

Photo courtesy of Mark Bockmann

NAME: MARK BOCKMANN

AGE: 34

RESIDENCE: BOULDER, CO

YEARS ADVENTURE RACING: 3

At first I wasn't planning to do the Balance Bar 24-Hour Race. It was expensive, and my fiancée Molly and I would have to find a third teammate. We usually race as a team of two. But as I read more about it on the Balance Bar website, I became excited about the race. It sounded like a spectacular course, with one standout section—whitewater swimming. We decided that if we could find a good teammate, we'd do it.

My friend Bill Wright answered my plea, although he is usually more interested in adventures of his own design than in organized races such as this. For example, Bill's the one who first thought up such exploits as the "Sanitarado," a one-day traverse of the six peaks above Boulder, starting at Mount Sanitas and ending with a steep bushwhack to the top of Eldorado Peak some twenty miles to the south. Bill was a bit concerned about the length and difficulty of the course, being relatively new to the sport of adventure racing. Knowing Bill's strength and boundless energy, I knew there was no way he'd be holding *us* back, and I tried to reassure him of this fact.

I signed us up in the nonelite division after a short period of indecision. With an unprecedented $60,000 up for grabs for the first-place elite team, all the big players would certainly show up. Nike/ACG/Balance Bar fielded two teams, with Ian Adamson captaining the second of the two, and Montrail, Earthlink, Balance Bar, and Epinephrine were all registered and ready for action. We'd be seriously outclassed if we entered elite. Plus, there was an amazing first prize in the nonelite division: a two-year lease on a Ford Explorer Sport Trac for each team member! It seemed too good to be true and too much to hope for, but it was fun to think about anyway.

Race day arrived before we knew it. Registration, gear checks, and cer-tifications took up the whole day Friday, and we scarcely had time to plot points on our maps and hit the beds before the alarm went off at 1:35 A.M. Saturday. With my nervous excitement I don't believe I got a wink of sleep.

Thirty-seven bleary-eyed teams climbed aboard buses to be carried to the start line at State Bridge on the Colorado River. We huddled in sleepy clusters on the bus, unwilling to stand around in the cold night air wait-ing for the 4:00 A.M. starting gun.

Finally the gun went off and we jogged up the trail in the dark. We turned uphill, and the pack quickly spread out. We had fourteen miles and four thousand feet of climbing ahead of us before we reached our first transition. Bill surged ahead, leaving Molly and me gasping for breath. He wanted to stay in contact with one of the front groups, but we just weren't going to be able to keep up at that pace. Soon we hooked a towrope up to Molly and started motoring ahead. I struggled to keep up, but we found ourselves not only staying in contact with the group in front of us, but leav-ing most of them behind, I noted in amazement as we cruised past elite Team Revo like they were standing still.

"Hiking uphill is my forte," Bill admitted modestly. What an under-statement!

Dawn arrived as we closed in on PC1 (passport control point 1). For the last half hour we'd been traveling with two teams—Timex and Salomon. We had been on good trails the whole time and were able to run every-thing but the steepest sections. A cameraman appeared up ahead—a sure sign that the PC was near. He asked us questions about the course and which team we were as he huffed alongside us with his heavy video cam-era. We suddenly hit a T-junction. Timex veered left, but I'd checked the maps earlier and knew the checkpoint was to our right. Molly handed in our passport and discovered we were in third place overall. We were absolutely thrilled at the news.

Energized, we charged up the trail just behind our friend Adam Chase with his Team Salomon. I was getting congratulated by my team for my navigation skills, and felt pretty good about myself at the time. But how does the saying go, "Pride goes before destruction"?

I had to pause to switch to a new map, and it showed us climbing up a hillside with few geographic features. At this point the trail had disappeared.

"Which way around this peak up ahead?" Bill asked.

I took a compass bearing. "We need to go farther south, to our right."

We cut straight across to a saddle. The other side looked nothing like the terrain shown on the map, and furthermore it looked like we were in for some heavy bushwhacking ahead. Salomon had gone left around the peak earlier.

I stared at the map, trying to make sense of the terrain. Bill took a look, too.

"You're looking at the bike section!" he exclaimed, and in fact he was right. This part of the map contained both the current trekking section we were on, as well as the next bike section. We had already marked both routes with a pen, but I was following the wrong one!

It's both frustrating and relieving to discover such a mistake. The frustration comes from knowing you've lost time, and the relief comes from finally knowing your whereabouts again. We made the best of it and were soon back on track.

"Track" in this case was an overstatement, as we found ourselves completely off-trail, scrambling up a steep hillside, climbing over an endless jumble of fallen logs, and stepping through marshy bogs and streams. Mere hours after we'd had enough, we emerged from the forest onto a perfectly smooth, well-used logging road. And it was headed in the right direction!

Soon we were trotting downhill to the first transition area. A number of teams were already there, and more arrived soon after us. I guess we should have savored our few moments near the front, because that time was clearly over. We quickly unpacked our bike boxes, assembled our bikes, grabbed some food, and pedaled off. Hordes of hungry mosquitoes had provided additional incentive to get out of the transition area quickly.

Luckily, after a short period of rolling terrain, this bike section headed rapidly downhill, dropping thousands of feet on its way to the Colorado River far below. We were making good time, flying actually. Well, Bill was really flying there for a minute when he hit something and crashed in singularly magnificent fashion.

He was okay, but both tires were flat. A quick analysis revealed two additional problems: First, he was running Schraeder tubes and we had only Presta spares, and worse, his tires were so old and worn that he had shredded one sidewall. The tube was visibly bulging out the side in three places. It would never last through the race!

"Bike maintenance is not my strong point," Bill said sheepishly.

No worries, we'd use the Presta tubes and hope they worked. And Molly saved the day with her quick-thinking solution: She used a Balance Bar wrapper to reinforce the tire's sidewall. She is so great at coming up with spontaneous and resourceful solutions. And it worked!

We arrived intact at the second transition area. Our next task was to load the bikes onto a truck and then clamber aboard an SUV for the "Ford Rally, Part 1." We had to direct our driver exactly where we wanted to go, which was PC4 in Kremmling. Along the way we pawed through the maps, trying to find the right ones before we missed any turns. Meanwhile, the whole team changed into wetsuits, packed our CamelBaks, and refueled while we nervously awaited the start of the whitewater swimming section.

It was Gore Canyon, as we had feared, home of some infamous Class IV and V rapids, as well as numerous stretches of Class II and III white-water. We grabbed our boogie boards and swim fins, loaded ourselves down with life jackets and full CamelBaks, and waddled into the flat brown water. We were in for a long, boring, cramp-inducing swim before we ever reached Gore Canyon.

How can I describe the slow torture of this incessant swim? Within half an hour my calves and hamstrings began to cramp painfully with each flip of my flippers. The water seemed to average about a foot and a half deep, making it difficult to get a full kick with the swim fins.

To break the monotony and spread the cramps more evenly among other muscle groups, I experimented with different methods of locomotion. The basic stroke consisted of a simple flutter kick, relaxing with my upper body on the board. I branched out from there with a sort of freestyle stroke with my arms, although this had the disadvantage of causing the board to creep out from under me, necessitating frequent adjustments. Soon I found that the "Sea Turtle" stroke worked better in this regard (using both arms in unison stroking out to the sides), but it was strenuous. For the shallow sections, I used the "Crab Crawl," digging my hands into the river bottom and pulling myself forward inch by inch. Other methods included the side-stroke (quite funny looking with a boogie board, I might add), and the "Reverse Heel Dig," wherein I faced backward, sat on my board, and pushed myself along by digging into the sandy river bottom with my heels.

All these techniques may have looked quite humorous to the casual passerby, but thankfully there were no casual passersby. It is worth noting at this point that Molly and Bill seemed to be having a much easier time with all of this. I believe I only saw them use the first two—more basic— techniques. Regardless, we eventually heard the roar of the river up ahead, and knew that our flatwater monotony was about to end.

The first rapid was a fun Class III run. We cruised through it with smiles on our faces. Then followed a long stretch of Class II, but soon enough the portages began. We had mandatory portages around every Class IV and V rapid. This required a lot of gear changes, as it's difficult to scramble over slippery rocks while wearing swim fins. It began to seem like every time we got into the water, we had to get right back out again.

But our spirits improved as we passed several elite teams along the way, including our friends on Team Salomon. And interestingly, Team Earthlink passed us on this section. Even though they were the ones passing us, we were psyched to have been ahead of Robyn Benincasa & Co. this far into the race.

We then arrived at the biggest swimmable rapid, a Class III-plus. Volunteers on shore gave us instructions on which lines to take, and said we had the option to portage it if we wanted. No way. We continued straight into the fray. Adrenaline pumping, we tried to avoid the biggest rocks and pick a good line as the current swept us through the canyon. We'd drop into a hole and get sucked under, but eventually the hole would spit us out downstream. Usually there was enough time to catch a breath before the next hole sucked us in. What a way to experience big whitewater . . . swimming headfirst down the river!

We made it! Laughing, we kicked slowly down the river below the big rapid.

Rounding a bend, the impressive ropes section appeared. An amazing array of cables was stretched all the way across the canyon. The volunteers said it had taken them a full week to build. At one end we climbed a rope ladder to reach the cables, then we tightrope-walked across the river using a chest-high cable for balance. It was a lot more strenuous than it looked. I reached the other side of the ropes and sat down on the cliff ledge, exhausted.

For me, there is a point in every long race where the adrenaline rush wears off and I suddenly become aware of how tired I really am. This was that point. The fatigue washed over my wet body like a wave. If I had known that we were twenty hours from finishing the race at this point, I'm not sure I could have continued.

The ropes were even more of a challenge for Molly. She has climbed with me on occasion, but her fear of heights is acute. She viewed the ropes section warily. In particular, she mistrusted the thin, threadlike safety lines that we clipped to the cables for backup. Pushing doubt aside, she inched her way across, fighting valiantly to overcome the strain and reach the cliff top to join me. Later, she admitted that was the toughest part of the course for her. "I wouldn't have made it without seeing you at the other side waiting for me," she told me.

After a quick rappel, we were back to swim/portage/swim mode again, but now the portages grew longer and the swimming sections shorter. A clap of thunder ripped through the canyon, and in a few moments we were huddled at the river's edge, holding our boogie boards like shields overhead as huge balls of hail pelted us.

Whack! A big one hit Molly right on the knuckle, causing her to wince. "Watch your fingers!" she yelled over the din of the storm. We tried to curl our fingers under the boards while still not losing our grasp, but each of us got nailed several times by the three-quarter-inch balls of hail.

The storm quickly passed, and as we entered the lower part of the canyon we were able to swim more. Unfortunately, this section contained a large number of rocks hiding just below the surface. Carried along by the swift current, my knee would smack a rock. The pain seared through my body, and just as it began to subside I'd inevitably smack that same knee again with another rock. Molly's and Bill's legs got abused in similar fashion.

Eventually we emerged from Gore Canyon and found the transition area, with kayaks waiting. The checkpoint volunteer informed us we were in tenth place overall! Not bad, but we had no idea if any other nonelite teams (competing with us for the Explorers) were still ahead.

The course continued another fourteen miles down the river to State Bridge, where we had started the race many hours earlier. This section had long stretches of flatwater interspersed with a number of rapids, some of which were rated Class III.

Our boats were Cobra Triples, made specifically for adventure racing and used in all the Balance Bar races. They are large, but they're comfortable and handle surprisingly well. We negotiated most of this section adeptly, working together as a team and trying to refuel and rehydrate along the way. On a few occasions we hit rocks that capsized us, but we were able to right the boat and continue without pulling ashore due to the boat's self-bailing properties.

At State Bridge we dragged our waterlogged bodies onto shore and created a wet, sloppy mess of gear at the transition area. Here we discovered that we'd incorrectly plotted the next checkpoint. Luckily Team Salomon caught up to us at that point and we were able to follow them up a steep mini-mountain to a 130-foot-rappel. After sliding down a ridiculously steep and loose slope back to level ground at the bottom, we hopped in a waiting Expedition for "Ford Rally, Part 2."

It was now dark, and we frantically tried to get organized for the next mountain bike section. Loading everything up in the SUV, we hit the road. Navigation to the next checkpoint could be difficult, because it was nowhere near any intersections or major geographic features. Furthermore, with the darkness it was difficult to see anything outside the vehicle.

Somehow we made it, but we discovered that another nonelite team had beaten us there! Thankfully one of the guys from that team came over and let us know they'd been hit with a seven-hour time penalty for skipping the swim. We therefore shouldn't worry about competing with them, he said. Such a nice guy, and he even offered us some chicken and ribs. For the moment, we were in first place in our division, but how long would it last?

Soon we found ourselves on our bikes headed uphill. The trail was rutted and overgrown, and within half an hour our progress ended at a private property gate. This definitely was not the right way! Resigned, we turned around and pedaled all the way back to the start. This time a handy ranch hand pointed us in the right direction . . . through an open gate that had previously been closed! If only it had been open earlier, we would have known it was the right direction.

Now began the longest and most difficult section. I started to get into serious trouble, getting that weak, woozy feeling I get when I'm starting to bonk. I handed the maps over to Bill, as I was in no condition to navigate. I tried to eat and drink some more, and Bill gave me several long pushes to help me up the hill. Before long my biggest problem became the sleep monster. I was having difficulty focusing, and I wobbled along on my bike in a half-asleep state. This continued for hours as we ground our way up the hill toward the checkpoint at eleven thousand feet. Bill continued as strong as ever, and Molly seemed to be doing fine as well, although I could tell she was getting tired.

We eventually came to the end of the road, quite literally. We found ourselves at the top of a huge ridge overlooking the Vail/Eagle valley, and the dirt road we'd been following ended right there. Clearly we were off-route again. I roused myself out of my narcoleptic state long enough to stare at the maps.

"It's this way," I declared, pointing to the east. Bill and Molly shrugged and followed. Our bike lights had died at this point and we were down to one LED light. Riding was out of the question. We trudged along, pushing our bikes toward what we hoped would be PC11. Half an hour later we stared through the darkness at a small glowing green object in a field, the checkpoint! It was all downhill to Beaver Creek from here!

Unfortunately our troubles were not over. Molly and I were now at the point of hallucinating. We both saw Bill walking up ahead with his arm around someone (whom, we did not know), when actually it was his bike. I noticed that there were hundreds of Quaker Instant Oatmeal packets growing in the middle of the trail, and then later realize it was clumps of grass. Molly saw a large barrel of honey with a tin owl perched on top. This weirdness continued until dawn.

Dawn! Yes, how great it was. As I stumbled along, I noticed Molly rolling past me with ease. How is she doing that? I wondered. Oh, she was on her bike. Wow, it was finally light enough to make out the trail. I hopped on my bike as well and soon we were riding through the frigid air toward the valley, still far below.

With Bill's navigation we successfully made it through the resort neighborhoods of Avon and up to the base village at Beaver Creek. At the transition area the volunteers told us we were still in the lead for the nonelite division. Foggy thoughts of driving a new car drifted through my head, but the race wasn't over yet.

Molly and I were moving in slow motion. We struggled to understand our final task. We were given one new map and told to plot the last three checkpoints. Next, we'd split up the team, each with a radio. Molly and I would find PC13a and Bill would find PC13b. Then we'd both meet at PC14 with the help of the radios and head to the finish in Beaver Creek village.

Our first checkpoint was a thousand feet straight up the ski slope. My right knee was giving me excruciating pain, and I could barely make my way up the mountain. Salomon, now on their way down the mountain to the finish line, waved cheerfully at us. Molly waited patiently with me while Bill chugged ahead. We both had altimeters to help us find the checkpoints, but still it was a difficult task, as we only had one map between us.

By the time Molly and I found our checkpoint, Bill had already found both 13b and 14 and was waiting impatiently. Team Timex was on the mountain and catching up rapidly! I gritted my teeth and plodded up the hill. We finally met Bill.

"Couldn't you hear the other teams on the radio?" he asked anxiously. "We're about to lose!"

He grabbed our hands and pulled us rapidly to the final checkpoint. One member of Timex was already there, with the others on their way. We signed in and limped as quickly as we could back down the mountain.

Frantic now, Bill kept trying to get us to go faster.

"Look, they're catching up!" he yelled. I looked up the mountain and saw Timex chasing us at top speed. Our fragile hold on first place was about to slip away, but we wanted those cars!

Sprinting to the finish, we crossed the line as a team. I could barely believe it was over. We had beaten Timex by less than three minutes, after twenty-nine hours of racing!

Yes, we had actually done it. We'd won the nonelite division and each of us would soon be driving a brand-new Explorer Sport Trac. Unbelievable!

And all I wanted to do was sleep.

I Am an Adventure Racer
by Nathan Lake
Team PureFit/Orca

I am an adventure racer. My skills are many, my needs are few: a long trail to run, a high cliff to climb, a fast river to ride, a good bike, and trusted teammates.

My sport is inherently risky, but risk taking is part of who I am. I consistently strive to know, understand, and prepare for those risks so that my team will arrive safely at the finish line.

I respect all athletes for their achievements, and the work and dedication they have for their sport. Having the ability to win is satisfying. Having the opportunity to participate is life.

Sometimes adventure racing is my life and sometimes it is just a hobby, but at my core I am, and will always be, an adventure racer.

Elf Authentique Aventure Race—Brazil 2000
Wanting It Bad Enough—The Journey

NAME: JIM MANDELLI
AGE: 43
RESIDENCE: NORTH VANCOUVER,
    BC, CANADA
YEARS ADVENTURE RACING: 9

L to R: Jim Mandelli, Cammy Ronchetto,
Dave Schmidt, Joe Wheeler

I'll take three teammates who are mediocre, funny, moderately talented, but really, really want it over three superstars any day! I have often stated this to my friends, who often chuckle at me. "Mandelli, what flipping planet are you from? You can't race with rookies. They'd drive you insane!"

Sometimes in life you actually get to test one of your theories! My chance came as the result of several freak circumstances coming together. Sit back and let me share my story—a story that helped me put this sport into perspective, form long-lasting friendships, and, most importantly, show the racing community and myself that it takes "wanting it bad enough" to figure out that "the journey" of the race is where it really is.

I distinctly remember *that* telephone call on a rainy bone-chilling March 2000 day in Vancouver, BC while sitting—okay, napping—comfortably at home on the couch in front of the television. Already depressed from pulling out two weeks earlier from a climbing trip to Lohtse in Nepal, I wallowed in self-pity, convalescing over a recent life-threatening encounter with some foreign blood virus that had accompanied me from somewhere in the Far East.

It was with that bleak picture that I viewed the world when a friend of mine, Joe Wheeler, excitedly called me to invite, nay "persuade" me to help navigate and lead their team in the Brazil edition of the Elf Authentique Aventure Race. "Jim," he exclaimed, "we'll have our entry fee paid for and be a feature team but I've got to get an experienced navigator before they'll agree to it. Besides, it's only fourteen days long (the longest distance race to date)—what could go wrong?"

Have you ever had that feeling like you were tied to two elephants, each going in the opposite direction, and you're being ripped apart, slowly, limb from limb? Well that pretty much sums up my thoughts. I had heard of this race six months earlier and at that time, while extremely excited with the race venue and the prospect of racing in the Amazon jungle, had ultimately decided to join the team planning to climb Lohtse, the fifth highest mountain in the world, nestled in the Everest massif.

Every once in a while life throws you a curveball, or two in my case. I had returned from a nine-week "vacation" in the Far East having traveled through Thailand, Malaysia, Korea, Borneo, and Singapore (the trip was awesome—thanks for asking!). Feeling like Superman upon my return, I entered and competed very successfully in the World Endurance Duathlon. Still on a high from that, I suddenly found myself wrought with high fevers and blood-freezing chills starting the next day. After two days of lying in bed and either sweating to death or shivering to death, Colleen convinced me (well—actually told me) to go to the hospital. After the obligatory poking and prodding, the doctor smiled at me and said "That's it—we're done!" Awesome, I thought, now I can get back home and lie down on the couch again before I faint.

Summoning all my strength (of course trying to hide the effort it took) I staggered up and started walking toward the exit door. "This way, Jim" was all I heard. Refusing to acknowledge, I continued to slowly walk to the door before Colleen grabbed my arm and gently led me deeper into the caverns of the formaldehyde-odorous hospital. Within minutes I was staring at my home for the next eight days—a clinically depressing hospital bed.

Well—to make a long story short, I had contracted a blood virus and had a temperature of 105 to 106 degrees for six days straight, and a blood pressure of 60/30 for most of that same period. The doctors must have had little hope for me because no less than twenty doctors a day came to look at me. As suddenly as the fever came, however, it left. The doctors admitted defeat and took credit for saving my life (yup—those extra-strength Tylenol pills they prescribed worked wonders!). But the real damage was not the fever as in the aftermath I was just a pathetic version of myself. I kind of looked like me, sounded like me, but had absolutely no energy. I'd walk one block and have to grab a stop sign pole or sit down. Two months later I was able to run for ten minutes without fainting. By March when Joe called, I had worked my way up to ten kilometers of running.

Back to the phone call and the elephants: of course I wanted to go! But all I was thinking was "Holy $#$&—how the hell am I going to race hard, navigate, and lead a team of virtual rookies to the finish line in the hardest race to date in AR?" Well—I did what any normal adventure racer would do—I lied to myself. A sane person knows the right answer. No, not us adventure racers. I told Joe my situation. Then I made a deal. "Give me the weekend Joe. I'll go out with friends, do a fifty-kilometer trek in the mountains of BC, and if I survive, I'll come." Joe and my other teammates, Cammy Ronchetto and Dave Schmidt, waited with bated breath until Monday when I made that call—"Okay," I replied, "let's get this rolling!"

For the next three weeks the seven of us (Joe, Dave, Cammy, and I as racers and James, Wendy, and Joe's sister as crew) came together to forge the most amazing friendships and complete successfully (fourth-place finish!) one of the most amazing journeys of our lives. To this day, over four years later, I can safely say that all of us reflect fondly on those three weeks—frequently using those memories as a crutch to strengthen ourselves when life seems to come crashing down all around us!

I was also quite intrigued with the chance to test my theory about taking a rookie team with tons of heart and soul through such an endeavor (although at the time I had no idea just how much heart and soul they were really capable of). Somehow I never doubted that we'd finish the full course. Showing up at the start seeing many of my friends, I recalled telling them who I was racing with. "Who?" they'd ask again. That only made me more excited about the upcoming journey.

I have often looked back on that race with complete and utter love for what our team (my friends) achieved! Joe had never done more than a thirty-six-hour race. Cammy had only done two five-day races. Dave, whom I had never met before, was in a similar experience bracket as Joe. Our crew was also in the same boat—lots of determination but never had crewed before. Each and every one of these racers taught me a ton about racing, the sport, and about myself.

Let's look at Joe for a minute. Joe had long hair that reminded me of a biblical figure. He was the messiest with gear, the slowest in the transitions, and the one who talked the most to locals. He looked like the least likely adventure racer. Did he drive me a little crazy at first? Damn right! Yet Joe was actually the one who had the sport figured out—not me! Joe had perspective on his lot in the race and why he was in Brazil. The Journey! He taught me to open my eyes to the wonders of the people and the land that we were racing through. I cannot begin to tell you how many times he amazed me with his ability to see things through the wide-open wondrous eyes of a child (not implying he was a child of course!).

One night on a horseback leg we came to a dark zone, and chose to stop in a village where Joe somehow managed to find a local who loved heavy-metal music as much as he did. He suddenly disappeared for a while, and it wasn't until we heard the music and Joe's voice from the second-story window that we solved the mystery. They must have talked and listened to Metallica for hours. We quickly rescued him from the Brazilian father who was trying to get Joe to marry one of his pregnant daughters. I think I got upset at Joe for disappearing but he didn't care—he had come to race hard and experience the journey, knowing he could do both.

Joe was also the calmest of the four of us. Cammy lost part of her rear derailleur at the start of a long bike leg. Without it she wasn't able to pedal—a potential race-ending situation. While I tried to jury-rig a new rear derailleur, Joe calmly took Dave with him back to the last village, showed the local villagers the part that was missing, and had the entire village out there looking for this piece. We found it and made new friends in the village, as they saved the day for us—The Journey!

For those who have not raced an Elf race before, it's pretty hard to imagine how difficult the race was. It's one of those types of races that you have to be there to really appreciate the pain and suffering of jungle racing. Enter Dave Schmidt—local comedian and all-around purveyor of charm and goodwill. Standing something like six-foot-four, Dave was the gentle giant. From the first time we met he was the one who was able to make light of everything, with an uncanny ability to create laughter when it was needed most. Without Dave, I doubt we would have been able to finish.

There is still one night that stands out in our minds as the night of all nights. We had been paddling in the mangrove swamps for what seemed like a million years. Arms were aching and falling off, it was Day 9 with four days left, and the race was down to four teams. It was pitch black and we had finally left the swamps for the coastline where we had to find a CP on one of the invisible dunes on one of the islands (there were many islands and many dunes). Those who have raced French races understand the teasing that goes on between the Americans and French. The Americans are always speaking English with a French accent, pretending to be the race organizers and teasing themselves. Well, Dave excels at this—so much so that he had Gerard Fusil, the race organizer (creator of the Raid Gauloises), in stitches. Well, on that paddling night Dave started yelling out in a very French accent, "Hello CP—where are you?" He'd go on for hours with this—we were giddy with sleep deprivation and laughed nonstop. Finally as we neared the real CP, in pitch-black conditions, Dave continued his charade when suddenly, from high atop a dune, came a desperate reply: "I'm over here! I'm over here!" We hadn't expected a reply and that started an uncontrollable fit of laughter that lasted for what seemed like hours. My stomach still hurts from the memory.

Dave helped me understand that you can laugh really hard while racing hard, but by doing so you get much more out of your teammates. He was more than a comedian. On a very swollen lake in the kayaks, we had to find the mouth of a very narrow river in the mangrove swamps. I'm a reasonably good navigator, but I have to admit being totally humbled here. Dave simply looked at the large swollen swamp as I pointed generally where I thought we had to go, and, like a bloodhound, he studied the minute flow patterns within the lake and within thirty minutes had us entering the narrow river. With darkness soon upon us, he saved us hours and hours of wasted time trying to find the river mouth. My lesson there was that even though I was brought onto the team to lead them through the race, you have to know when to step down and trust that others will step up to the plate!

Anyone who did this race will immediately tell you the number one reason why teams dropped out. Foot Rot! The ability for any team to remain in a jungle race revolves around the team's ability to endure an unimaginable amount of foot pain. The question is not *if* you will get fungal rot in the feet but *when*. We, like all the teams out there, suffered tremendously. After Day 1 we witnessed team upon team pulling out because of bad feet. We talked at length about it during the race. We felt it nonstop. It was so intense that it became debilitating. There were never thoughts of anyone on this team pulling out—not vocally anyway! This team understood that pain was simply a constant reminder of the final

goal of this race—The Journey! My favorite phrase is that "pain is tempo-
rary." I can't remember if I used it in this race but that philosophy has
come in handy in many races!

Cammy was utterly vital in keeping this team on the racecourse. Her
ability to endure pain selflessly and her ability to treat all of our feet on the
course was, without doubt, the only reason we stayed on the course. In the
end, we remained in the race because we had agreed ahead of time to suffer like we never suffered before, and suffer we did! I look back on the race
and actually think that it got to a point where we gained strength in seeing the others around us fall like flies. It's not that our feet were any better. It's just that we all agreed that in only a few more days we'd be able to
get off our feet and relax!

Cammy was also our "horse expert," having several horses at home
available to her on a regular basis. She took a lead role in caring for the
horses while helping each and every one of us learn to handle and become
one with our trusty steeds. During the horseback-riding leg, which
spanned three nights and three days, Cammy and I worked very closely,
trying to push the pace in over one hundred degree, sunny, unbearably
humid weather as she told me when the horses needed food, drink, and
rest. This may have been a rookie team but I'll tell you—everyone was
working so well together it felt and looked like we had been racing together for years.

As the jungle storms, the worst in twenty-six years, ravaged the course
and the heat wilted our horses, many if not all teams were forced to sur-
render at least one horse after it refused to continue. We were also a victim
of the "tired horse" syndrome. As a result, we were forced to have one person (alternating) run the last fifty km of the horseback leg. Our team
maintained their composure as we witnessed some very experienced racers become angered, frustrated, and even abusive to their horses. However,
never did I experience such an attitude from the rookies! Our race philosophy was simple—"It is what it is." I feared that someone on the team
might buckle under the stress and strain but they never did!

In this race we faced twelve hours of darkness in the Amazon jungle.
That's an awfully long night being stuck out on the trail so we distinctly
planned the day and pace so we'd end at a village each night. A village
meant cold drinks and a warm cooked meal by the villagers. Sure, it also
meant lots of distractions from the curious villagers (and less sleep), but we

overwhelmingly voted for a dry concrete floor over a wet jungle floor crawling with fire ants. We all also relished the idea of meeting the locals scattered throughout the Nordeste region of Brazil—The Journey!

Our next challenge was a three-hundred-foot rock monolith. It was the first time that technical rock climbing would be part of a race. With five pounds of mud on each foot, we slimed and slithered our way to the top of the rock. We reveled in the 6:00 A.M. early-morning mist over the jungle floor below, before another hundred-degree day dawned. Intoxicated by each other's company, we celebrated Cammy's fortieth birthday, a day she and our team will never forget!

After the seven-hundred-foot rappel that followed, we entered what I affectionately call the Heart of Darkness. The heat was unrelenting, the torrential rains never-ending, and the fungal rot in our feet was growing exponentially. The navigation was tricky, especially at night as trail upon trail meandered everywhere across the seriously outdated and often wrong maps. But again, this team continued to surprise me with their enthusiasm. We laughed, we cried, we sang, we joked. Dave would entertain us with tales when we got sleepy. Somehow, even as our rotting feet reduced us to hobbling shadows, this team continued to move forward. We continued to witness teams pulling out of the race, and we continued to climb in the ranks.

With three hours of much-deserved sleep and repairs to our battered feet, we happily jumped on our bikes expecting a welcome relief having just been on our feet for over forty-eight hours. Boy was I wrong! This mere eighty-five-mile bike leg took the lead team over thirty-six hours. Need I say more! Our feet took such a hammering it was laughable. We did actually bike for a while before the sand in the road reduced us to a walk. Sand in the socks and shoes, combined with jungle rot, is comparable to someone taking sandpaper and rubbing it continuously over, for example, a sunburn!

Seriously, it was fine until we found ourselves hauling our sorry asses and bikes up three thousand feet of densely vegetated jungle. The vines caught every pedal and handlebar as we crawled our way higher, watching each other slip down two feet for every foot of gain on the mud rivers posing as trails. At least it was still hot! We enjoyed summiting the mountain and being able to ride a little bit before the inevitable sand walk. This bike leg was a forty-hour ordeal, and if you factor out the hundred degree days and the sleep deprivation, things went quite well. Two-thirds of the way into the bike leg, in 115-degree heat, Cammy was fading quickly. We shared towing her and taking her pack as we struggled to get her to the next town, Bom Principio, where it was time for us to take a break and recover. We rode into the town and found four other teams (or partial teams) congregated around the Brazilian team (they spoke Portuguese)— ordering cold Coke and chicken with rice for everyone—we enjoyed the local company while pounding back several Cokes.

As the sun started setting, we still had forty-five kilometers to go to the TA. Weary but feeling revitalized, we set out thinking four hours to go— a reasonable guess for the distance. But once again, we failed to account for the sand, and the mud, and the sand, and the mud! By 3:00 A.M. and nine hours later we rolled into the TA at the edge of the Rio Parnaiba. Our feet had not recovered at all. In fact, our feet were even more hammered and infected than before since one-third of the bike leg involved hike-a-bike sections. Cammy once again worked her magic as did our support crew, as we laid our heads down and they cooked and nursed us back to life. We were emaciated but still moving forward. The team was in great spirits. We suddenly heard while at camp that we were now in sixth place as teams everywhere were dropping out from heat exhaustion, fungal rot infections, and just too much pain. Secretly inside I feared what this was doing to our team, as I knew we were already pushing our limits. Would seeing other very experienced racers pulling out give sufficient justification to quit? They never gave indication of such thoughts and I never queried!

My fears eased once we pushed off in our kayaks for a 115-kilometer paddle through one of the largest mangrove swamps in the world. Knowing that our feet would have a reprieve from trekking, the only real obstacle was surviving the extreme fatigue. No problem, except that Dave excelled at sleeping as soon as he got into the kayak. What an incredible team effort that ensued for the entire paddle as we struggled against time cutoffs to paddle kilometer after kilometer closer to the Atlantic Ocean and the final cutoff. We were close to the cutoff and I struggled to get more speed out of all of us. We were tired but we kept to a regular fifty power strokes and fifty recovery strokes attempting to catch valuable minutes. With about ten kilometers to go I stated the inevitable "we missed the cut-off!" We all looked at each other—we had worked so very, very hard and were down to only four teams on the course. I think we all started to cry inside, when Gerard pulled up in a boat and informed us of the new cut-off time—we'd make it easily if we just paddled normally for the next ten km. The smiles were infectious—and Gerard could see it too!

Once again we laughed and cried at the same time. We looked like refugees—Dave had lost about twenty-five pounds by then. All our faces were gaunt and drawn. Dehydrated, hungry, with our feet barely able to hold our frail bodies up, we couldn't have been happier. We paddled the remaining ten km to the start of the last bike leg—a relatively short sixty km dirt road and sandy beach ride. Other than overcoming an abnormal amount of flats, pushing our bikes through long stretches of sand dunes, and Joe becoming heat-exhausted, the ride was relatively uneventful.

All I could think of were two things. First—I could not believe that after nearly eleven days, we were going to start the trek through the dunes! The magical dunes—the signature event of this race! Followed closely by thoughts of how the hell are we going to trek sixty-four kilometers through the sand dune desert when we're literally hobbling?

The last trek was a bit of a blur for me. It was ironic that after the team had relied on me for so many days it was now my turn to ask for help. I faded badly in this section. As the sole navigator, I just didn't have this section dialed. We nailed the first CP, before I lost it. With forty-four kilometers ahead, the pain in my feet was too much and I navigated us to nowhere! We were lost in a sea of dunes! The team gets huge kudos for helping through this stretch. We finally stumbled our way to the end of the trek before we all wearily fell at the foot of the kayaks—our second-to-last event of this race. I think the only thing that drove us at that point was knowing that we were one of only four teams to complete that magical trek and, most importantly, there was absolutely no way that we'd let each other down.

We gained strength and spirit as we paddled and sailed our way to the finish. By the end, after thirteen days and four hours of racing, we finally realized that our journey was over. But was it?

This Journey has continued on. Some of us have and will continue to use this race as the barometer to not only measure other races but also measure other events in our normal lives. There was no way we could have completed this race without the determination and want that this team had. I have never seen another group with so much love for racing together and enduring to finish. I love each and every one of my teammates for the Journey they allowed me to share with them!

I have always said that anyone can do these races and be successful. And when I say anyone I mean individuals who are motivated to compete and of reasonable talent. You may not win the event but is that what it's all about? For the elite—definitely. But for the Joes, Daves, Cammys, and Jims—the race embodies much more than just the finish line. Let's face it—life's finish line is not that attractive. Those who figure out life realize that it's your time spent on this planet doing things you enjoy that is special. So why would you do a fourteen-day race and *not* enjoy the journey as well?

I can only wish that each and every racer out there has had their Elf race! It is a memory that will last a lifetime.

Internal Chaos of Creation

NAME: TERRI SCHNEIDER
AGE: 43
RESIDENCE: SANTA CRUZ, CA
YEARS ADVENTURE RACING: 10

Photo courtesy of Terri Schneider

I was ecstatic to learn that I was diagnosed with leptospirosis. After many pints of my blood traveled cross-country in several heats, to be housed and inspected at the Centers for Disease Control in Atlanta, they finally unveiled the cause of my misery. Whew.

This internal bacterial infection, obtained from crawling through the frosting of animal excrement covering all microenvironments that Borneo offered with open wounds, bites, and infected cuts, had my white blood cell count in the five-digit range. I was subsequently battling fevers that pushed the thermometer mercury to its summit for several days. My organs were under attack, and due to severe pain in my legs I did not venture past my hospital room door for three days. Walking to the bathroom became its own novel urban adventure. Juxtaposed to visions in my mind of the pristine waters of the islands of Borneo, my hospital room walls left me feeling like a wounded caged wolf.

Will I do other expedition-length races in peculiar, intriguing countries you ask?—You betcha. But we'll get to that.

Chosen for the Eco-Challenge Sabah 2000, this inimitable environment attracted seventy-six co-ed teams of four people from twenty-six nations. All had designs on penetrating, and exiting intact, this raw, ancient, and at times hostile blotch on the earth. We were Team Hi-Tec composed of David Kelly, Karen Lundgren, Jacques Boutet, and Terri Schneider. If we didn't have what it took physically plus a very sound mind we wouldn't make it out of this place.

The triple overhead canopy jungles epitomized the fringe of what a human body could safely inhabit for any length of time. Even given advanced technology in cameras, video, and internet play and the plethora of media at this event, it was impossible for "them" to authentically capture what we went through in the bowels of this country. One had to feel it to truly experience it. The natives of Borneo say there are ancient spirits that inhabit the jungles. I believe.

To say that we sweated profusely in the jungles is a gross understatement. Rather, water visibly poured off our chest, head, and back until our clothes filled with this fluid and stuck to our bodies like wet sponges. Within a few hours after the event start, we were filthy. After a day we resembled homeless people in a wet T-shirt contest, and that was our existence for many more days. The insects, spiders, and vegetation were seemingly on steroids and oddly shaped as though props from a B-rated sci-fi movie. Vines and trees laden with spikes reached out to rudely grab clothing, hair, skin, and ankles. We did not just walk through these areas—we muscled through in full-body-contact hiking. Tarzan would be proud. Donning full-fingered leather gloves we clawed, groped, slithered, and swung our way along using abundant vegetation and an occasional dangling reptile. It was endless and invigorating. The trees stood as ancient dwellings for hobbits or elves, as their trunks rose and twisted from the earth. Majestic in a mystical sort of way.

At night, the definitive black in the bowels of the jungle descended upon us. Noises projected from insects, birds and animals, ranging from a visit to a video arcade, to the power tools of a crazed, unrelenting carpenter. Each noise would build upon each other as we hiked along until the pitch was deafening and vibrated through our bodies. Then abruptly it would *stop* as we hiked up next to its source. A moment would pass and then the frenzy would begin again.

I am convinced we were being watched and followed in the jungles at night. Oddly, it was comforting. "They" were as curious of us as were we of them. In the confines of the battle in my hospital bed, post-race, back in the pristine U.S. of A., I longed for this far-off nightly extravaganza. It seemed to make more sense than needles and fever delirium.

Let's talk about leeches. Omnipresent, persistent, aggressive, unflappable, icky leeches. Heading into our first big jungle-hiking section of approximately fifteen-to-twenty-plus hours we were committed to pushing through without stopping. *Leech motivation,* we labeled it—and it worked. The earth was alive, and severely infested with leeches and countless other beings. If we stopped for one minute we would find several of these wormlike critters on our legs. They squeezed through clothing, shoes, gloves, and zippers in search of heat—a commodity we abundantly provided. They flung themselves off branches onto our faces and necks and attached at instant touchdown. Karen and I were motivated by leeches and by God we hiked our butts off to get out of predominant leech territory.

What these jungles had to offer were the most difficult hiking sections I have undertaken to date and a raw and wild beauty that was unparalleled. We viewed iridescent and vibrant-colored butterflies with foot long wingspans, and wild orchids in a vast array of sizes and shapes. The smell changed up from rich wet, damp earth to clove or chamomile essence. Every cell in this place was moving and thriving in a pecking order that seemed natural and in balance yet in a constant state of critical mass. Oxymoron? No. Jungle repose? Yes! We did not belong there, yet we were privileged to have visited for even a moment.

We crawled/climbed through caves laden with bat guano, paddled endless miles of crystal-blue, tepid, dangerous, open ocean in boats that appeared to be a project from my nephew's high school wood shop class. We mountain biked over elephant droppings, steep, rocky hills, rain and mud. We swam, rappelled, and hiked on feet that looked like they had been sitting in a bathtub for three days with a sprinkle of meat tenderizer, and dirt, rocks, and grit ground into their skin. Then we paddled some more and swam some more into relentless headwinds and star-filled lightning storms in lucid blue waters.

As Apsley Cherry-Garrard stated so poignantly and eloquently in *The Worst Journey in the World*, "Exploration is the physical expression of the intellectual passion."

Amen.

The event was based out of Kota Kinabalu (KK) on the northwest coast of Sabah, a four-plane, twenty-eight-hour air ride from San Francisco. We started the race on the southeast coast of the state in a town called Semporna, a ten-hour bus trip from KK.

Off mainland Borneo and Semporna, numerous islands sprinkle the ocean. Some large, rocky, and densely jungled. Some with fine, pristine, white sand beaches the length of which you could stroll across in a moment. All were surrounded by warm, unpredictable waters. Our journey simulated an extended treasure hunt on land and sea in a 350-mile maze of salt and fresh water, sand, mud, jungle, and rock. The islands were stunning and everywhere we went it was hotter and more humid than anywhere I'd experienced on this earth.

In a prologue and to allow the teams to get to know their perahu boats, we sailed from Semporna to Pulau Bum Bum to sleep on the beach of this small island the night before the official race start. Some boats sank before they arrived. Some, like ours, broke. All teams were making frantic adjustments/repairs to boats throughout the night before the official start.

Our first task was to split our team in two and choose by lottery who would paddle and who would hike/coasteer. After the initial start we collectively sailed/paddled to our first island, Gaya, dropped off two teammates (David and me), while the boat (affectionately named Dude) and Karen and Jacques would make their way to PC7. David and I temporarily inhabited the island as we swam, ran and scrambled our way around the steep jungle-infested land, bagging intermittent PCs.

In the frenzy of getting off the boat in a timely manner David and I forgot to get our map bag, which also hosted our passport. David noted our error halfway through our swim and began a wild chase in choppy seas to try and find Dude. I went to shore with his pack and readied his shoes and gear while I waited pensively. David came to shore sans maps and we proceeded ahead hoping Karen and Jacques would notice the mistake and bring us the maps by boat to PC2. They did. We shook off the error and advanced.

The fate of our team lay, at this point, in David's and my ability to move through this island quickly as it could potentially take us upward of twelve hours to complete this segment. The paddlers would take approximately two hours to get to their destination where we would join them.

David and I moved well, wearing one-piece Lycra suits and leather gloves to protect our skin from the coral, thorns, and rocks. I felt like a playful grinning ninja slinking through the jungle doing the full-body-hiking thing, body fresh, strong, senses keen. Hike, swim, jog, hike, swim, jog, we moved up quickly and found ourselves in sixth place in no time.

David and I got back to the boat, cut, bruised, filthy and with big holes in the backsides of our groovy Lycra skin suits from sliding down muddy slopes. With big smiles and team high fives, our first grand adventure was behind us. Despite two large errors we landed in ninth place for the day.

After a few more hours of paddling and grinding our mud-laden butts into unforgiving wooden boat seats, we dropped Karen and Jacques off, in the dark, to hit "their" island for more coasteering/hiking adventures while David and I waited pensively on this new island shore for their return. Day broke to the distressed faces of Karen and Jacques coming down the beach. They informed us that the passport had been lost. There was a brief moment of quiet as each of us went through our own internal attitude adjustment in knowing what this meant. Another error. No choice but to let go and move on. At the next transition area/gear resupply we would do time in the form of a six-hour penalty for our lost passport.

At any point, half of our food for the entire race was carried on our backs, while we hauled double digit pounds of water. Our motto quickly became—if we don't have it, we don't need it. In an environment where it was impossible to keep up with water loss from sweat—that was a tough one to swallow . . . or not. At 7:00 P.M. we rolled away on our bikes loaded with thirty to forty pounds or more burdens.

The mountain bike had enough tough, steep, hills thrown in and a few sections of gratuitous hike-a-bike in calf-deep mud just to wear us down and mess our bikes up a bit. Our packs grew heavier as the miles rolled on, but our early sleep break paid off and we passed several teams lying napping on the side of the trail. We noted the elephant dung on the dirt roads and tried to imagine the size of a creature that could lay turds that cast shadows by our headlamps. Impressive.

Then David got sick. Vomiting and projectile diarrhea plagued our strong captain and navigator. In this hellishly humid climate he was shivering uncontrollably from some unknown internal inhabitant. He hung tough as the night passed, and with the help of some antibiotics and a couple of rest breaks, his discomfort waned and he was solid again. Adventure racing is one big mood swing—especially when you're dealing with four moving targets for microscopic predators.

Finishing the ride, we shoved our filthy, muddy bikes into their cases and readied ourselves for a jungle hike of epic proportions. The raw and brutal "Lost World" would give us repeated big wet slaps on our stoic, unflappable, adventure racing faces. This race was the real deal. Forty teams would not make the cutoff time coming off the bike onto this hiking section. They would face unranked status, and a shortened course to the finish line.

Covered in dirt, blood, mud, and sweat ground into our skin, clothing, shoes, packs, and scalps, our bodies appeared to be decaying due to moisture and lack of adequate calories. The stench was stifling. We had hit that point in an expedition race when animal survival, and all that that implies, is status quo.

For most repeat adventure racers, getting hyper down and dirty is appealing in an anomalous, primitive sort of way. I believe it is one of the quintessential issues that offers that open door of knowing those who have from those who have not been there. This particular race venue was bringing out the best that this primal essence had to offer.

The appeal is the contrast between absorbing oneself in a task regardless of the challenge it offers, while intermittently desiring the existence in which most humans reside—comfort. Repeat adventure racers thrive on both. The contrast and the entrenchment in both are equally appealing and affirming. If I embrace sleeping in the dirt, while filthy, with equally filthy people who embrace the same, I exponentially appreciate sliding fresh from the shower into clean, cool sheets—undeniably more than the folks who take showers each day while still being relatively clean. The change-ups feed us. Contrasts offer a much stronger appreciation for each, and a chance to take neither for granted. The splendor of dirt reveals the genuine beauty of being clean and comfortable.

That said, we were psyched that our next task submerged us in water. Downriver we swam with our packs, shoes, and clothes—no helmet, no padding, and no form of propulsion except whichever shoe-laden leg or loose arm we had available to kick or pull us around. What we'd surmised to be a refreshing dip in the river turned out to be a threatening lesson in damage control.

As we hit the first rapid, I caught a toe on a protruding rock, which pulled my legs under me to face down just before a small drop-off. Wham!—before I could get my feet back downstream, I slammed my body on a rock, knocking the breath out of me and injuring my rib cage. Karen in turn slammed her knee on a boulder, severely bruising her knee cap and quad. Given the level and speed of the water we were often sucked into rapids before we had a chance to pull over and scout. There were a myriad of sweepers, rocks, and holes that threatened our ability to safely and quickly maneuver our pack-burdened bodies.

David and I, being the folks on our team a bit more comfortable getting around in water, paired up with Karen and Jacques and took on the role of scouting rapids and picking lines through the river. To safely move through challenging areas we would take turns swimming ahead to scout, and would yell and/or give hand signals to the rest of the team. Even given our methods and experience, this seemingly straightforward episode became one of the most potentially dangerous situations we had undertaken in an adventure race, and the first time I thought I had lost one of my teammates.

Jacques and I had buddied up and were moving into a swift section of river. Obstacles required us to swim river left to avoid a large boulder in the middle of the river, which was attached to the shore by a log river right. The log had numerous projections of branches and debris that were visible above waterline. The water hitting the log walled up and was then powerfully sucked under its girth.

I urgently motioned Jacques to move river left while I kicked and stroked hard to clear the boulder and attached sweepers. As I popped my feet forward at the last second to deflect the large obstacle I looked over to see Jacques hit the log with his pack flailing about and get sucked under by the force of the current. What lay beneath the surface was an unknown. I yelled his name through the wad of dread accumulating in my throat and lunged around the boulder's width. All the while I knew that if he were trapped beneath the log my efforts in trying to free him could be futile. I visually groped and then saw his head pop up on the surface one hundred yards downstream. Whew.

After the top fifteen teams went through this river section, the race closed it down. All nonswimming teams were required to hike around this section or were driven in vehicles. No pads, propulsion, or helmet made the safety of this caliber of river swimming questionable at best. Coming out of the water, our depleted, dehydrated, fatigued bodies were borderline hypothermic. Though 85-degree water is comfortable at worst, submerging a 98.6-degree body into it for five plus hours will draw the body temp down. So yes, in Borneo, we were shivering from cold.

Next? You got it, more paddling. We were introduced to our indigenous sampan canoe, seemingly fresh off the set of *Xena, Warrior Princess*: strong, buxom, moody, unpredictable. Our river-paddling section would prove to be a roll of the dice with a bit of skill, followed by a lot of hard work.

Hitting a dark zone (enforced stop) immediately, we found a pristine yet bug-infested stretch of white sand beach to lay our heads for some sleep. Dreaming of a long luxurious siesta, it started to rain. We flipped our behemoth boat tilting it on its side to be used for a cramped, damp shelter. What had promised to be a night of slumber proved to be a wet and miserable flopping fest.

The following morning downriver, we cleverly portaged our four-hundred pound vessel to the edge of shore at the base of a waterfall. Our next task was to ferry out into the current and attempt to swing her bow around in the rapid in order to hit a narrow, rocky chute straight-on. David, who was guiding the boat from the stern, and I from the bow, discussed our strategy briefly in typical adventure racing conversation style:

Terri: "Do you think we can ferry out and swing her around without tipping over and/or racking the boat on the distant shore rocks?"

David: "I don't know."

Terri: "Okay, let's do it then."

End of conversation.

I drew the bow out into the rapid's mouth. The river's force swung us around hurriedly and the unstable hull of the boat caused us to pitch and rock until we came face-to-face with a massive boulder. We frantically backpaddled to stall our forward motion, biding time to clear the mass of our boat and looming rocks. Made it. Big rush. Love that.

The personality of this river changed many times with the subsequent personality of our team. We had moments of peaceful silence, the synchronicity of our strong strokes stimulating us enough to stay awake, only to be countered by bouts of deep, profound laughter, life-affirming stories, and songs. These moments prompt a smile when brought to mind months later while daydreaming of far-off places. The team seemed to come alive in this boat sharing simple, pure adventure, the kind that only teammates or fellow adventure racers thriving side by side in the trenches can appreciate.

Steep, cliff-lined shores changed to sloping, sandy beaches speckled with forty-foot-high wild fig trees. Crisp, brightly colored birds followed our path and monkeys played in the branches above. This became the Willy Wonka River for its chocolate color and seemingly magical qualities. I threw alphabet cookies in the water to emphasis our theme. In this delusion we attempted to create a better situation of the fact that we had to drink this mucky water.

It was grand to get off our feet but the effects of trauma and hot sun leisurely swelled my feet like sausages roasting on an open pit. I took my shirt off to air out my skin while my teammates oohed and aahhed at my swollen heat rash. The next few days "The Rash" would spread to my inner thighs, ankles, and stomach. Along with our bites and wounds, we appeared prime candidates for a smiling leper colony.

Back on land at night and lacking headlamp batteries, we moved snail-like to a jungle PC. I was sleep-bonked, food-bonked, and foot-bonked. For me, the pain had become momentarily unbearable. My heart wanted to press on but the foot rot and blisters said rest. It was a challenging moment for our team.

We decided to sleep an hour and have the doc nurse my feet. He used a syringe to drain my blisters then taped up the heels and toes that were affected. Once my feet dried out a bit they were "doable" and I shoved them back in my shoes. Though we had been out of the top ten for a while we still remained—unflappable. The finish line was a ways off and if endurance sports have taught me anything it's that a whole lotta stuff can happen in a few days' time. We pressed on.

This hike started benignly enough, as we shuffled packs and gear around distributing weight to those who felt the strongest. David and Karen became the grunts as Jacques and I focused on walking. If you have ever played in sleep deprivation while under physical duress you know that it is an uncomfortable prospect at best. The effort exerted in trying to keep one's eyes open is unlike any other effort I have experienced, in an intense, miserable, despicable sort of way. And there's that lure that can stop movement. It's the knowing that at any moment you can close your eyes and be down for the count. Inner voices argue:

"Why not? Just lie down and close your eyes. Go ahead, you can do it."

"You're weak. Pathetic. Keep moving, keep moving."

"Just slide to the ground. Your pack is a perfect pillow. Lay your head back. Just for a minute. It'll only be a minute."

"Keep moving, this is your main objective. Be strong."

While doing battle in your head, your eyes are half closed and you are still hiking.

As we came into PC23 I started to sob. The tears became the metaphoric steam released from the metaphoric pressure cooker. My feet felt as though they had been beaten with a baseball bat and it took all my energy to keep focus. David worked with our new set of maps. Jacques tried to get himself together. Karen scurried around to organize gear and give me hugs. She gave me jobs to do like putting batteries in headlamps. I struggled to see how the batteries were organized in each lamp. I'd fall asleep mid-lamp-recharge, wake up, continue in my efforts, fall asleep again. I found out later, I was good entertainment value for Karen. The crying eased the stress while the rest of my brain spat obscenities on this weakness. Not only did the finish line call—so did a top-ten placing. My need to sleep angered me.

I was not conscious of anything of importance. Except that the decision to press on was what I wanted and fought for. If that small glimmer was all I could grab on to then that must be enough. My teammates provided the rest as they tossed me in the bottom of the boat to take a nap, and on we went. After a fitful struggle I slept. Twenty minutes later I woke with a tear-stained face, sat up, and started paddling. Back in the game. The struggle enthralling. The result? Even more curious given my complete misery and emotional demise only moments before.

Given the opening, the mind can step forward to harbor and nurture perceived essential goals. In this nudging, we are offered opportunities to witness new faces of selves to whom we had not previously been introduced.

"Hello ugly self, pleased to meet you and the lessons you will force down my throat."

What emerges, if we look deeply, is the proverbial butterfly from the proverbial cocoon of life throwing us dark challenge. And on we fly into the unknown—higher and stronger—*if* we choose. It's always and only a choice. Ours for the taking. There's always more for which to dig, if we choose. Even lying in a cramped heap on the floor of an archaic wooden boat, I knew I was still in the game.

We paddled one of our last legs into a storm and headwind on a liquid treadmill hosting chop and headwinds. I concentrated on lateral shorelines, willing them to move backward as if to solidify forward progress.

Having battled to tenth place with relative grace, ninth was within striking distance. Our next destination was our final hike to a village and the caving and ropes section. I had lost my hat along with some other gear to the adventure racing vortex lost and found, and acquired banana leaves to protect my head from the beating sun as we trudged along the road.

This small village was known for harvesting bird eggs from the roof of the cave to sell in general Asia. The nests and eggs were said to bring a strong price. Their value?—an aphrodisiac.

At the base of the cave we donned climbing gear, crawled through bat guano and mud to the foot of two ascents, which brought us through an opening in the top of the cave. Picking our way like moving solar panels along a knife-edged ridgeline to a four-hundred-foot rappel, we arrived at our final jungle-hiking section.

Much to Karen's and my chagrin and that of everyone whom we came across including event media and race personnel, David and Jacques never changed their clothes the entire race except to don bike shorts. Oddly impressive. I changed clothes once midrace and still could not stand the feel of their filth and stench on my constantly wet, rotting skin. Completing our final jungle hike, and like a slightly maddened soul, I ripped my clothes off. On we went, underwear, hiking shoes, backpack.

Common adventure racing power nap: Sit down with pack on—wherever you happen to be, road, dirt, rocks, scree, mud—no matter. Slide butt down a bit below pack to the chosen surface and tilt head back to use pack as a pillow. Within seconds you are in REM sleep. Set an alarm, ten to twenty minutes, you're good to go. Stand up, hike on, very efficient.

So there we were: underwear and all sleeping in dirt that generations of native villagers had inhabited for their entire lifetimes. Upon waking, we would leave them behind to their simple lives while we paddled to some vague goal we deemed important. Back to our baths, pedicures, lattes, and impeccable life stuff. Coffee shop daydreams bring me back, knowing the villagers still reside there and perhaps remember a strange maddened woman with big, tired blue eyes, sleeping in her underwear on the side of the road.

Some of the folks in Borneo live in homes above the water. They are not houseboats but longhouses—wooden homes on stilts out in the middle of the ocean and their seaweed crops. We floated through crops and stilts, darkness, lighting, and wind to our distant shore and finish line that would not get closer. I closed my eyes and counted strokes. My internal negotiation involved closing my eyes and paddling, then opening them to check forward progress when I hit the thousand-stroke count. The harder we paddled, the farther our shoreline seemed to get, until in one abrupt moment it was upon us and mixed emotions flowed. The reality that our adventure had suddenly ended sunk in. The pull for hugs from friends, cheers from the crowd, and hot showers drew us back to civilization and that contrast thing.

We were tenth place in arguably the strongest field ever assembled for a race of this length. Not bad for a few disheartening days and our share of mistakes. Adventure racing is a novel, intimate experience in a viscerally deep sort of way. How privileged I am to share this gift with such quality people.

In a piece by Paul Theroux in which he speaks of an epic paddling adventure around Cape Cod, he describes a conversation he had with an animated family member.

". . . it was as if he was on an instant touched with lucid insanity, the exalted chaos of creation."

The words remind me of a place many of us curious types decisively choose to go time and again. Perhaps in our minds and hearts, intermittent lucid insanity is what we seek in life—like an itch that needs attending or a craving satisfied. Perhaps this internal chaos helps unveil the raw pieces of self—the artistry of being, the authentic inner beauty, the fringe we strive to find in ourselves and hope to see in others. Perhaps. I'll wager so.

Leptospirosis? I'll be back again. That internal chaos of creation thing calls . . .

The Evolution of a "Misadventure" Racer

NAME: MAUREEN MOSLOW-BENWAY
AGE: 42
RESIDENCE: POWHATAN, VA
YEARS ADVENTURE RACING: 8

L to R: Steve Riley, Maureen Moslow-Benway,
Bill Moslow

In 1995, I watched the very first Eco-Challenge being televised on the Discovery Channel and as I sat there absolutely transfixed, I knew that one day I would compete in the race. The Eco-Challenge embodied everything that I loved—athleticism, endurance, camaraderie, teamwork, adventure, the outdoors, and exotic locations. I viewed the Eco-Challenge as being some sort of athletic nirvana and believed that the successful completion of the race would be the ultimate accomplishment of my athletic career. In short, I became obsessed.

Even though I have been an athlete pretty much my entire life, over the course of the next few years, I began to prepare in earnest. I had always been a runner, but I started to run ultramarathons. I learned how to navigate and got to be quite proficient. I even became a navigation instructor for the Sierra Club. I also got into mountain biking and started competing in numerous endurance bike races. Eventually I started competing in off-road triathlons and sprint adventure races as well. My husband, Bob, my teenage son, Matthew, and I competed in a Hi-Tec Adventure Race outside Pittsburgh and wound up finishing in the top 10 percent. By 1999, I finally felt like I was ready to start competing in multiday adventure races.

The first multiday race I did was the Endorphin Fix, a two-day race in West Virginia organized by Don Mann and Odyssey Adventure Racing. My team consisted of my husband Bob, Brian, Steve, and me. Brian and Steve were co-workers of mine who had become good friends over the course of several years. We got to know each other extremely well and had spent days and weekends together mountain biking, kayaking, rock climbing, and camping. We even spent a few long nights together in various hospital emergency rooms, waiting for one another to get stitched up.

Like most Odyssey races, the Endorphin Fix started at midnight, so racers got to experience twenty-four hours of sleep deprivation only six hours into the race. As we lined up at the starting line, we were a bit nervous, but overall pretty confident in our abilities. This confidence lasted for all of about thirty seconds after the starting gun went off. As we rode our mountain bikes down the hill, Brian suddenly shouted out that he couldn't see. Unfortunately, he had never tried to mountain bike with his fully loaded backpack on before, and as a result he could not lift his head up because his pack was pressed against his helmet. We wound up stopping and completely reloading his backpack and by the time we fixed the problem, we were in last place. We continued riding and awhile later, Brian once again called out that he couldn't see. Unfortunately, Brian was the only one of us who wore glasses and it was incredibly humid. As a result, his glasses kept fogging up. He couldn't see with his glasses on and he couldn't see without them—not a good situation. He wound up taking them off, which led to many godawful, bone-crunching crashes because Brian couldn't make out the rocks and logs, especially at night. Things then went from bad to worse when Brian's bike light died. Now he literally couldn't see whatsoever.

Thank God for sunrises. The new day breathed new life into our battered team and Brian could once again see! We finally finished the mountain bike leg and started the canoeing portion of the race. Brian and Steve, who are both decent paddlers, were in one canoe. Unfortunately, Bob and I, who thought we were decent paddlers, were in another. Let's just say there wasn't one single rapid that Bob and I got through without flipping our canoe. I was sitting in the front of the canoe and, in addition to paddling, my job was to look out for rocks, logs, and other obstacles. Much to my chagrin, I discovered that I had direction dyslexia. In the heat of the moment, I couldn't quickly figure out what side was right and which was left. So poor Bob paddled and tried to steer while I shouted out insightful commands such as "rock right, I mean left, no I mean right." Usually, by the time I figured out exactly what I meant to say, we had crashed into the obstacle and tipped our canoe. I could tell Bob was getting annoyed, so my next technique was to not say anything until I had worked out the exact location in my mind. That resulted in me blurting out "rock right, go left" approximately one nanosecond prior to impact. Steve and Brian would just watch, totally bemused, as we once again tipped over. Everything, and I do mean everything, we owned was drenched. My turkey jerky looked like soggy roadkill and my iodine pills had stained everything I owned a nasty brown. Finally, the end was in sight. We had just one more rapid to get through and we'd be done. I had the obstacles located and the correct line identified. I ordered Bob to go left. He responded, "I got the line, babe," and proceeded to go right. Naturally, we immediately hit two half-submerged rocks and did an "endo" in our canoe. By the time we swam over to the checkpoint, dragging our canoe behind us, we were not exact-ly experiencing marital bliss.

From there we started the trekking portion of the race. We started off well and hiked for hours, and hours, and hours. By 1:00 A.M., twenty-five hours after the race began, and thirty-seven hours since we had last slept, we were absolutely exhausted. In fact, we were so tired we laid down on a dirt road and set our alarms for twenty minutes. I think it took us all of twenty seconds to fall asleep and twenty minutes later when our watches started beeping, I felt amazingly rejuvenated. Unfortunately, Bob didn't. He woke up and the first words out of his mouth were "This is stupid, I want to sleep." However, we continued on. Shortly thereafter, Brian got debilitating leg cramps. At first it was just his quads, then it was his quads and calves, and then ultimately his quads, calves, and feet were cramping simultaneously. He was absolutely miserable and we quickly were becom-ing that way as well. We were extremely frustrated because we were approaching the cutoff time for the next checkpoint and for the life of us, we couldn't find it. We weren't alone—there were a number of other teams with us and they were every bit as confused. Finally, time ran out and we were disqualified. It was my first-ever DNF and a humbling expe-rience, even though we were in the middle of the pack by the time the race ended. I have to admit, I felt much better about the entire situation when I learned that only six out of the forty-two teams completed the race and over half of them had already done the Endorphin Fix at least once.

The Endorphin Fix taught me many things, but the first and most important lesson I learned about adventure racing was to expect the unex-pected, because things are invariably going to go wrong. Believe it or not, this can be good news, because for the most part, misadventures are what turn ordinary races and outings into adventures. After all, if everything went as planned, it would be just another run, paddle, or bike ride through the woods. However, if you have the blind leading the dyslexic, it turns into a real adventure. I learned that it's important to be able to laugh at the many misadventures that we've experienced while training and racing, even though, to be perfectly honest, many of them didn't seem all that funny at the time they were happening. However, looking back, those are the moments that are forever etched in my brain and those are the memories my friends and I still talk and laugh about years later. The Endorphin Fix also taught me one other invaluable lesson and that was that under no circumstances would Bob and I ever take a whitewater canoeing vacation together. I'm pretty sure if we did, our marriage would wind up as rocky as whatever river we were paddling.

After the Endorphin Fix, Steve and I were more psyched than ever to do an Eco-Challenge, but unfortunately our team was down to just two people—Steve and myself. Bob had absolutely no desire to suffer from sleep deprivation for days on end and Brian's fun meter, as well as his quads, calves, and toes, had been totally pegged out! We needed two more teammates and fortunately, we found one right away. My brother Bill had successfully completed several Eco-Challenges and was dying to do another one. So we entered the lottery for the Eco-Challenge 2000 race in Borneo and amazingly, we got selected. I approached my employer, Booz Allen Hamilton, about possible sponsorship and very generously, they agreed to pay our entry fee and donate enough frequent flier miles to get us to Malaysia. Thus, Team Booz Allen was born! We eventually found a fourth teammate, John, a former Army Green Beret who specialized in water operations. The four of us trained incredibly hard for months and by late spring, we were ready to test our readiness to do the Eco-Challenge by competing in a four-day adventure race called the Mega Dose.

We had initially registered for the Mega Dose as a four-person team, but two days before the race, Bill's wife went into premature labor and he was unable to participate. Instead, Steve and I entered as a two-person team and John registered as a soloist with the understanding that we would do the race together. Our adventure began in May 2000, when we arrived in Natural Bridge, Virginia. Don Mann, the race director, got up and gave a pre-race briefing. There were three things he said during this presentation that really stood out in my mind. First, he advised he was eliminating the requirement to carry fleece and cold-weather gear because it was going to be a beautiful weekend in the Blue Ridge Mountains. Second, he stated he was shooting for a 50 percent completion rate for the race. And third, he spent twenty minutes introducing various competitors. For those of you who don't know me, let's just say that I'm not very easily intimidated. However, looking around the room, I never saw such fit people! To be honest, I was secretly thinking Team Booz Allen might be in over our heads.

The race began under the Natural Bridge at 12:30 A.M. with a twenty-eight-mile mountain marathon. Our team was one of the few who chose not run it. We figured that we would make up the two to three hours later in the race, when everyone else's legs were "fried." Instead, we hiked it at a brisk pace and it took us seven hours. When we arrived at the canoe leg, we were in forty-seventh place out of fifty-five teams. From there, we got into the canoes and paddled forty miles down the James River. We decided it was fastest if the three of us were in one canoe, so we dragged the empty canoe behind us. It took us the better part of the day to paddle the forty miles and overall, it was pretty enjoyable. After we finished the canoe leg, we hopped on our mountain bike and began the first of *many* steep climbs.

Unfortunately, less than two miles into the mountain bike ride, John's rear derailleur disintegrated and he was out of the race—there was simply no way to ride the 140-mile mountain bike course without being able to change gears. The only positive thing was that John was registered as a soloist, so Steve and I could go on without being disqualified. Steve and I then pedaled for hours, climbing steep jeep roads and rapidly descending bumpy logging trails. After a while, night fell and it was very difficult to see. At one point, we realized we were almost ten miles off course, so all in all, we had a "minor" twenty-mile detour. Around midnight, I was getting extremely tired and was afraid that I would fall asleep while riding. It was around this time that I started hallucinating and over the course of the next three days, I had to see and hear literally hundreds of things that didn't really exist. Worst of all, it was around this time that an imaginary radio began to play in my head. For the next forty-eight hours, I heard the song "Afternoon Delight" over and over again! Could you possibly imagine a worse song to have playing nonstop in your head, especially when the absolute last thing you're thinking of having is a little afternoon delight—how about a hot shower and a good night of sleep instead? Eventually, around 3:00 A.M., we arrived at the checkpoint and discovered we were now in twenty-seventh place.

After two hours and fifteen minutes of fitful sleep, we awoke, cold and damp. We hopped back on our bikes and started riding uphill. Several of the climbs were simply too steep to ride, so we wound up hike-a-biking. We rode up and down mountains all day long and late in the afternoon, we arrived at the bike/hike transition checkpoint. It felt great to finally get off the bike and to start walking. Unfortunately, it was about this time it began to pour and it continued to rain pretty much nonstop from then until the race ended several days later. So much for the beautiful weekend in the Blue Ridge Mountains!

After a brutal eighteen-mile hike in the pouring rain, we arrived at the next checkpoint. Teams had to be at this checkpoint no later than 6:00 A.M., or they were disqualified. We arrived around 4:00 A.M. and I believe we were in fifteenth place. There were a number of teams there who had decided to drop out due to the cold and exhaustion and it was obvious that more than half the field was going to get eliminated at this checkpoint. Steve and I tried to sleep for an hour or so, but we were too cold and wet to do so.

By this time, we were ready to get back on our bikes, since our feet took a major beating the night before. Unfortunately, we immediately started another steep climb and had to hike our bikes. This day we continued to spend hours climbing long, steep jeep roads and then minutes rapidly descending them. However, the highlight was that we knew we were going to be passing through Buena Vista, Virginia, a small town that reportedly had a Subway restaurant in it. Talk about obsessing over food— I absolutely could not get the vision of a Subway Super Club out of my mind. It definitely kept me going. After all, there's nothing like a little "afternoon delight"!

Shortly thereafter, we dropped our bikes off at a checkpoint and started another fourteen-mile hike up to the top of Bluff Mountain. It was steep and as usual, it began to rain again. Once we got to the top, we had to bushwhack our way eight miles down the backside of the mountain. I think this was the most difficult part of the entire race. There was no trail and we were following a very rocky, wet, slippery ravine. I can't even begin to remember how many times I fell. Suffice it to say, that I had dozens of bruises on my butt and legs from this section. It took us eight *long* hours to get down the mountain to the climbing site. We got there at 2:00 A.M. in the pouring rain. We sat down for about an hour trying to recover and warm up before we started climbing. First, we had an eighty-foot ascent using jumars. Once on top, we were hooked up to a Tyrolean traverse that was strung 250 feet across the ravine. I had never done a Tyrolean traverse before and I have to admit, the first half is easy (gravity rules) while the second half (pulling your weight back up) is exhausting. I remember being quasi-stuck, about fifty feet from the end thinking to myself this is "nucking futz! It's 2:45 A.M., I'm exhausted, cold, tired and I'm hanging eighty feet in the air above a gazillion rocks." Fortunately, I eventually made my way across and then rappelled eighty feet back down to the ground. From here, we had to turn around and bushwhack our way eight miles back up the ravine. This was definitely the low point of the race for me, because I knew exactly what we were in for.

Hours later, we made our way back up to the top of a ridge and then had to follow a nicely groomed hiking trail down to the next checkpoint. By this time, I was hallucinating quite frequently. I heard an army drill sergeant calling out cadence and was seeing wild animals and French châteaux. It's amazing what your brain does to compensate for lack of sleep. The only good thing was that around this point, the radio in my head stopped playing "Afternoon Delight." We walked down the hill, both of us exhausted, cold, wet with throbbing feet. You could tell we were starting to lose it mentally. I literally fell asleep while walking and didn't wake up until I crashed into the ground. Eventually, we arrived at checkpoint 14 and found out that we were the sixth place team—just about everyone else had dropped out. Needless to say, we were pretty psyched! The race officially was supposed to end in an hour, and it looked like nobody was going to finish it within the time limit. An hour later, the race ended and we later found out that only one competitor, a professional mountain biker soloist, officially finished the race with thirteen minutes to spare. That was one team out of fifty-five—Not exactly a 50 percent completion rate! Even though we didn't complete the course, it was a great confidence-boosting experience. The Mega Dose was by far the toughest athletic competition that Steve or I had ever done and it certainly prepared us for the Eco-Challenge.

Like the Endorphin Fix, the Mega Dose taught me many things, but the most important lesson I learned about adventure racing was that the race doesn't always go to the swift. Sometimes just going slow and steady and not quitting is the way to do well in a race. To be honest, when we started, my only goal was to successfully complete the race. I would have been thrilled to finish in the top half. And after looking over our competitors, never in a million years would I have imagined that Steve and I would be in sixth place, well ahead of many world- and national- class athletes, by the end of the race. It just goes to show how far a little luck and a lot of determination and perseverance can take a team.

Three months later, Team Booz Allen arrived in Borneo ready to race. We were well trained and in the best shape of our lives. As it turned out, it would be necessary for us to draw upon all of the lessons learned in our earlier races.

Our race had an almost disastrous start. The day before the race officially began, all of the teams had to sail native perahu canoes to an island that was the starting point. These shabbily built, unseaworthy boats were overloaded with gear and drinking water. Bill, Steve, John, and I had all of one afternoon of sailing lessons on the Potomac River, so we weren't exactly America's Cup contenders. Anyhow, as we neared the island, the boat next to us began to swamp. There were television crews filming this and I said to my teammates, "Hey guys, we can be heroes. Let's go help them." Well, no sooner did we turn our boat in their direction than our boat also completely swamped with water, as did many of the other nearby boats. We all jumped overboard and tried to collect as much of our gear and water as possible before it floated away. We wound up swimming and dragging our boat at least a quarter mile to the island and we lost about a third of our issued water supply. Needless to say, this episode knocked the wind right out of our sails, literally and figuratively.

The race began the next day with a sailing leg. It went reasonably well and we reached our first checkpoint in approximately eighteenth place. Steve and John had a separate leg to do and as we waited for them, Bill and I found a local native and paid him to reinforce our boat. We raised the sides and covered the front part of the boat with some plywood. It made a huge difference. Later that evening, as we were still waiting for Steve and John, the race directors advised that squalls were moving into the area and they wouldn't recommend sailing at night. After our earlier near sinking, I had absolutely no desire to be out in a perahu in the South China Sea in the pitch dark in the middle of a storm. John and Steve returned around midnight and after talking it over, we decided to get up at 4:00 A.M. and head out before daybreak. Most of the other teams also opted not to go out in the storm. Anyhow, we were up by 4:00 A.M. and were one of the first teams out. Unfortunately, there was no wind so we wound up paddling the entire way to the next checkpoint. As we arrived, we realized that unbelievably, no one on our team had checked us out of the previous checkpoint. In the Eco-Challenge, each team carries a mandatory passport that must be stamped when the team enters and again when it departs a checkpoint. So needless to say, we had to turn around and paddle all the way back to where we had just come from and then turn around and paddle back. We lost hours. Let's just say this wasn't one of those misadventures that we were laughing about at the time—things were a bit tense on the boat.

Eventually, we made it to land, where we suffered through the mountain biking and jungle trekking portions of the race. The mountain biking was brutal and many teams were disqualified on this leg. It was incredibly long and about halfway through, it turned into a total quagmire, with mud so deep and so thick it was impossible to pedal or even walk without having your shoes sucked off. When we finally made it out of the mud, the mountains began. The jungle trekking was even worse. It was muddy, slippery, and steep and leeches were everywhere. As I trekked along, I could feel the leeches in my shoes. They would crawl through the mesh in my hiking boots and then after biting and sucking the blood out of my feet, they would get so bloated they couldn't fit back out. So instead, I could feel them curled up all over my feet and periodically they'd get squished. All of us had blood oozing out of our shoes.

The leeches also made it extremely difficult to sleep at night. In a "what the hell were we thinking" moment, we decided to forgo getting the hammock tents the race officials had recommended and instead purchased six-dollar survival blankets made out of aluminum foil. After all, we were going to be at the equator competing in the Eco-Challenge. How cold could it possibly be and how much sleep would we get during the race? The answer was it got plenty cold and we didn't get hardly any sleep because we were freezing our butts off trying to stay warm with useless blankets that were filled with leeches and ripped to shreds after all of one day. About four days into the race, I would have given my right breast to have had one of the hammock tents.

One particular night during the jungle trek is forever etched in my mind and pretty much captures the essence of what the race was like. It was about Day 4 or 5 of the race and Steve, who was probably the strongest member of our team, got sick and started bonking bad. He was exhausted and couldn't go on. After some debate, we decided to cross the river then stop and rest for the night. Naturally, it immediately began to rain. We had to use a zip line to cross the now torrential river, and lightning was flashing all around. When we got to the other side, we were drenched, chilled, and basically miserable. Steve and John found places to sleep, but they were in the rain. Bill found a large tree that had fallen over and he and I crawled under it. It had to be at least six feet in diameter and although we were cold, at least we were dry. We started a fire to try and warm up and immediately discovered that we were lying on top of an ant hill. We literally had thousands of ants swarming all over us, but luckily they didn't bite. Shortly thereafter, John joined us and the three of us lay down and tried to sleep in an extremely uncomfortable root hole while we had ants crawling all over us. To make matters worse, John took his hiking boots off and put them next to the fire to dry out. Somehow, one of them fell into the fire and the tongue and front part of his boot melted. We wound up duct-taping his boot to his foot for the rest of the race.

Each time we did a leg of the race, I kept thinking to myself *it can't get worse than this* and somehow it always managed to. I dreaded sailing more than any event. If there was no wind, we had to spend countless hours paddling in the hot sun making slow progress. If there was a wind, we were in constant danger of having our boat swamp. At one point, we tried using our "secret weapon," an extra spinnaker sail we had brought with us. During one sailing leg when the wind was really blowing, we raised it up. We flew along for about one minute before our mast snapped in half. We paddled to a nearby island and tried to fix the mast. Just as we thought our race was over, an Eco-Challenge race official boat passed us by towing an empty perahu from a team that had been disqualified. Miraculously, they allowed us to swap masts.

This went on for days—ten to be exact! We were the thirtieth place team (out of seventy-six) to cross the finish line. But as we crossed it, I had mixed emotions. The Eco-Challenge was brutal and far more difficult than I had imagined. I had lost over ten pounds, had two serious staph infections, approximately four hundred leech bites, and I had somehow contracted lung flukes, yet in a way, I was sorry that it was ending. The Eco-Challenge had consumed my life for so long and had become such a part of me, I wondered what my life would be without it.

Like our previous races, the Eco-Challenge taught me many things, but the lesson that clearly stands out above all others is that the journey is the destination. In my mind, I had made the Eco-Challenge out to be the Holy Grail, and believe me, it was an incredible experience. We had a lifetime of highs and lows in such a short period of time. We survived, and at times even thrived in some incredibly difficult conditions. We got to do some absolutely amazing things and for a brief moment, we got to experience what it feels like to be a celebrity. It was a heady experience and one that I will take with me to my grave. But looking back on it, the Eco-Challenge was just the icing on the cake. What were truly special were the years and the experiences that led up to Borneo. Once I made my mind up to compete in the Eco-Challenge, I found myself doing things I had only dreamed about and pushing myself far beyond my established limits. For example, I learned how to whitewater kayak and consequently paddled on beautiful rivers all over the mid-Atlantic. I hiked mile after glorious mile and fell in love with night hiking, especially on full-moon-lit nights with crystalline ice covering the bare branches of trees. I learned how to really ride technical mountain bike trails and spent weekend after wonderful weekend riding through spectacular scenery, forging incredible bonds with people whom I will be friends with for the rest of my life. I learned how to rock climb and found myself five hundred feet up a sheer cliff face. I entered all sorts of endurance races and got to see new places and meet new people. I started a corporate Adventure Club that has grown to over three hundred members. We do everything from ski in the Alps, to ice climb in the White Mountains, to parachute out of airplanes. I came to realize that I am far tougher than I ever imagined and that I can accomplish anything I set my mind to doing. I know myself so much better—both my strengths and my weaknesses. As I sat in my family room watching the inaugural Eco-Challenge, little did I realize what a wonderful, life enhancing experience it would be. Yes, the journey to Borneo truly was the destination.

The Beast in Me

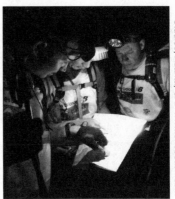

NAME: MICHAEL SHEPARDSON
AGE: 38
RESIDENCE: DES MOINES, IA
YEARS ADVENTURE RACING: 5

Michael Shepardson on far right

The beast in me has had to learn to live with pain
And how to shelter from the rain   —Johnny Cash

There is no truth in adventure racing. Your stories become tainted with your teammates' experiences during the eternity of an expedition race. Vague nighttime recollections are riddled with hallucinations and false memories. Miles warped, most unremembered, others taking days to complete. My race has been distilled down to less than a dozen distinct miles that I still carry with me. The remaining miles were sweat out of me, before melting into the ground behind. Those memories became one with the trail, just as I did for those three days. Here are the miles I still carry with me, the ones that will be with me forever. This is the true story of my first attempt to finish an expedition-length adventure race.

Adventure racing is a grueling test of one's stamina and determination but to describe the physical challenges would be to only give you half of the equation. Einstein has shown us that the motion of a body cannot be measured unless there is another body to gauge the motion against. It is only from the perspective of this other body that there is motion. The same is true of the race ahead of me. Without a perspective against which to judge my trials and tribulations, you may fail to comprehend my joy, my pain, and, ultimately, my accomplishments. To measure a man's journey, you must know where he began.

I begin in the Plains States, where the world is flat. There are no mountains outside my window, I don't drive past trailheads on the way to work, and the only rapids on our rivers are dams. I'm a flatlander from the Midwest. Adventure racers do not live here and I am not an adventure racer. I'm an accountant who is past his prime. I'm on the downhill side of life and I've lost control of the reins. My life is speeding downward and I'm frightened by the certainty that awaits me at the bottom of the hill. I must stop the relentless progression of time, if only briefly. Racing does this for me.

When I race, I become the living, breathing incarnation of my childhood dreams. Before I strode off my parents' doorstep into the swampy morass of responsibility, this is how I wanted to live my life. Racing is my alternate reality where I become primitive nomad, crusading knight and Marco Polo, all rolled into one. My journey takes me through the empty portions of maps where cartographers disguise ignorance with sea monsters, walls of fire, and cities of gold. Once I dip off the map into uncharted territory, time ceases to have meaning.

My expedition race begins five years earlier on a couch in my living room. I'm watching the Eco-Challenge Morocco with the usual mix of awe and respect when Australian racer Jane Hall speaks to the camera. "To many people, it appears that the racers are superhuman, but they're not. They're just a whole bunch of average-type guys and gals who want to get out there and have a go." At that moment, Jane Hall steps out of the television screen and joins me on the couch. She sizes me up, looks directly into my eyes, and tells me that I am an adventure racer.

I spend the next two years trying to exorcise the ghost of Jane Hall with extremely lucid arguments against racing that are well buttressed with facts and logic. Still, her words haunt me. She will not return to the television set from whence she came for one reason: I believe her.

That I believe Jane doesn't change the fact that I have none of the skills required to even think of competing in an adventure race. My salvation comes in the form of an ex-Navy SEAL named Don Mann. Don runs an adventure race training camp designed to fill the chasm between "aspiring adventure racer" and "actual adventure racer."

Don motivates with a whisper, not a roar. He channels his military tough love through a Zen master persona. I've actually seen grown men break into tears upon receiving one of his bear hugs at the end of a race. Like a loving father, Don motivates with a fine balance of patience and expectation. His four-day training camp teaches all of the disciplines required to finish an adventure race and, more importantly, imparts his students with the confidence that they can finish. He completes his balancing act by sending his new racers on a two-day adventure race designed to break them.

When I walk into Don's camp, I am a neophyte, scared and alone. When I walk out, I have a new perspective on life and two of the best friends a man could ask for. The three of us arise from a scrap heap of a team that doesn't last through the first night of the two-day race. Anna and I bravely push on when the team disintegrates. Although he drops out of the race, Mark continues as our unofficial support team. He shows up at the checkpoints the following day and his encouragement buoys our flagging spirits. Well after midnight on that second night he is still up, trolling the roads of West Virginia looking for us. He finds us cold, wet, lost, asleep on our feet and yes, broken.

Mark shepherds Anna and I into his car and back to our beds. In so doing, the three of us make an unspoken promise that I hold as dear as my wedding vows. Somehow we three castoffs from other teams form a bond that lasts to this day. I've never raced without them and probably never will.

Adventure racing is like parenting. Until you have done it, you can't appreciate the challenges and you can't imagine the rewards. The short races we did in our first few years were like taking your nieces and nephews for the weekend. You get a taste for parenting, you can probably tell if being a parent is your cup of tea, but it isn't remotely like having children of your own.

Perhaps that is why Jane Hall still haunted me. She hadn't told me to take the kids for the weekend. She had told me to "have a go." To live in the woods, sleep in the woods, be the woods! Jane wasn't going to leave me alone until I stepped up to the challenge of an expedition race.

Having sampled the buffet of shorter races available, I felt Don Mann's were the toughest I had experienced. This is the type of race I was after, a true test of body, skill, and character. Don's big boss race is called the "New Balance Beast of the East" and this year it is in North Carolina.

That is where I stand now, breaking bread with two old friends and one very welcome new acquaintance. To complete our four-person team, Anna has produced a physical specimen that I had previously assumed only existed in men's fitness magazines. Standing before me, with nary an airbrush in sight, is a picture-perfect physique with a very stoic personality. If there is anything this team needed to round it out, it is a picture-perfect physique and a stoic personality. Dave is welcomed with open arms.

The four of us share a few final words as friends before we cross the starting line and become racers. In life, you know who you are and generally how you will feel each day. In adventure racing, you don't know from hour to hour. One moment you make a brilliant navigational coup de grâce that avoids seven miles of bushwhacking. An hour later, your teammates are force-feeding you GU in hopes you'll stop complaining that Santa Claus is stalking you.

During an adventure race, you will be the hero and you will be the goat. Somehow you must come to terms with that and handle both states with grace. It is impossible to adequately prepare for uncertainty so you must simply set aside your concerns and "have a go." Which is what we now do.

As the starting gun sounds, we take our first steps into this unknown psychological melodrama. The first night blurs past like an impressionistic video on MTV accompanied by the steady beat of pounding feet. With dawn comes Proud Rock. It has a nondescript formal name, which I forget as soon as I hear it, but I have given it a moniker more befitting its stature. Proud Rock is a hulking brute of a rock that pushes up four thousand feet above the vegetation. It wears a crown of trees pushed back on its head to expose its mighty face. It is that face that we will soon be rappelling down. Fear becomes palpable as we peer through the trees at this freakishly oversized boulder.

The brutal hike up Proud Rock dulls our fear. We drive up the rock relentlessly, trying to stay ahead of our fear. The four of us march in grim silence for over two hours to reach the crown of trees. At the top, our plan is to have Anna descend first. She is the most skilled and fearless climber on our team. We hope that seeing her successfully descend will raise our spirits but the plan doesn't have a chance. As Anna's small frame dips out of view, her confidence goes with her.

The rock face itself stretches down nearly five hundred feet into the fog but the crown of Proud Rock commands a view of the entire valley. It is breathtaking. Literally. I have to force air in and out of my lungs. Anna descends with grace and poise but the fear that chased us up the mountain catches us before Anna clears the rope. In my mind I know that Anna has made it down and that I will too, but the cowardly critters churning my stomach cannot be quelled by reason. When it's my turn to take the rope, I begin chanting my climbing mantra:

"Don't look down.Breathe.Don't look down.Breathe."

Climbers on either side of me speed by as I inch downward. I celebrate their passage by pancaking against the rock face in front of me. Sounds halfway between grunts and involuntary curses escape my lips as I struggle to ensure the rest of my descent is not one long scream.

By the time I reach the base of Proud Rock, the rest of the team has done a quick map check. We can make the cutoff time at the river if we push hard. Buoyed by the adrenaline from the rappel, our pace is strong. We know that we are going to the river. Going "to the river" means going downhill and it's downhill all the way. We break into a jog. We pass people. With each team that we reel in, we feel stronger.

Huge, pregnant drops of rain hammer us as the next checkpoint comes into view. Dozens of people are huddled under a park shelter. All we have to do is pick up our bikes and race down the final hill to the river. It's going to be close and there is a chance we will make the cutoff. I don't know it at the time, but this is the turning point. Even as I dare to dream of finishing in the "Pro" class, the seeds of our destruction are being planted.

The faces that peer out of the shelter look oddly out of place . . . too young, too clean. They stare at us as if we've just invaded their planet. I know this look. I had the same expression the first time I saw adventure racers. Like a puzzle, the logic slowly pieces together in my mind: "These people have never seen adventure racers before. Ergo: This can't be the checkpoint." We have fallen in with a high school field trip and based on the sideways glances and hushed conversations, it is obvious that we are much more interesting than whatever it is they have come to see.

We are not at the checkpoint nor is there any hope of us making the river cutoff. On the way to the actual checkpoint, the rain beats any remaining joy out of my body. Upon arrival, we celebrate missing the cutoff by giving our bodies some badly needed sleep. The checkpoint proves to be a horrible location for a power nap. There is a constant din of support personnel greeting their arriving teams, adventure racers calling for gear, and, worst of all, vehicles pulling in and out frighteningly close to the nylon tent wall that separates their tires from my head.

I sleep fitfully but it is sleep and I am refreshed by it. Mark rouses us with a hearty, "Ride, Beer Nuts, Ride!" and we steer our bikes onto the course. Anna was unable to sleep but she and David are physically stronger than Mark and me. Our team seems to have found a balance and we pedal with renewed vigor. Mark and David navigate confidently as we pass several teams. Only tired batteries and dimming lights slow our pace.

When Mark's bike light fades to black, I ride in front of him so that he can leech off the beam from the powerful headlamp I've been conserving. Suddenly I hear unprintable words spew from Mark like machine-gun fire. He catapults over his handlebars and I hear the dull thud of flesh on rock. His cursing resumes, a mix of anger and fear. I hurry to him and when his face catches the beam from my headlamp, I let out an audible gasp. Half of his face is oozing fresh blood. I look away.

Blood weakens me but I know that Mark is scared and needs to know if he's hurt. I look again. His teeth are bloody but intact. His flesh is ragged but not torn. To our mutual amazement, Mark is not seriously hurt. Later, the details of the crash will reveal themselves to us in the form of large greenish black bruises that develop on Mark's arms and legs. Mark will never complain about his wounds. By the time their pain begins to surface, it will have been buried under the layers of more urgent suffering.

With this second dawn we trade our biking shoes for hiking shoes and set off down the trail. Within minutes, Anna begins pinballing off the rest of us as we walk. We debate Anna's need for sleep versus the senseless waste of daylight hours that sleeping entails. The sound of Anna's head smacking into a sturdy tree branch resolves the issue. As much as we hate to burn daylight, Anna needs sleep and she needs it now.

Several more teams pass us as we lie curled up by the side of the trail. We discovered a wormhole through time and space when we missed the river cutoff and were driven to the next checkpoint. Now there are dozens of fast teams behind us, but it feels good to be in the company of other racers.

The trek ahead of us has been aptly labeled the "death march" by race organizers. Oddly enough, I have very pleasant memories of this section. With some sleep under our belt, conversation blooms. We talk about aspirations, literature, and memories from our youth. There is an undercurrent of humor as my affection for my teammates grows with every step.

We are unanimous in our appreciation of the trail. It is steep and challenging but as an appetizer it is very enjoyable. It would make for a very agreeable day hike but as with any meal, the first bite is always the most appealing. By this time tomorrow, we will have had more than our fill of the death march.

We have taken to betting foodstuffs on the exact time the next rain shower will arrive. While these games bring flashes of joy to our dreary trudging, the rain begins to take its toll on our bodies. Our support vehicle blew a tire the night before and Mark was not able to get a dry change of clothes. His feet have been exposed to constant moisture since the rainfall on the first day. The steep descent begins to tear at the saturated soles of his feet.

Mark's case of trench foot is a stark reminder that we aren't doing minor league races anymore. We are in the major leagues now and the injuries we are facing can only be acquired by extended exposure to harsh conditions. The soles of Mark's feet have taken on a pale white pallor and are ridiculously wrinkled. He has a blister protruding from each foot that looks like a sixth digit. A poor-fitting shirt has chafed his underarms raw and since he was unable to change into a fresh pair of shorts, his rear end isn't any better.

The ensuing night proves almost unbearable for Mark. His chafing turns bloody and his entire foot oozes puss when we change the bandages. At some point during the night, the irritation from his drenched shorts becomes excruciating and Mark strips them off. In a halfhearted attempt at modesty, he ties a shirt around his waist. When we encounter another team he ties on another shirt to cover the view from the rear. The "Adventure Racing Kilt" is born.

Sleep is no longer determined by physical need. We bed down when we become disoriented; we wake when another team blunders into us or the rain comes. I have vague, half-remembered recollections of Mark's face, lit by flame and framed in a veil of aluminum space blanket. Mark would later confirm that he'd become frustrated by the persistent cold and tried to create fire. He faced two challenges, the soaking rain and his own fragile sanity.

Picture a grown man scrambling around on all fours, using his blast furnace of a butane lighter to make kindling out of anything lying on the ground. Frustration mounts as his waterlogged environment fails to combust until he finally falls upon his own gear. Digging into his pack he frantically pulls out a plastic bag whose original purpose is now forgotten. Flame slowly curls the bag until the foul, unnatural odor of the smoldering plastic finally brings him to his senses. This is how the scene plays out in my mind as I struggle to my feet and step past the scorched remnants of a plastic bag.

While I'm thankful that Mark was not carrying the maps during his fevered attempts to create fire, the maps are not serving us well. They indicate that we are to follow the blue trail but the map's maker did not distinguish between the turquoise-blue trail and the sky-blue trail. We choose the turquoise trail. We are wrong. We follow the sky-blue trail until it forks. We choose the left fork. We are wrong.

We must certainly be in last place by now but still we run into other racers. A team of two comes down the trail toward us. Their navigator has the crazed look of a prospector who has spent too much time in the mountains. He has dedicated hours to searching this trail and its tributaries. He insists that this is the wrong trail and it goes on for ninety miles before reaching a trailhead. We put our faith in David's navigation and push on. An hour later that same team catches us from behind. Their navigator shrugs an apology as they shoulder by.

By the end of the death march, we are barely moving. Mark has the look of a prizefighter caught against the ropes. He is battered and bruised, or rather, his feet are blistered and torn. He is beyond feeling the pain. It has stripped him of rational thought. He is living on instinct and his instinct tells him to keep moving. I can't bear to watch anymore. I know that Mark's pride won't let him stop fighting but for his sake, I throw in the towel.

I am no longer racing through a fantasyland filled with sea monsters, walls of fire, and cities of gold. I am not a nomad, a knight, or Marco Polo. I am a father who is a long way from his family. I am tired and I miss my wife, my children, and my bed. For the first time, this journey feels long.

Mark, Anna, and I have moved on. We have mentally checked out of the race and into the hotel room that waits for us. David decides to ride on from the next checkpoint. I have read in physics books that Mr. Newton and his apple demonstrated gravity is constant and measurable, but adventure racers know gravity is an ever-fluctuating force. Gravity has a more tenuous hold on David and as the rest of us succumb to gravity's pull, David's bike floats away with each sinewy thrust of his powerful legs.

David's favorite memories of the race lie ahead of him but I'm not envious. He has my respect but my race is over and I have reached my finish line. There is no ribbon to break, no cheering crowds, and no bleary-eyed hug from Don Mann. Unfortunately, that doesn't make it any less real.

For the past seventy-two hours I lived my life in the pursuit of a single goal and I have come up short. But there is no lingering disappointment because I didn't come here to finish a race. I came to escape the bonds of time and for three days I have lived my life gloriously free of obligation and responsibility.

As I slowly drive past the ghost of Jane Hall, we nod to one another. It is an acknowledgment that I will be back to have another go but that she can let me rest in peace until that time. Time has once again begun its inexorable march forward and as life speeds up, I bask in its embrace. I came here seeking solace from my everyday life but now I'm eager to return. I'm excited by the prospects of a life where the passage of time is measured not by checkpoints, but by birthday parties, summer vacations, and Christmas dinners.

Perhaps this is the real truth in adventure racing. That the common man cannot truly appreciate the splendor of everyday life without having spent some time in its absence?

I return from most vacations wanting more: more sand, more sun, more food, and more fun. I return from this race with an appreciation of all that I have and the wholeness of my life. Absence truly does make the heart grow fonder. That applies to your family, your possessions, and your purpose in life. My life is truly blessed and leaving that life behind allows me to bask in its everyday glory when I return. If you doubt the grandness of your life, heed the call of Jane Hall!

From "Atta Girl" to Adventure Racer

NAME: CHRIS RUMOHR
AGE: 43
RESIDENCE: RESTON, VA
YEARS ADVENTURE RACING: 5

My name is Chris Rumohr and I, like so many other women in this country, wear many hats. I am a single mom of one son who is currently serving in the United States Coast Guard and is stationed in San Diego. I am a paralegal who has worked in civil litigation in northern Virginia for over eighteen years. I am a volunteer member of the Shenandoah Mountain Search and Rescue Group and I am an adventure racer. Being an adventure racer, in and of itself, is not so unusual. However, what is unusual is that I have *never* been athletic in my entire life and I didn't catch the adventure racing fever until I was thirty-nine years old!

To be honest, my first foray into adventure racing happened quite by accident. I had decided it was time to do something different in my life, so I set my sights on completing a triathlon. One day while I was online looking for a local race to train for, I came across the website for the Inaugural Western Maryland Adventure Race, which just also happened to be one of the very first adventure races in the Washington, DC, area. Images from the Eco-Challenge television shows I had watched for a couple of years came rushing back, and I thought to myself, "Why not?" I registered that day.

I trained as best I could by myself for this five-hour, two-person-team, sprint race. As it turned out, I lost my teammate at the eleventh hour. This was the first lesson I learned about adventure racing—that often just getting to the starting line with your full team intact is as difficult as the race itself. Discouraged, but not ready to throw in the towel, I solicited and received special dispensation from the race director to race solo—which I did and the rest, as they say, is history. Despite finishing in last place, I was hooked. The following year, I trained and prepared even harder for the second running of the race, and wouldn't you know it, the same thing happened! I lost yet another teammate at the last minute but went on to race solo. Once again, I successfully completed the race, but finished in last place. However, the third time was a charm!

After chuckling over the fact that I had to make my own chocolate chip cookies for post-race finishes, since I seldom ever crossed any finish line in time to enjoy the post-race festivities, a top local-area adventure racer put a bug in my ear about how nice it would be if I actually finished a race in time so that I could enjoy the food at the end! To add credence to his idea, he suggested that we team up for the third running of the Western Maryland Adventure Race. I was amazed and intimidated since I knew he was then trying out for a team that would be competing in the New Zealand Eco-Challenge. Why on earth would this caliber of adventure racer want to race with me? Well, against my better judgment, I accepted his offer. His physical strength and team strategy showed me what it was like to look back and have athletes behind me. What a kick in the pants that was! We went on to finish this race in style and in the top thirty!

I have a couple of wonderful memories from that third race. One memory was that of me hoarsely yelling back to my teammate on one of the trail run sections that I couldn't catch my breath, to which he, without missing a beat, calmly stated, "Don't worry about it, Chris! I've got your breath back here and I'll give it back to you at the finish line!" At that, I found enough wind to laugh to myself for quite a while. My other favorite memory was on the paddling section. After starting off on the canoe leg with a lot of energy, my teammate asked me to look behind and tell him what I saw. I turned my head back and there were literally dozens of canoes way behind us! That was my first taste of being up front. I had never seen people behind me in a race before! Suddenly, that day my goal went from just finishing to finishing in front of as many other teams as I possibly could.

In the meantime, buoyed by my success at Western Maryland, I went off to hone my fledgling adventure racing skills in order to do better with race finishes. My training circle grew and I started posting my training schedule online and was often joined by five to ten people for regular training outings in all disciplines. I also contacted Odyssey Adventure Racing and volunteered with that organization to get a front-row view on the ins and outs of adventure racing. Furthermore, I supported an awesome team, The Lumberjack Specials, during the Beast of the East, a five day expedition adventure race. That in and of itself gave me more experience than a year's worth of training.

It was at this time that my son Michael enlisted in the Coast Guard and headed off to boot camp. I was so distraught at what he might have to endure and overcome, that I decided to put myself through boot camp the very same week. I signed up and completed the weeklong Odyssey Adventure Racing Academy, which culminated with the Endorphin Fix, arguably the toughest two-day adventure race in America.

By this point in time, I had gained some fundamental knowledge of racing and had my "Atta Girl" persona firmly established. Having lots of heart and desire, but still lacking the technical skills necessary to complete a race and still be able to walk the next day, I was often given the cheer of "Atta Girl" as I stumbled or dragged myself across the finish lines of dozens of endurance mountain bike races, off-road triathlons, and orienteering meets, usually at the very back of the pack. As I was "atta-girling" my way through these events, naturally I had a few tales of woe, which I affectionately dubbed my "loser stories."

One of my favorite of these stories happened at a mountain bike race in Slatyfork, West Virginia, in 2003. The short of it is that my teammate and I lived to tell the tale that follows. The long of it is that the Wild 100 is a hundred-kilometer mountain bike race comprised of unmarked single-track, double-track, and fire road trails, which you navigate just like an adventure race. I teamed up with a friend who flew in from Chicago to race with me. We had attended the same Odyssey Adventure Racing Academy class, and had decided that this race would be a great opportunity to catch up and test our newly acquired skills!

The race went well for us—at least it did at first. We navigated flawlessly. We overshot CP1 by about a quarter mile mile because . . . well . . . it was early and I didn't get my coffee before the race started. The day went great. It was very hot and humid as is typical for August in West Virginia. As we approached CP3 we found several racers milling about discussing their map. We all teamed up together and navigated ourselves to the checkpoint where we ate lots of great food, including yummy pudding (my new race food of choice), drank naughty Coca-Colas, and transitioned out of CP3 fairly quickly. We left CP3 around 3:45 P.M., determined to make it to CP4 before 6:00 P.M. The five guys we came in with decided that their race was over and rode back with the race volunteers to the camp. Smart men!

Due to mechanical difficulties, many endos, the hot sun, trail conditions, and other assorted trials and tribulations, we slowed way down and did not make it to CP4 before six. In fact, we did not make it to CP4 until nearly 8:00 P.M.! Not knowing any better, we decided to go ahead and finish up the race unofficially. Our plan was to get to CP4, where our bike lights and cold-weather clothes were staged for us by the race management, and continue on at night to the finish. Never say die, right? Right!

By the time we arrived at CP4, the volunteers had left, leaving us two gallons of water but no lights or food or warm clothes. We mistakenly thought our lights would be at CP4, when in actuality they were staged at CP5, which had also closed down and gone back to base camp. Now we were stuck in between a rock and a hard place. It was decision-making time and I made the decision to keep moving forward since we had about three and a half miles of tough hiking, but it would eventually lead us to a better trail and then after a couple of miles to a gravel road that would lead us to CP5 and then back to camp. In hindsight, this was a very *bad decision*!

I naively thought I could navigate that in the dark. What I didn't realize is just how dark the woods are in West Virginia on a cloud-covered night. As the light faded we were reduced to navigating by feeling the trees for the plastic blue diamond trail markers. A few minutes later, we could not find the next tree short of running into it, and then were totally unable to find the next blue diamond. At 9:04 P.M., there was nothing we could do but stop and bivouac for the night. We had been out for approximately fourteen hours by that time and were cold and wet. We had bike shorts and sleeveless jerseys on. We had one space blanket (thank God) and light rain jackets. That was it. We wrapped up in the space blanket and hunkered down for a long, long night. I don't remember which one of us said it, but just as soon as the words "It can't get any worse than this" were uttered, the storms started rolling in.

We weathered three severe electrical storms that night right below the ridge. Lightning came at us sideways! The thunder was so loud that we couldn't hear each other as we huddled for warmth. It rained so hard that at one point I looked up and choked on the amount of water coming down. Sometime during that storm I yelled over the thunder to my teammate that I was concerned that we were covered by a metal blanket during an electrical storm, to which she optimistically lied, "Oh it's not metal, it's Mylar." It rained on and off (mostly on) for over nine hours. We spent the night shivering and shaking violently and we alternated lying down, standing up, and squatting in an attempt to keep warm and to stay out of pools of water that were accumulating on the ground. We fell over twice when we fell asleep standing up. I tried to find the trail markers at 4:30 A.M. and again at 5:45 A.M. with no luck. It was 6:25 A.M. before there was enough daylight to hike/ride off that ridge and back to camp. We hiked on the trail, which was now a creek with mud and water in places up above our knees. We eventually arrived back at camp a little after 8:00 A.M. to very relieved friends and to the shock of other racers who had finished the night before—no one could believe we weathered the storm on the mountain that night.

As miserable as that night was, I learned a lot from the experience. First, I discovered I had many loyal and caring friends who spent the night scouring the mountains looking for us. Second, I developed a great respect for my teammate Sarah Boardman. Sarah went through that horrible, cold, wet night never complaining once! We actually laughed like school-girls each time the storm would rage on us and joked how this was one hell of a way to spend time catching up! At one point, I felt her tucking in the sides of the space blanket around me to make sure I was covered even though she was not. Now, that is a team player! And finally, I learned that no man is an island in the sport of adventure racing. Sometimes the best decision is to know when enough is enough.

This certainly was not my only "loser story." I have had many more, but one thing I've learned is that if you try hard enough and long enough, you will also have once-in-a-lifetime experiences that make all the dirt, blood, sweat, and tears worth it!

For example, the past two years have held an incredible amount of suc-cess stories as well. I was able to work on my navigation skills and felt more in control of my technical abilities, race strategy, and gear. I was able to test my faith in those skills in several races. In March 2003, my team and I placed first in the bootleg adventure race "Josh's Diet" held in the beauti-ful Blue Ridge Mountains of Virginia. This race was created for and named after the race director's "rescue" of his younger brother, Josh, who had gained a few pounds while at college. I had done this race in 2002 and crossed the finish line dead last. And even though we came across last we were proud of ourselves because we had successfully navigated all the way to the finish line! In 2003, the race was held in extreme winter weather, making the difficult course even more challenging. Snowfall had measured into the feet the week prior to the race. Sleet, snow, and freezing rain helped level out the course and made it an all-out gut fest. Finishing in first place in those conditions was quite an accomplishment. Then just two weeks later, my team placed second overall at another bootleg race called "The 24 Hours of Elizabeth Furnace" in Virginia's Shenandoah Valley. This Rogaine-style race allowed for creative strategies from all who participated. Needless to say, navigation strategy was key in determining how long we would be out in the mountains, and that was very important seeing as the race director had decided to push the "cold as crap" button on his RD Weather Control Device around 1:00 A.M. Saturday morning.

Despite freezing temperatures, my team had a blast with race strategy after the checkpoints were released and I was confident that our navigator had come up with the best possible plan. We made the decision to run to the first checkpoint and were the first team to get there. We then returned to the start to pick up our bikes, whereupon we rode on fire roads with numerous stream crossings for hours. Our team saw several other teams and near the summit we even hid in the woods so that Team Forward Progression, our main competitor, would not know where we were. It was so cold, my shoes froze to my feet. We all were concerned about the effect the cold was having on our wet, frozen hands and especially our feet, so at one point we all sat on the ground in a triangle and put our feet under each other's shirts to warm them out of a danger zone. After this short break we were back on our bikes and heading toward Burnshire Bridge. Team Forward Progression finally caught us near the top of Burnshire Hill and they were relieved to finally know our location. By this time I was exhausted and my two teammates had to talk me all the way up the mountain. I think my body was finally paying me back for the initial, all out sprint during the first two hours of the race. Several painful hours later, we finally reached the finish line in a surprising second place!

On January 22, 2004, I had another success story that will be forever etched in my mind. That January, I decided to jack my winter training up a notch by accepting an invitation to do a winter ascent of Mount Washington in the wild and beautiful White Mountains of New Hampshire. Mount Washington is renowned for having the world's worst weather and despite its rather nonimpressive size, it is one very dangerous mountain. Dozens of people have lost their lives summiting its six-thousand-foot peak, and Himalayan mountaineers routinely train on its slopes.

I went to New Hampshire with a group of adventure racing friends and as luck would have it, we picked one heck of a day to climb the mountain. The sustained wind speeds were sixty to seventy milesper hour with gusts up to ninety-five, and the winds at the summit were over a hundred. At times, we literally had to crawl on all fours or scoot along on our butts because it was impossible to stand up. To make it even more challenging, the temperature was in negative digits and the windchill went down to eighty degrees below zero at times. Climbing that mountain, on that day, was one of the most difficult, yet one of the most memorable experiences of my life. I don't believe anyone knew just how frightened or exhausted I was. In fact, I was crying underneath all of my cold-weather garb, but fortunately nobody could tell. Besides, the wind was absolutely deafening— I couldn't even hear myself think. I drew upon every ounce of skill and stamina I had gained during my years of adventure racing. In fact, I now know that if it wasn't for my adventure racing experiences, I would never even have attempted a winter ascent of Mount Washington, much less have succeeded!

Adventure racing has enriched my life in so many other ways as well. It has brought to me bonds and friendships that are lifelong and important. It has taught me to differentiate between significant and insignificant problems. The lessons learned in life translate to adventure racing and quite so in the reverse as well. Finally, the adventure racing lifestyle answered the often asked question when life tests your patience and/or physical or mental limits, and leaves you wondering, "Now, was that experience really necessary?" When you cross the finish line with your team, you realize that all those experiences were not only necessary, but mandatory for success in life as well as adventure racing.

These days find me busier than ever. I still work in law but spend many hours growing the sport of adventure racing. It is a labor of love. I have been called the Ambassador of Adventure Racing. Remember posting my training schedules to friends? Well, that little e-mail list has evolved into The A List—the national capital area's largest clearing house for adventure racing training and race information that services hundreds of racers in the area and nationwide. I am also in the process of helping local government agencies organize an expedition-length race that will cross their state. Additionally, I continue to host and manage adventure racing clinics at various outdoors stores in the DC metropolitan area and I provide consulting services to local outfitters to aid them in providing proper gear and informational services to adventure racers. Adventure racing has indeed become an integral part of my life.

I started adventure racing five years ago and have raced, directed, co-directed, created, supported, consulted, and volunteered in and for literally hundreds of races since that time, culminating with qualifying for the 2003 Nissan Xterra World Championship in the over-forty division. I simply adore and am fully involved in all aspects of adventure racing. I believe the lessons learned from adventure racing are positive and life changing. Adventure racing has given me the opportunity to witness first-hand many top athletes on the same course as my team, but just as important I have had the privilege of also witnessing the unsung heros—the everyday ordinary human beings transformed into superhumans with a seemingly limitless capacity for endurance, flexibility, and an ability to adapt to a particular condition and overcome challenges, all with grace and humor. I am also inspired by other "women of age" who have gone before me, and there are many more than you would think. I have come to realize that it is not in spite of, but rather because of the passing of those years and the sheer accumulation of knowledge and all sorts of experiences gained during that time that we've become formidable athletes in the difficult, ofttimes grueling, multidisciplined sport of adventure racing. These experiences have forever left an indelible mark on my perspective and how I conduct myself in my everyday life. My advice for anyone sitting on the fence is, "If I can do it, anyone can!" Do not let self-intimidation stop you from anything you desire. I started this journey as an "Atta Girl," but I have become an Adventure Racer, and for that I am immensely grateful.

The Territory Ahead: The Bear Necessities

NAME: DAVID P. KELLY
AGE: 39
RESIDENCE: FAIRFAX, CA
YEARS ADVENTURE RACING: 10

I grew up exhuberant in body but with a nervy, craving mind. It was want-ing something more, something tangible. It sought for reality intensely, always as if it were not there.
—*John Menlove Edwards, "Letter from a Man"*

The Alaska Wilderness Classic is a grassroots, no-hype race that rotates every several years to another remote corner of the Alaska wilderness. This particular year it went from the tiny coastal town of Hope (population seventeen; initially built a century ago around the Russian bride trade for lonely Alaskan men during the Gold Rush) to Homer (population twelve hundred; also called Land's End given its position at the end of the Alaska Highway and the southernmost portion of contiguous Alaska). The "Classic" is a wild and woolly adventure meant for those who are native Alaskans and have already tested their mettle in the woods and wild land-scape as a natural course in their everyday lives. However, that sentiment wasn't entirely airtight as there was at least one "outsider." After seeing an advertisement for the first Eco-Challenge in '94 while sitting with a group of friends in Hawaii, we all agreed wholeheartedly that this new sport sounded like great fun, and that we should all race together in the Eco-Challenge Utah '95. After spending the next four years racing, learning not only the nuts and bolts of a sport that had limited history but also learning how to accommodate this thing called adventure racing into my life and psyche, the Alaska Wilderness Classic showed up on the radar screen in '98 as something compelling, intriguing, and absolutely needing to be done. So I, along with my good friend and racing cohort, Alaska native and civil engineer Jacques Boutet , decided haphazardly to make the few hours' drive from Anchorage to Hope to begin and finish a race we would never forget.

Bear sign sprinkled the landscape. Every turn was accented by scat, trails blazed through thick underbrush, and wide deep prints embedded in mudflats. When we first saw her, she was a half mile away: over one thousand pounds of muscular golden sheen rippling in the early-morning sunlight. Flanked by two cubs, she wound her way along the thin talus shoreline of the lake at the terminus of the monstrous Skilak Glacier. She was right in our intended path. These were ingredients every expert and book says to avoid in the Alaskan wilds.

It's become increasingly clear to me over the years: It is not variety that is the spice of life. Variety is the meat and potatoes. Risk is the spice of life. I believe there are two basic approaches to life. You can mire yourself in precautions as you endlessly try to avoid and outwit fate: trying to create a perfect scenario for a long safe life. Or you can let it fly. Each has its own downside. In the precautionary approach, you might be stuck with a long, boring, uneventful flatliner ride on the stream of life. To me, there's more risk in that proposition than letting it fly. It's a matter of choice. You take risks. You search. Sometimes luck is with you, and sometimes it is not. The important thing is to be willing to take some risks along the way, rather than turning toward safety and comfort within your personal zip code.

If you are into adventure racing, you spend much of your time being wet, cold, tired, hungry, and frightened. You take risks, and you fail occasionally. In order to get through the demands, you have to have a deep burning passion to do so—racing is hard. (To paraphrase an old Nike slogan: "You've got the clothes. You've got the shoes. You can dribble the ball. But have you got the love, baby?") Adventure races are too long, and life is too short, to not have "the love." When you decide you want to get to the finish, you need to decide how to overcome the barriers along the way. You choose the right teammates to give you the best chance to succeed. You learn the appropriate technical skills, and select the right equipment and clothing for the conditions. You train enough to know your physical limits. You select the best possible route to get you through safely, methodically, and efficiently. You try not to expose yourself to more risks than you can handle—something you rarely fully know until after the fact. In the back of your mind you remember that there will be other races if this one refuses to cooperate. And you're driven by a burning passion.

But to compete at the top, you have to be willing to take some risks. And you have to be willing to fail occasionally. That means pushing your and your team's comfort zones and limitations. That doesn't mean do-or-die situations should be sought out. It doesn't mean you should constantly be riding the edge of your limits. You don't have to live *on* the edge all the time, to still gain knowledge *of* the edge. However, you do have to flirt with it a bit—dangle your arms and legs over the edge a bit, perhaps—to perform well. In the safest possible adventure race there is substantial stimulus from probable and present danger. To know your limitations and to keep within them is the essence of decision making. A comparatively weak team, aware of its weak points and keeping within their limits, can outlive and outperform the strongest team that proceeds indiscreetly.

To keep going day after day under mind-numbing and heart-sickening strenuousness requires a bigger, more powerful faith than in oneself or in any concept of superiority. There are some simple truths encountered in an adventure race. Sometimes the harder the race, the more truths reveal themselves. I believe adventure racing reveals us as we *really* are. It doesn't show us who we *think* we are. It doesn't show us who we *want* to be. In an adventure race there are few places to hide from your true self—in all of your splendor and ugliness. And there is an incredible raw intensity in that simple fact—a fact that makes it both rewarding and scary as hell. The Alaska Mountain Wilderness Classic offered an incredible venue to reveal some of these truths and offered a fix to any hubris we were hanging on to.

Traveling hyperlight, it would take Jacques and me five days to complete the 150-plus-mile course of the Alaska Mountain Wilderness Classic across the Kenai Peninsula by foot and small packraft. We were given a start, the town of Hope, where we started with one bare toe dipped in the ocean's water. We were given a finish, the end of the dock at the end of the Homer spit. The route was up to us. Twelve maps, a compass, experience, and our intuition were our beacons. The course and terrain conjured up words like: *awesome, majesty, rawness, intensity* and *fear.* We knew that with minimal safety net, and the inherent challenges of the terrain, we would have a few opportunities to potentially kill ourselves. We were short on food, clothing, bivy and safety gear. We were sent off with reassuring words, "If someone don't show up at the finish within eight to ten days, a search and rescue party might—but don't count on it—be sent looking. Have fun!"

In preparing for these races, it's always a good idea to consult the experts about some of the objective dangers of the area. Through reading and conversation, I generally learn quite a bit from others. In Alaska's case, I learned that grizzlies were one of the daunting regional hazards, and reading what the experts had to say I learned a lot about these bears (aptly given the Latin name *Ursus arctos horribilis*). I learned how to spot a grizzly. It's that big muscular hump-shouldered creature that can reach up to sixteen hundred pounds (that's almost ten of me, and someone advised me long ago, don't screw with anything ten times your size) and can stand eight feet tall. Grizzly bears don't attack humans that often, unless they feel threatened—particularly if one feels as if its cubs are threatened. But on rare occasions they will attack for no apparent reason other than a quick and easy snack.

Griz have large feet with nonretractable claws and huge omnivorous appetites. Their claws are designed mainly for gathering food and for taking swipes at things. Their teeth are for killing and tearing off hunks of meat. The best way to encourage a grizzly to attack is to run. Giving chase is one of their prime sources of entertainment. At thirty-five miles per hour, they also can run a lot faster than puny, fleshy, slow-moving two-legged man. If you get caught, remember they also enjoy wrestling—something they're quite good at. So playing dead often, but not always, discourages the grizzly, which leaves looking for more fun elsewhere. Fighting back (unlike with the black bear) encourages it to fight back. Grizzlies have also been known to cheat in wrestling: often biting and scratching, particularly to your head and neck. If it is really hungry, the griz will eat you. The bear is hungry. You are food. It's a simple equation called Darwinian Math. And they don't always bother to kill you first. They just grab hold of something and start munching. Often they'll go for your soft underbelly. With their claws, and a quick swat, they can rip you open like a stubborn bag of corn chips. You may have the exceedingly unusual opportunity to feel yourself being ripped apart and watch the meal, which is you, in progress. Any way it happens, the bear wins, and you lose.

These portentous words of expert advice and wisdom were running through my head as I chirped on my little orange bear whistle—better to have her hear us and skedaddle. But the half-mile distance and our position downwind didn't do much for the acoustics, or our situation. My intuition told me this was probably not so good. Why do we have intuition? Intuition is quite important. It reminds us to be frightened when we may be too stunned to remember why should be in the first place. Our problem lay in the fact that the only pass over the mountains within too many miles lay just on the other side of those grizzlies. As the climber and adventurer Yvon Chouinard says, sometimes you simply have to take "big, hairy risks." This particular risk was looking larger than life, and getting bigger and hairier with each step. But damn it, we were approaching our third day and in a serious race mode. As we stealthed down the narrow shoreline, we eventually lost sight of our three furry companions. Like true believers, we convinced ourselves they must have heard us and scampered off. We beat our mental chests with pride and accomplishment. "So far so good," said the man after falling forty stories of a fifty-story building.

There is at least one time in every adventurer's life where you realize this is for keeps—no more nerf-life. In this pessimistic moment you get that sharp acidic taste and an inner tightening that comes with *knowing*, not just mildly *thinking*, you might not get out of this. Twenty minutes and a mile later, as we rounded a large talus pile, there towering over us was our thousand-pound pissed-off grizzly making it abundantly clear that she didn't want us in her backyard. We had entered into the arena of true life or death. Things like nature, mountains, and grizzlies, for that matter, have little respect for credentials. They don't care who you are, where you've been, what you've done, or how much money you make. They become great equalizers in many ways. Right then, we were puny little fleshy nobodies—and we knew it.

Wearing the startled looks of Spanky and Buckwheat, we froze. Only a few yards away, the goliath grizzly gnashed her jaws and lowered her ears. We stared at each other for a few miliseconds that dragged on for three eternities. Now, I know what every bear book you read and every expert will tell you about what to do in a grizzly encounter such as this: *"Do not run!"* And this is precisely where secondhand advice and firsthand reality meet head-on. What did we do? We ran our butts off. After slamming my ankle into a basketball-sized rock, I proceeded to limp-run for a quarter mile, trying to keep up with the speeding Jacques, who apparently had done more homework than I: Jacques understood the adage, "Always go out in the grizzly country with someone slower than you." When Jacques did finally stop, I caught up to him in a pile of sweat and breath. It was, once again, dilemma time: Keep on running and go around many miles, or go through the grizzly. We had all of twenty breaths to think about it before, off to our side in the cover of thick slide alder, came that liquid nitrogen spine-chilling "ROOOOOAAAARRR" of the stalking bear. Off we were again, this time for half a mile before we finally came out into a large enough clearing by the end of Skilak Lake. We were stuck between a glacial lake, a pissed-off grizzly, and the conviction that we were in a race and further retreat was not an option.

I remembered the childhood rule: "Can't go over it, can't go under it, can't go through it, guess we better go 'round it." Seven minutes and thirty-five timed seconds later we had blown up our mini-packrafts with puckered lips and pumping lungs. We paddled and flailed our way toward the pass, cautiously winding around raft-popping glasslike shards of floating ice and irritable grizzlies to the base of the glacier. We frantically hopped out, and on the run deflated the rafts and crammed them into our packs. We didn't stop until we had bashed through two thousand vertical feet of slippery slide alder and loose talus slope. In an exhausted heap on a rocky outcrop overlooking the massive glacial valley below, after rolling into our fear and rolling back out, Jacques and looked at each other and pealed into uncontrollable bouts of crazed laughter that echoed up and over the Kenai mountains and down through the valleys of our fears. Right then I remembered Chouinard's corollary to "take big, hairy risks": "Adventure comes when you screw up and you get yourself in a fix and have to fight your way out." We were definitely in the realm of screwed-up adventure.

Throughout the Classic, we were worn down by: the constant motion; a single fifty-five-hour sleepless stretch; the constant battle to stay as warm as we needed to, to stay as dry as we could; the raw hamburgered feet; the excessive swelling from taking too many anti-inflammatories; and the need to keep moving up and down mountains, through dense alder and chilling glacial streams, twenty-three hours a day. For the brief times that we lay down for rest, and even occasionally for some long-needed sleep, I had nightmares about that grizzly. I smelled her musty coat and felt the tremble of her roar. Each time we lay down, my body quickly fell into deep muscle-twitching shivers. Metabolism is a less effective warming device when your body is slowly consuming itself for food. While moving I daydreamed of us reaching the finish line, excitement driving me past exhaustion. At those moments I looked around, considered just how biblically awesome, hostile, and beautiful our environment was. I wondered which one was the real madness, the daydreams or the nightmares. And I loved every single moment of it.

Adventure racing isn't about *being at* the finish. It's about *getting to* it. The finish line is a necessary formality and finally crossing it can be anticlimactic. Sadly, once you're there, the journey is over. And the only real losers in an event, finishers or not, are those people that can't take the gift of the learned lessons home with them and continue to learn from their experiences.

I feel a great affinity for wild places: The priceless rewards will always be the challenges and beauty offered. Going there makes me feel a part of something infinitely more rewarding than what I've left behind. What I see and experience in the wild moves me in ways that nothing else can. The Classic, during the days of the midnight sun, was the vehicle for simple motion and pure form, with the basics of a start and a finish and everything in between. We saw massive glacial valleys with towering fairy-tale mountains rising through the mist on either side. Looming granite walls and spires looked so close we could caress them, only to realize they were spread five miles across. Dall sheep pranced up impossibly vertical worlds of rock as regal moose tended their young on gravel stream bars. And the grizzlies: When they weren't eyeballing us, we watched them feed their young on spawning salmon struggling on their final death march up stream. Wide-winged bald eagles soared above it all. Incredible!

In the final twenty miles of the race, limping along, suffering from mild hypothermia, but still with that elated yet dumbed-down grin, we were passed for first place. Well, as they say, "Some you lose." We had been cold, hungry, exhausted and frightened. We didn't win the race, but I did win a few lessons from the Classic: lessons about taking risks, about pushing oneself to the limit, about wilderness travel through Alaska, and about the life altering power of nature. I was reminded that the wilderness, ever remorseless, can be indifferent to mortal ambitions, and that the games played here can be hers alone to call. Above all, I learned a great deal of humility.

We reached the finish line of the Classic hobbling on wobbly, unsteady, aching, and swollen ankles and knees, sleep-drunk. Despite the chilling wind and bulletlike rain blasting my body and face, I opened my eyes in wide rapture and gazed away like a blissful Buddhist monk. I thought: For the rest of my life I will be trying to regain this feeling.

I wanted movement and not a calm course of existence. I wanted excitement and danger and the chance to sacrifice myself for my love. I felt in myself a superabundance of energy which found no outlet in our quiet life.
—*Leo Tolstoy*

Coast to Coast:
Face-to-Face with Fame and Danger

Photo by Will Ramos — www.0bounds.com

NAME: CAROLINE BROSIUS
AGE: 36
RESIDENCE: WASHINGTON, DC
YEARS ADVENTURE RACING: 7

When I first heard about adventure racing, I was drawn to the competitive team aspect of the sport. At the time I was racing sprint kayaks, which by its very nature is an individual sport. After the Olympic Trials in 1996 and the disappointment of not making the U.S. team, I decided that the singular pursuit of one sport was limiting in many ways. I wanted to continue to compete in athletics, but diversify my training and seek more overall balance in my approach to competition. Adventure racing seemed like the perfect solution—I could utilize my paddling skills, expand my existing cross-training interests, and learn new skills as well.

The first year I got involved in adventure racing, I competed with one of the up-and-coming racers in the Washington, DC, area. Our goal for every race was the same as it had been while racing my kayak—win or place in the top three. We placed second in my second adventure race, the Raid the North, in June 1998. It was an extraordinary experience, but not just because of how well we placed. The way feelings of pride, joy, happiness, exhaustion, and frustration were so completely shared by the team, made it a very memorable experience. Finishing second was almost . . . secondary.

Over the course of the next few years, I truly came to love adventure racing. I liked the fun and enjoyment I got from training on my own and pushing myself to always get a little bit better, a bit faster and a bit smarter at race strategies. I enjoyed training and racing with other people and sharing countless unforgettable experiences with my friends. I also valued the lessons I learned. For example, adventure racing taught me that sometimes competition isn't always about me doing my personal best: it's just as important to help someone else accomplish their own goals. Furthermore, I discovered that a successful race wasn't always defined by what place I finished. Some of my best and most memorable races weren't necessarily the ones with the highest finishing places. In fact, one of the most unforgettable adventure racing experiences I ever had occurred in 2002 when I was offered the opportunity to enter the Coast to Coast Adventure Race as a soloist.

The Coast to Coast is a three-day race that entails paddling, hiking, mountain biking, and climbing across the state of Florida. To make matters even more interesting, Jeff Westerfield, a friend of mine, was producing a television film about the race and asked if I would consider being one of the highlighted athletes. I agreed, even though it would be the first time I would be competing as a solo racer. Although I had no doubts about my physical abilities to finish the race, I was concerned about the extra challenges soloists have to face, particularly since any problems I would encounter would be televised for thousands of people to see.

Fortunately, I was able to convince my friend Emily to serve as my one-woman support crew. Emily was a godsend and I can't say enough good things about the wonderful support she provided both before and during the race. So in late May, we loaded up my truck and drove south to Florida. After two days of buying last-minute supplies, checking gear, packing, and repacking, we were ready.

The race began on the Friday before Memorial Day weekend at 6:00 A.M. with a twelve-mile paddle along the Florida Barge Canal before entering the Crystal River. The Crystal River truly deserves its name. The water is beautiful, clear, and fairly deep. The bottom is white sand with various dark green grasses. I even saw a couple of manatees. This section went fairly quickly and as I neared the end, I discovered where the boat "recovery test" and the mask and snorkel drill would occur.

I had practiced righting and getting back into a canoe on the Monday prior to the race, so I was pretty confident I had it figured out. So I secured my pack and gear as best as possible and then flipped my boat over. Unfortunately, the only thing I hadn't accounted for was having bow and stern float bags. The stern one turned out to be more of a hindrance than a help. As I was trying to climb up from the stern of the boat, over the inflated bag, it pushed the boat farther into the water, hence letting more water into the boat. I managed to find the air tube and deflate the air bag, but not quickly enough. I ended up in the boat, but up to my waist in water. I realized after a futile few minutes of trying to bail or pump the boat out that I was going to have to reflip my boat and completely pump it dry. I proceeded to spend the next fifteen minutes floating beside my boat in the nice, comfortable river, pumping the water out of the boat. By now, several teams I had never seen passed me, did their test, and proceeded on. Argh! Once the boat was emptied, and the bag had deflated, I was able to quickly climb into the boat and paddle to shore, where the mask and snorkel test was staged.

The mask and snorkel test required participants to follow a line down into the river to a depth of about nine feet. Attached to this line, by plastic cable ties, were Styrofoam cards with team numbers on them. The task was to find your numbers, cut them free from the cable ties with your knife, and return them to the checkpoint monitor, who would then punch your passport so you could proceed. I have to say there was something a bit disconcerting about the thought of having people diving around in murky water with knives, searching for numbers, against the clock. As far as I know, no one was stabbed and it was actually a pretty fun event.

At this point, the downside of being a soloist became apparent. Only one member of each team had to dive for the number tags, while the remaining teammates could be moving the boats up and over the dam that we had paddled to the base of. Since it was only me, I did the swim and then had to drag my boat up the grassy slope and over to the launch site on the upstream side of the dam. A short paddle later, I was at the first transition area.

Fortunately, Emily was waiting and was able to help me get out of this area quickly. While she took care of the boat, I took care of getting my passport checked and showed the mandatory gear that was requested. This wound up being the first of several times I had to pull my cell phone from its waterproof package and prove that it had batteries by turning it on. I decided that since I had lost ground and the bike ride was only ten miles before another paddle section, I wouldn't change clothes at all. I found Emily with my bike, grabbed my helmet, gloves, and pack, and took off down the road toward the next checkpoint, bound and determined to make up time.

The bike section was along a busy, two-lane, fifty-five-mile-an-hour road. Just after I passed another soloist, I saw a truck pass something in the middle of the road. At first, I thought it was a bird or roadkill. However, as I got closer, I realized that it was a turtle. There was no way I was going to leave a turtle sitting in the middle of this road, race or not! So I pulled my bike over to the shoulder on the other side of the road, ran out to the middle, grabbed the turtle, ran back, and set him down. Meanwhile, the soloist I had just passed went by, looking at me like I was crazy. I jumped back on my bike and passed him again within a couple of minutes, still feeling good about rescuing the turtle. I managed to pass a couple of other teams as well, so I was quite happy with how things were going.

The next checkpoint was the beginning of the next long leg of paddling. I dumped my bike, gulped some water, and was on the river as quickly as possible. I knew that the paddling sections were the one portion of the race where almost no one would be able to beat me, and where I could make up the most time. Sure enough, over the course of the next few hours, I passed several teams and moved back up to about twentieth place or so.

At the next checkpoint, I got ready for the first of two extended trekking sections. Emily and I carried the boat to the truck and I got changed while she fixed me food and helped me get my gear ready for the next few hours. We were already ahead of schedule and were very excited with how the race had gone so far. Shortly after I headed out on the trekking section, Jeff took several shots of me walking and jogging along, as well as interviewing me about the first few hours of the race. Several of the nearby racers nicknamed me "Hollywood." We wound up hiking together for the next 12 or so miles. The walk was along some of the various trails that cross central Florida in an area known as the Florida Greenway. Reportedly, this land was originally going to be dredged and used for an east-west water canal. However, the canal had never been built and instead, the land was turned into a recreational area for hikers, horseback riders, and mountain bikers. It was a wonderful trail, except for the heat, the sand, and the horseflies.

We arrived at the next checkpoint about an hour or so before sunset. Emily had once again outdone herself. She had found an awesome site and had all the gear and food set up and ready to go. As I changed out of my sand-filled socks and shoes and prepped my feet for the next section, she cooked up a feast and we went over our plans. As I left the comfort of the transition area on my bike, the sun was setting and the reality of facing a trail alone, at night hit me . . . I could get really, really lost! This fear rapidly disappeared, though; as I was locating the first trail heading east toward the climbing site, I met Team Hornet, a group of four Marines. I asked if they would mind if I rode along with them, since we were headed in the same direction. I think we all figured we would separate as the need arose, but we wound up riding together all the way to the climbing site.

"Where in the world is there anything to climb in Florida?" was one of the questions I had asked when I first looked into doing this race. Well, it turns out that they like to dig a lot of big holes called quarries and we were given the opportunity to do a Tyrolean traverse and an ascent in one of them. The Hornets and I arrived to find a bustle of activity in a half-lit pit as the teams that had arrived before us were sliding across the traverse, suspended about thirty or forty feet above the ground, between the two sides of the quarry. At the same time, the other teams ascended (or scrambled using ascending devices) up about a twenty-foot crumbling cliffside. As I was doing my ascent, Jeff made sure that everyone knew who the solo female racer being filmed was by asking all the teams waiting their turn if they would shine their headlamps up at me as I climbed. Nothing like a little pressure to perform!

After the fun time in the quarry ended, Team Hornet and I headed out on the second half of the bike section. Unfortunately, one of their team members was suffering from the heat, so they told me to take off and try to follow some of the other teams whom we had seen leaving the quarry site. I had my maps in hand, but soon caught up to two, two-person male teams. I figured I would ride with them as long as I could. This is where I learned my first lesson as a soloist—believe your own navigational instincts and don't get caught up in another team's navigation panic attacks.

The next checkpoint was at a campsite, and reportedly the bike trail we were on led directly there. In reality it didn't and after unsuccessfully trying to find it via the trail, we finally decided to bike-whack our way through the woods to a nearby highway. We wound up at the back fence of a trailer park. Since it was almost midnight, and we were basically coming through people's backyards, we made a lot of noise and made sure our bike lights and headlamps were turned on. We eventually figured out we were three miles south of where we wanted to be. Then to make matters worse, I got a flat tire just about a half mile from the checkpoint.

At this checkpoint, we decided to stay together since we already had been through so much that night. They were happy because they had moved up fifteen places, while I was a bit bummed that I had dropped thirteen. However, knowing exactly where we were and exactly where we were going lifted all our spirits. We had a relatively straight and fast ride along well-marked and paved roads under a full moon.

When we arrived the next checkpoint, I had a message waiting for me from my friends from Team Hornet: "Next time, stick with the Marines." They had apparently recovered and passed through the checkpoint ninety minutes ahead of us. Let's just say, I was not amused. However, I knew that part of the next leg was another major paddling section and to begin it, all the teams had to portage their boats over a mile to get to the put-in at the river. The teams had to carry their boats, but since I was a soloist, I had a nice little set of wheels to put under my boat. I knew I could make up a lot of time and suffer a lot less misery than the teams, so I was already plotting what I would say when (not if) I caught them later.

Shortly after putting in, I noticed round, glowing eyes on both sides of the river. A friend of mine, who had once lived in Florida, had warned me about the "red eyes"—which belonged to alligators—and advised me to watch out for them. I had taken her advice with a grain of salt, figuring that I wouldn't be paddling anywhere I would be exposed to that many alligators in the first place. Boy, was I ever wrong! On both shores, there were the glowing eyes. It must have taken an hour before I would admit to myself that maybe these glowing yellowish eyes actually belonged to the same type of creature that my friend had been telling me about—alligators! Once I admitted I was alone, at 3:00 A.M., in a carbon-fiber canoe, with nothing but my mandatory two-and-a-half-inch pocketknife and whistle for protection, I had my first bout of nerves.

To make matters worse, it was extremely difficult to navigate because I couldn't see. Within fifteen minutes of putting in, the only light available to show me the water, let alone where the river was headed, was the setting full moon already behind the overhead canopy of trees and my headlamp, whose batteries were dying. This was not enough light. Ironically, I had conscientiously tied my halogen flashlight to the rear thwart of my canoe just before pushing off, thinking that I could get it "if I wanted to." Well, after watching the glowing eyes, I decided that even though I desperately wanted my flashlight, it just as well could have been back in the truck with Emily. There was absolutely no way I was going to try getting to the other end of my canoe to untie the light, nor was I going to go to shore—not with all those eyes!

As I paddled along fluctuating between being annoyed at myself for tying the light in such a stupid spot, and scaring myself with visions of hitting an unseen log and being eaten by an alligator, I rounded a corner and found, to my relief and amazement, a couple of fishermen floating along in a johnboat. I paddled up to their boat and asked if they would please untie my flashlight for me. They didn't say a word but untied the light and then wished me a good evening. Although I felt much more reassured having my nice, bright halogen flashlight, I now wondered how the heck I was going to use it. I was in a canoe with a kayak blade and needed both hands to paddle. I didn't have any way to attach the flashlight to the boat and I wanted to be able to scan the environment. My solution ended up being to hold the flashlight in my mouth. What I sight I must have been! I had a headlamp perched on my head, I was wearing two layers of Capilene and a rain jacket with a hood up for warmth, and now I had a six-inch, neon yellow halogen flashlight sticking out of my mouth . . . all the while paddling down a gator-lined swamp. Too bad this was never captured on film.

Later I heard that folks who paddled this section during daylight said it was beautiful. However, as one who paddled 99 percent of it alone, in the wee hours of the morning, all I can tell you is I was *never* so glad to see the sun rise. What began as a basic night paddle that looked straightforward and simple on the maps ultimately turned into a night that changed my perception of me and what I am capable of accomplishing.

And just as the sky was beginning to brighten and I was about a mile from the takeout, who should I come across as I rounded yet another bend in the river but Team Hornet. They were adrift and half asleep in their two boats, which were sitting side by side. As I paddled up to them, they said, "Hey, it is us and we are lost!" To be honest, I had spent part of the time paddling thinking of all the humorous things I would say when I found them again, but at this point, they were so funny, and so tired, that I just said, "Hey! No you aren't lost! We are only about a half hour from the camp!"

I was relieved to finally get out of the boat and after a short bike section, Team Hornet and I began a very long twenty-one-mile hike. The navigation wasn't challenging since we were following a well-marked trail—it was just long and all the same. The trail was described as "scenic" but after a couple hours of sand, dirt, pine trees, low bushes, and more pine trees, I decided that I had had enough of this version of "scenic." Several hours into the trek, we decided to lie down under some trees and sleep for forty-five minutes. It's amazing how much a short nap can help after being awake for thirty hours.

At this point, Team Hornet and I formally introduced ourselves and began to talk. Roger was the tall silent point man, who was the captain of the team. "Baggy," also known as Brad, was a talker and joker who made the entire walk and events much more fun. He and I at least managed to entertain each other. I don't think either of us is genetically wired to be able to remain silent for more than fifteen minutes. Mike and JR rounded out the team. All are married, have children, and are somehow involved with the Hornet airplane, hence the team name.

The trek went on for hours and hours, and wound up taking twice as long as we had predicted. By the time we finished, Roger and I were both out of water and very dehydrated. When we finally got to the next checkpoint, I told Emily that I needed to rest for a couple of hours. Not only was I dehydrated, but I had also developed some sort of crazy rash that stretched from my sock line up to the top of my thighs. It hadn't particularly bothered me during the walk, but once I stopped, it exploded. My legs were very, very hot, and the rash was red and blotchy and somewhat swollen. Naturally, the film crew was there also and dutifully filmed the mystery rash as well as all the other "wonderful" effects that thirty-six hours of racing, sleep deprivation, and dehydration have on to a body. I wound up spending three hours at this transition area, basically eating myself into a coma. When I finally got moving again, I was relieved to know that "all" I needed to do for the next three to four hours was paddle a boat again. At least this time I was prepared with the idea of "river" and "dark," alone in a canoe. Or so I thought.

I launched about 9:30 P.M., just as full dark set in. There were a couple of tricky things to watch out for in the beginning of this section, but I had studied my maps prior to launching. I actually had to pull out my compass to determine which of two equally small, dark, and tree-covered streams headed southeast. Meanwhile, Team Hornet and a couple of other teams had launched while I was eating and sleeping, since they didn't want to be on the river at night again. However, I knew I could make up time and catch them now that I was rested and fed.

This paddle was much more intense than the first night. For one thing, there were *a lot* more glowing eyes, and these eyes also liked to follow the boat, or swim across in front of the boat, or swim toward the boat and then disappear underneath it. At least the eyes the night before had stayed still. Once again, I followed my navigating-on-the-water method by keeping the open canopy above, locating the banks, staying in the middle, and avoiding the debris. The first third of this section had much more debris strewn than the previous river. Several times I had to stop my boat, back-paddle, and inch my way around and through downed trees. At one point, I decided that the alligators had specifically pushed logs and deadheads into strategically located spots, where the current would naturally push you, so that unwitting victims, paddling alone, would run into them and be tipped into their waiting jaws. I was determined to outwit them.

After an hour or so, the river opened up. It was lined on each side by tall trees, and had large lily pads stretching ten to fifteen feet from shore. Within these lily pads, and on some of the banks and low-lying trees, were more glowing red eyes—a lot more. I kept trying to remember everything I could about alligators and kept thinking about big teeth, dinosaurs, the fact that they have survived forever and were fast in the water.

Since the river had opened up, I was able to take advantage of the full moon and had turned off my headlamp and was just cruising along in the fastest part of the current. I was paddling along, finally relaxed and comfortable and following the lazy zig and zag of the river, when I spied a set of glowing red eyes gliding across the lily pads from my right. I had become accustomed now to the fact that the red eyes did swim and move, so didn't think too much about it. The eyes approached the bow of my boat, and then sank below, and I paddled over the swirls where they had been. I was waiting for the boat to be hit from below (insert *Jaws* music here) and then telling myself I was just imagining things again, when suddenly off the bow to my left, there was a loud smack and the ripples from the tail of the alligator bounced my boat a bit. I started to paddle faster, and kept an eye on the left, when about three feet to my left this gator did a body slam, lifting most his body and tail out of the water, splashing me and sending more waves to rock my boat. He must have been about six feet long. Finally, he had one last big splash at my stern to send me on my way. I realized that I had just been warned by an alligator and decided I would stay farther away from the lily pads so I didn't "disturb" any others.

I arrived at the checkpoint at the time I had predicted and Emily was there on shore, waiting for me. We carried the canoe up to the truck for the last time and I sat down and chowed down on eggs, oatmeal, bacon, doughnuts and hot tea! It turned out that after finishing their paddle, Team Hornet had eaten and gone to sleep and were still in the checkpoint. Baggy came over to find out what my plans were and it looked like we were going to be ready to head out at the same time for one last forty-mile bike ride followed by a beach run/hike along the Atlantic Ocean to the finish.

It was now about 3:00 A.M. on Sunday and I had been racing since 6:00 A.M. Friday and only had about seventy minutes of sleep. The first ten to fifteen miles of the bike ride were slow and steady. Everyone was tired and fighting to just stay awake. The bike was fast and flat, except for one portion where we had to slip, slide, and walk our bikes along a sandy fire road. This is always fun to do, especially while half asleep and having the occasional hallucination. Once the sun rose, though, it got hot again very quickly. We followed the roads to the last transition area, where we dropped off our bikes and changed into our beach walking clothes and got more water, more sunscreen, and final instructions from the film crew. I was to walk up over the "cliff" (about a four-foot drop), pause while they caught it on film, and then scramble down to the beach and walk out to the ocean and head south toward the finish. It was the most theatrical shot of the entire race. After two or three takes of me approaching and then heading down the beach, Team Hornet and I teamed up one last time to do a fast walk down the beach, seven and a half miles to the finish line.

It was a gorgeous morning. The ocean swells were running pretty big; it was partly cloudy and there was a storm about a mile off shore. We passed quite a few early-Sunday-morning beach walkers and sunbathers, who looked at us, all filthy, bedraggled and decked out in our hats, glasses, backpacks, and race tops and asked, "Where did you come from?" We dutifully bragged about how we had just crossed the entire state of Florida, and were headed to the finish line.

And then—it was *over*! As I crossed the finish line, I felt a mix of emotions.

I was relieved because I could finally stop.

I was thrilled that I had finished the race and completed it faster than I had hoped.

I was pleased because even though I had done the race solo, I had made many friends along the way.

And I was proud of what I had accomplished. I wound up finishing fourth out of the eight soloists and placed thirty-seventh overall (out of the sixty-three teams entered).

Yet part of me was sad that it was over. It had truly been an amazing, once-in-a-lifetime experience and one I'll never forget!

Adventure Racing Is . . .
by Bill McBlaine

Adventure racing is:

A. A multidiscipline endurance sport emphasizing outdoor skills, teamwork, and perseverance.

B. One- to seven-day events that rob you of your self-esteem and outdoor skills confidence.

C. A great way to get away for a weekend and return sore, broken, and broke.

D. An incredible team sport where you rely on your team, your team relies on you, and you find out what you're made of.

E. A sick and twisted "sport" where race directors conjure up insane routes and sit back and enjoy the misery they inflict on otherwise sane participants who actually paid money and traveled long distances to do this.

F. A multiday sporting event where you learn that your best runner has a blister and can't run, your best biker has a broken wheel and has to push the bike, your navigator has a headache and is lost, your team lost a piece of mandatory gear, and the so-called weakest person on the team is pushing and towing your team toward the finish line.

G. All of the above.

Team FRED
Sharing the Gift of Adventure Racing

NAME: MARC BENDER
AGE: 50
RESIDENCE: RIVERSIDE, CA
YEARS ADVENTURE RACING: 9

Photo courtesy of Marc Bender

Genesis of FRED

It all started in '95 at the Hi-Tec off-road triathlon at Lake Castaic in LA. My wife, Carla, had been doing triathlons for years and decided to team up with a couple of my cop buddies to try this "new thing." I just went to watch and cheer them on. I was a couch potato. The only thing I had ever done to improve my aerobic capacity was to quit smoking two packs of Lucky Strikes every day.

Twenty minutes before the start I was approached by a couple of guys I knew from Ontario Police Department. They said their third teammate hadn't shown up and asked if I would fill in so they could still do the race. I was in no shape to contemplate it, but, being unclear on the concept of "team," I agreed to go to the starting line with them, so they could leave me behind and do the race.

That's what happened. We started out and after the first one hundred yards I never saw them again. But I continued on as long as there were people behind me. At the finish line there were still about twenty teams behind me (out of about two hundred teams that started) and I felt like Lance Armstrong winning the Tour.

That's when I started to get infected with the AR bug.

I got a couple of guys from work and we did a couple more of the Hi-Tec races. Then one of the guys saw a flyer for the Walkabout, a forty-eight-hour race in the Ortega Mountains of Orange County, right in our backyard. We went out on a ten-mile "training hike" before the race and figured we were ready.

We showed up to race in cotton T-shirts, cotton sweat socks, down jackets, military-issue backpacks, big leather hiking boots, a huge military folding compass, and a bag full of PowerBars. We were all undercover nar-cotics cops so we looked like a bunch of dope-addicted Hell's Angels. We got some interesting looks from the other teams, usually including a puz-zled little smile.

Here is where FRED was born. The term *Fred* was used by Carla's friends in the road cycling club to refer to a guy who was doing something dumb. Like the guy who gets his first set of clipless pedals and falls over the first time he comes to a stop. "Nice move Fred." Or the guy who gets squirrelly in a pace line: "Hold your line Fred." It expanded to be used any time somebody did anything goofy. Buying warm beer, putting gasoline in a new diesel truck, driving into a carport with bikes on the roof rack . . . well, you get the picture.

When we looked at all the other teams, then looked at ourselves, we christened ourselves Team FRED. It can also stand for Fools Running in Every Direction.

We went into the race with no idea what we were doing, no training, no navigation skills, no decent equipment, and no food. We wandered through the course and crossed the finish line dead last in forty-seven hours and thirty-six minutes. We were bloody, blistered, dehydrated, cov-ered in poison oak, famished, and sleep deprived. Then we learned that only seven other teams had finished the race. "Hey! We made top ten!"

I was hooked.

Carla and I started doing several twenty-four- to forty-eight-hour-long races per year. We had a blast racing together but it soon became apparent that she needed to be on a faster team. In cool weather, it was hard for her to stay warm at FRED's pace. So she got her own team together, Team SAGA, and was very competitive.

Just getting to the finish line was enough of a challenge for me. This became the goal in every race. Reaching that finish line was the only rea-son to show up for a race. If we were last, that was okay. If we were short-coursed, unofficial, unranked, penalized, or came in after the awards cer-emony was over and everyone had gone home, that was okay too, as long as we made it to the finish line.

I've never been an athlete and was not likely to become one due to my racer profile.

Name: Marc Bender

Age: 50

Sex: Yes

Height: Just a hair over five six and three-eighths.

Weight: Mostly in the belly

Training schedule: Works an average of one hundred hours per month in overtime, has a ten-year-old daughter who is very active in competitive gymnastics. Tries to squeeze in a marriage, and almost never has time to train.

Training diet: Due to crazy schedule, just grab whatever is available. Seems to be able to schedule a regular intake of beer (when off-duty, mostly).

Motto: "Have a bunch of fun and get to the finish line, no matter what."

Becoming the Pied Piper

I then discovered that one of the hardest things about adventure racing is getting a whole team to the starting line. Aside from paying for the race, getting to the race, getting the gear to the race, and getting a support crew for the race, I had to find three other people to do the same thing.

Gear Rule: No matter how much gear you have, the next race will require a piece of gear you don't have yet.

I was able to recruit a few people from work, but most of them looked at me like I was crazier than the last time they talked to me. I found SCARABS, a Southern California web forum for adventure racers, and started inviting newbies to race with me. They would usually do a couple of races and one of three things would happen:

1. They would be so thrashed they vowed go back to doing triathlons.

2. Their wife/husband would complain of "time away from the family" and refuse to issue a "kitchen pass" allowing them to race again.

3. They would catch the AR bug and decide to be competitive, which meant looking for a faster team.

So it evolved that I began to have at least one newbie at every race. So far, seventy-seven people have done their first race as a FRED. (In this count I have included nine who had experience in short races and did their first expedition-length race as a FRED.)

These newbies have provided the fodder for the funniest things that have happened at races. Many of these things are only funny now that some time has passed.

Please keep in mind that I'm not complaining or criticizing anyone when I tell these stories. It's just part of the FRED experience.

The protagonists in the following anecdotes are all newbies and names have been changed to protect the innocent.

We are walking down a hot trail on Day 3 when a black wasp the size of a sparrow starts buzzing our heads. Everybody is swiping at it with gloves, hats, and whatever, except for "Ben," who begins to lecture us in kind of a bitchy way like, "Quit being pansies and just ignore it. It will go away. You're just making it worse, it's not gonna just sting you for no reason." Suddenly the wasp dives into Ben's chest and blasts him right through his shirt. He screams like a girl and falls to his knees as we are laughing so hard we can't help him.

Getting ready for a big hike I tell "Rick" to lube his "sensitive areas" with Vaseline to prevent chafing. He informs me he is "all man" and only guys in San Francisco put Vaseline on that body part. "You'll never catch me doing anything like that." Thirteen hours later he comes into the finish line walking as though he is holding a beer keg between his knees.

Not long after I start doing the Cal-Eco I learn that any racer who completes the five-race series will be awarded the coveted "Golden Carabiner." I wasn't likely to win any races but I set my sights on that biner.

It's the first Cal-Eco of my second season of the "Golden Biner Quest" and I have two newbies. The race starts with a long downhill single-track on the bikes. Halfway down, the female newbie, Bernice Pearson (true name, I have to give her credit for this one), falls and dislocates her knee. It's bent pretty weird and she's hurting . . . a lot. I jump off my bike and start telling her, "Oh, that's okay. This happens all the time. You'll be fine. I can fix you right up." In my mind I'm seeing that gold biner slip out of my grasp for another season, right? I pull out the first-aid kit. My first-aid kit consists of Motrin and duct tape. I give her a handful of Motrin and go to work with the tape. I get her knee wrapped up pretty tight and tell the team we're moving out. They're looking at me like I'm loony, like somehow I might have missed the fact that our girl is seriously injured.

We prop her up on a bike and start pushing her down the trail. We do pretty well for about two miles until we come to a steep area and she sort of gets away from us. Bernice goes sailing down the path and crashes into some bushes. I feel like crap for not taking better care of her, but when we get to her, she's able to stand. The second crash knocked her knee back straight! She walks around a little, then jumps on her bike and says, "Let's go." I act like I expected this to happen but actually I can hardly believe it.

We end up finishing the race in thirty-sixth place. Guess how many other teams finish the race? Right, thirty-five.

Another Cal-Eco and two more newbies. "Rex" appears to be in pretty good shape and is very enthusiastic. He turns out to be a nightmare. We start off on foot for a long hike and Rex starts telling us how "bitchin'" he is. I start pushing us a little faster, hoping he'll run out of breath, but it doesn't work. We hear about every cool thing he has ever done. After several hours I ask him if he knows what the word *tedious* means. He says "Sure," and starts telling us about his IQ, extensive vocabulary, yada, yada, yada. We get to the kayaks and I put him in the other boat. We're going into a stiff wind on flat water in those inflatable yellow Sevlars. It's very slow going and hard work. Rex tells us he is a great swimmer and is adamant that he can pull the boat, swimming, faster than we are able to paddle. I tell him to just keep working and we will get there eventually, but he persists until I've just had it with him and tell him, "Go ahead. Jump out of the boat and pull it." He thanks me, jumps from the boat, and begins flailing around as the kayak drifts away from him. I let him go for about five minutes until he was good and thrashed, then we pick him up and continue to the next transition area. I think this will humble him a bit but it is not to be. He's just as bad on the bike. Getting to that finish line is the longest thirty hours of my life.

My next misadventure takes me to the jungles of Brazil. I've decided to bring a filter pump for water after getting violently ill in the XPD race in Australia, where I drank some water treated with iodine tablets. I give the pump to the newbie and tell her, "I want to keep this with us all through the race." She puts it deep into her backpack. Two days later we are on a monster trek and it's a hundred degrees. We run low on water and I see no water on the maps. I find a small pond and ask her for the pump. She says, "I didn't bring the pump. Nobody told me to bring the pump." I donn't know her well and we haven't slept yet and she was getting a little "edgy" anyway so I decide not to argue about it. I pull out some iodine tablets I brought "just in case."

Two days later we're in a transition to kayaks and I tell the team I want to put the race-issued radio in the dry bag. She reaches into her backpack and hands me the filter pump. I give her a puzzled look and it goes like this:

Me: "I thought you didn't bring this."

Her: "You gave it to me at the start and told me to keep it with us."

Me: " I remember that but two days ago you told me you didn't have it."

Her: "What in the hell are you talking about?"

And then the light goes on.

Me: "You think this is the radio, right?"

Her: "That is the radio."

I can't answer. I'm looking at the water filter pump and trying to imagine it as a radio. I'm rescued by another teammate who handed me the real radio.

Her: "What's that?"

Me: "The radio."

Her: "I thought *that* was the radio."

Me: "I know that now, but I'm not sure I understand it."

Her: "Well, I've never done an adventure race before."

Me: "I guess that should explain it. Let's go."

From an expedition race in the jungle of Brazil to a forty-eight-hour race in the Sierras, the newbies keep me on my toes and never knowing what to expect. "Omar" has done several orienteering competitions and wants to get into AR, so I invite him along. We've been given the coordinates for the checkpoints about three hours before the race so I'm plotting the CPs, marking our course, cutting and laminating the maps. Omar is looking over my shoulder and from his comments, he seems to have a grip on where we're going. He starts working on me to let him navigate and after a while I give in, figuring I can get us out of whatever trouble he might lead us into.

The first leg is a twenty-eight mile bike ride. The first six miles are a steep, steep downhill on fire roads, a short section of flats with a maze of trails, then no apparent trail along a river for fourteen miles to a twenty-eight-hundred-foot climb that looks like it's going to be a hike-a-bike.

At the starting line I make sure everyone has the mandatory gear. Then "Omar, you good with the maps?" Omar says, "All good with the maps, boss."

We take off at midnight and fly down to the bottom and get into the mess of trails. We stop and I look at Omar. He's looking at the trails. I'm wishing he was looking at the map.

Me: "Which way, Omar?"

Omar: "I don't remember."

Me: "Remember what."

Omar: "Which way to go."

Me: "Maybe a gander at the map will help refresh your memory."

Omar: "I didn't bring this section of the map."

Me: "You brought the wrong map?"

Omar: "Somebody took the maps out of my backpack."

Me: *"What?"*

Omar: "I thought I had the maps. Somebody must have taken them out of my backpack and forgot them."

Me: "Somebody."

Omar: "Yeah. Somebody must have."

Since we're not going to ride back up that hill, I take the lead and head in the direction I *think* we need to go, from my memory of the maps. There are tire marks heading in many directions so I know several teams are going the wrong way. There's a group of about seven teams at the next intersection and we blow on by with confidence. They follow.

We find the river and there's no trail so we start to hike-a-bike up the boulder-covered riverbed with the other teams still following. They don't know we have no map. They are following me because I'm pretending I know what I'm doing. There are sheer cliffs on both sides of the riverbed so I feel confident we aren't passing the trail up the hill. It is very obvious when we get there as the way up is a fresh fire break. We climb straight up to the CP/TA, meet our support crew, and get the maps out of Omar's gear box where "somebody" put them, and got ready to set off on a trek.

Omar: "Where's the map?"

Me: "Right here in my hand."

Omar, reaching out: "Let me see it."

Me: "No way."

Omar: "Then how am I gonna navigate?"

Me: "I think I'd feel more comfortable if I handle that responsibility."

Omar: "You said I could navigate."

Me: "I'm sorry, buddy. But the most important job a navigator has is making sure "somebody" doesn't take the maps out of your backpack and hide them in your gear box. I'll handle it from here."

"Omar" pouts all the way to the finish line.

I always get a big kick out of racers who get lost and tell me later, "My compass wasn't working right." I tell them the story of when I was a little kid and was sawing a piece of wood. My grampa was beside me and I said,

"Grampa, this saw saws crooked." He said, "Boy, it ain't the saw."

Haw haw, I'm a funny guy right? Well, I'm two days into the second Primal Quest at about 2:00 A.M. and I'm looking for the mouth of a cave that goes straight down into the ground. There's tall brush with occasional large igneous rock outcroppings. I take a bearing and begin walking. I walk in what I think is a straight line and forty meters later I'm ninety degrees off my bearing. I walk back to the last point, take the bearing again, and start walking. I pick out a star on the horizon and head for it. Fifty meters later, I'm still walking toward the star but I'm sixty degrees off my bearing. I'm tired but not *that* tired. I spend about an hour trying to figure it out before it occurred to me that the cave I was looking for and the piles of rocks around us were caused by volcanic action and the rock is filled with iron. So I let go of the compass and use the stars and find the cave in short order.

I don't make fun of people anymore when they tell me their compass messed up.

The Final Piece

Team FRED had participated in the Cal-Eco series for several years and become friends with the promoters, Dan Barger and Maria Burton. They knew that I enjoyed bringing new people into the sport, so about an hour before the start of the Cal-Eco in South Yosemite I was approached by Maria, who asked me if I would allow a solo racer to stay with my team. She was worried about allowing this person to go out on the course by himself. I already had three newbies on my team and it was like herding cats just getting them to the start line.

I was thinking, "If she's worried about letting him on the course, why would I want to add him to the chaos I'm already dealing with?"

Reasons to refuse:

1. I might have already bitten off more than I could chew with three newbies in one race.

2. I had a responsibility to my teammates. They had paid their money and put all their trust in me to get them to the finish line. It wouldn't be fair to them to take on a possible liability.

3. The guy might be a jerk.

It didn't make any sense to agree to her request, so I looked Maria straight in the eye and kinda grooved for a minute on how cute she was and said, "Sure! No problem." She took me over and introduced me to

"Larry the Solo," who had flown in to California for this race, his first attempt at AR. He ran a 5K last year representing his total athletic experience.

He seemed like a nice guy but . . . .

Larry was in his late twenties, a little chubby (who am I to judge?), wearing leather Reebok court shoes, blue jeans, two cotton T-shirts, a big cotton sweatshirt with a hood, and a backpack the size of my couch. Next to him is his bike, leaning on its built-in kickstand! There is a flashlight duct-taped to the handle bars and a 6" piece of foam rubber duct-taped on top of the seat.

I am in such big trouble. This guy is FRED squared, or maybe cubed, or maybe to the power of twelve.

Another classic case of a pretty girl talking me into doing something I know I shouldn't do. I'm the only guy to ever have that experience, right?

Well, we're at the starting line and I'm giving my recently enlarged team of novices some last-minute pearls of wisdom when the gun goes off. Larry takes off like a bullet and is with the front of the pack. I figure he'll last about a mile before he bonks and I find him lying on the side of the trail.

Well, guess what? I never see that guy again until the finish line.

On Day 2, one of my newbies goes hypothermic. We had to swim a few miles in some pretty cold water, but that isn't the problem as we all have wetsuits. A one-hour bushwhack in the middle of the afternoon, in our wetsuits, sweating our *&#^%s off and that's when he succumbs to the cold. Go figure. So we miss one checkpoint (penalty, not DQ) and get him to the TA. Get him dry and warmed up and continue on.

When I finally see Larry after the race, he tells me he took off at the start thinking we were ahead of him. He kept going hard trying to catch up to us before giving up and following other teams. He did that swim section in his cool surfing Jams, but decided at the end of the swim section that he had "had enough." At that point he was still several hours ahead of us.

This is such a great example of why we shouldn't "judge a book by . . ." I think that adage holds true for AR more that many other sports. I've seen plenty of lean, mean, ripped-up, badass looking athletes at the starting line and had the pleasure of stepping over their bodies later along the trail. And I've seen plenty of people who looked like they had no business even thinking about racing get to the finish line twelve hours ahead of me.

That's part of the beauty of AR.

Another big part of that beauty, for me, is that it takes me back to the freedom of childhood. Remember when you were a kid and your friends would come to the door and say, "Hey, let's go play," or "Hey, let's go ride bikes"? Back then we didn't need to schedule playtime, didn't need to find out where we would go or how long we'd be gone or all that crap. We'd just go play. So now I get these phone calls from people who say, "Hey, you wanna go do the Four Winds at Lake Mead?" or "Hey, let's do Primal Quest." And I just say, "Yeah. Let's go play!"

The most rewarding thing about AR, though, the thing I am most addicted to, is overcoming my limitations. To realize those limitations are self-imposed. I've done fifty to sixty races and in almost every race there was a time when I wanted to quit. When those demons sat down on my shoulders and started whispering in my ear, saying things like, "You're too old, you're too fat, you're just beating yourself up for no reason, you don't have to be doing this, you're going to ruin your knees, you're lost, this is stupid, just lie down and take a nap, you could be kicking back with a beer right now, you've done enough, you can't go on, you're spent, you're done." So I just take another step or spin those pedals one more time and then one more and I end up at the finish line. To this day I've never crossed a finish line without a little lump in my throat.

The world used to look so much bigger to me. Mountains looked so much higher, rivers faster, water wilder. But now that I've been over mountains, down rivers, and across deserts, I've learned there is no limit to what I can demand of my body. That feeling, the epiphany of realizing that pain doesn't matter, that heat or cold doesn't matter, that hunger, thirst, lack of sleep, blisters, chafing, heartburn, poison oak, confusion, disappointment, none of it matters if you decide to take another step, dip that paddle one more time, keep going you will get to the finish line.

That is the gift I give to every newbie I bring across the finish line. I know that the world, for them, just got smaller, easier to conquer. They've learned something new about themselves, and as I hold their hand across that finish line, and I see that little buildup of moisture in the corner of their eye and that big swallow, I know that their life has changed too.

I just can't get enough of that.

Anatomy of a Race from the Belly of the Beast

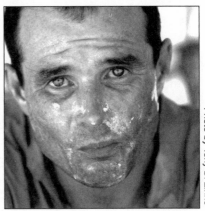

Photo by Tony Di Zinno

NAME: ROBERT NAGLE
AGE: 46
RESIDENCE: CAMBRIDGE, MA AND
   THE WHITE MOUNTAINS OF NH
YEARS ADVENTURE RACING:
   FROM 1994 UNTIL 2001

• Tar trees, wait-a-while vine, saltwater crocodiles, hairy caterpillars, stinging trees, the deadliest of deadly snakes, yada, yada, yada. Enough of this already! While the competitors at the 1997 Discovery Channel Eco-Challenge are held in thrall by another display of the dangers northern Queensland poses, we leave the room with our maps to go over the course in more detail. We've heard this scare-mongering before, let's concentrate on the racing. Tactical decision #1, not-so-smart move #1.

• Later that night, we estimate our food requirements for the first stage of the race. In the 1996 version at British Columbia, we'd run out of food on one of the mountain stages and survived for the last twenty-four hours on rationed gels and pilfered blueberries (we were pilfering from bears— I guess they didn't like our smell as they readily gave way). Imagine five bedraggled athletes counting down the minutes to the moment we could share (all five of us) a single PowerGel. That's right—twenty-two calories every ninety minutes. Not a very healthy ratio and one we certainly weren't going to repeat this year. We load our packs with dehydrated food, PowerBars, fruitcake, and a potent powder mix of dried milk and geriatric meals. Tactical decision #2, not-so-smart move #2.

• Ten hours into the race—we're in the bottom third of the field. This has never happened before. Briefly we ponder, "What the hell is everybody doing? Why are they going so fast?" Sure, the navigation is easy on this stretch and the going isn't arduous (ankle breaking at times but no real elevation to deal with and open terrain to move through). But how could there be so many teams ahead of us? Screw them—we'll just go at the pace we know we can maintain for seven days. Strategic decision #1; in fact, strategic rule #1 (make your own race).

• Thirty hours into the race—we're really having fun in the inflatable 'yaks. Narrow twisting stretches with branches and fallen logs everywhere. Occasionally a small rapid. It's dark (it'd be dark in some spots even during daylight). John and I are improvising strokes when the flow increases, picking the more aggressive lines whenever we can. We're not moving very fast ('cause the river generally isn't) but we're definitely not losing time on this stretch. Are those crocodile eyes over there? Ah, who cares, they're probably only freshwater crocs. First fun time of the race.

• "Holy shit, what was that?" John is on his feet behind me in the 'yak as I struggle to keep it upright. I affect calmness but John insists something dropped into the boat. It's a snake, he's convinced (we've already had four close encounters with snakes in the first thirty-six hours). I change his mind for him—we paddle on. Ten minutes later, he leaps to his feet again—"It's wriggling behind my back!" This time it's hard to be blasé—when John gets animated, he can move mountains. But I'm either Mister Cool or Mister Naive—eventually I calm him down and we paddle on. Later as day breaks, we find the culprit—not a deadly snake but a small fish. He wasn't imagining things! Memorable incident #1.

• After forty hours, we reach the first rope section: a good-sized rappel that runs out over a waterfall at the end; a short ascent on the slimiest rock you can imagine. Then a whitewater swim around the base of a waterfall, from which we clip into ropes and ascend up beside the waterfall. Adrenaline time—arm-pumping time. The only hesitation comes before the leap into the water for the swim—but at least it's not brass monkey cold. More fun.

• At the top, we gather briefly to dry our gear (no point in lugging wet stuff). The heat of the sun on the rock is vicious and it seems to take mere moments before our harnesses and packs are dry. The navigation from here looks a little trickier. John takes a cursory glance at the map and leads us away. After a while, we catch one of the other favored teams—their navigator is rather bookish in his approach, methodical, careful, cautious. He trots to the head of the line to confer with John. "Looks like we figured out a similar route—what bearing are you on?" John looks up: "I'm not using a compass." Their navigator replies, "But what are you aiming for?" John answers, "Nothing in particular, I'm just getting us to the checkpoint with the least possible work. Someone else has the maps." The next question forms silently but goes unasked. Dumbfounded, their navigator leaves. We press on, picking up speed as we go. And dreaming up the land as he goes, John leads us to the checkpoint. Display of genius #1.

• The next section is equally tricky on the map. We haven't had much rest so far—we've tried twice but each time the nighttime cold awoke us. The sun is setting now but the land retains the heat of the day. We decide to get a solid "comfortable" rest before the hard work ahead. As we skip away off the trail and hunker down on a sandy gulch, we hear other teams coming through and pressing on. After a luxurious two hours, we rise, thoroughly refreshed. Smart tactical decision.

• Once again, John's navigation is superb and we find the checkpoint quickly. Somehow we've leapfrogged into third place. The route to the next checkpoint is even trickier in the dark—a fainter-than-faint trail around a series of spurs. Andrea is astonishing as she smells out the path—it's invisible, yet she scarcely hesitates. An hour later, we're in second place.

• The next thrill is an enormous Tyrolean traverse, rigged across an entire valley. A gnarly descent to the rope finds us in the lead. So as we leap out over the valley, we savor the astonishing sight. In the predawn illumination, the Herbert River is far below. The ride is astonishing. Fun squared.

• In the early light, we tramp along by the riverside. Crocodile prints are everywhere. We joke and josh about the course rerouting necessitated by sightings of two enormous saltwater crocodiles here (originally teams were to have canyoned along the Herbert River). Suddenly Andrea vehemently asserts the presence of a large crocodile. Keith confirms the presence of not one but a pair of crocs observing us from the water. We don't waste any time. Memorable incident #2.

• Even though we're now moving faster than most other teams, we are still overburdened. Our food supplies are, to say the least, ample. The effort has not been as strenuous as anticipated. As we reach each checkpoint in turn, we dispense food favors to the tired volunteers manning them. They're pleased to have it and we're pleased not to.

• Blencoe Falls is a spectacular water spill over twelve hundred feet high. The most demanding test on the ropes is to ascend this. The cascading water is deafening, the climb thrilling. Grueling work, especially on the last section when the ropes fall vertically from an overhang. Pausing to rest, we dangle in midair, surrounded by water, looking out over a magnificent scene illuminated by the early-morning sun. A sight never to be forgotten. Truly memorable moments!

• On the first mountain bike ride, we know that it is impossible for us to complete it in time to start the rafting section. Because of the danger, the river can only be rafted in daylight—arrive too late and you have to wait till dawn (hence it's called a dark zone). But the clock keeps running and other teams can wipe out a ten- or twelve-hour lead by catching you there. We resist the temptation to push too hard on the bike—the chances of making the cutoff are too slim and the attendant risks too great. But we maintain a brisk pace with the minimum of interruptions. Arriving in the middle of the night, we are able to get a solid four-hour, comfortable sleep—few other teams will have this luxury. Another good tactical decision.

• The Tully River is a blast! None of us has ever rafted so technical a river before. Every moment in the raft is spent working—turning hard, shifting weight, moving off rocks. This is probably the best true test of teamwork in the race—unspoken efficiency is the key to moving through the rapids with the minimum of fuss. Not only do we have a blast—we beat the time standard set by a raft full of guides the day before the race started. Tons of fun. And the fun is doubled because no other team has caught us in spite of our being held at the dark zone for six hours.

• "Stretch" is an Aussie character—a cross between an American cowboy and a denizen of the Outback. He's surrendered his horses to the race for our use on the ride through the rain forest. As we're the first team through, he decides to accompany us. In the moonlight, he sings, tells tall tales, and regales us with facts about the rain forest. His horses are magnificent—trained on multiday treks through the Outback, this is a "walk in the forest" for them. What a memorable day! Just one magnificent experience after another.

• The second mountain bike ride has river crossing after river crossing. In the dark, the depths are unknown (waist- to chest deep), the footing is tricky, and we begin to grumble. We're tired and each of us, in turn, zones out for a while. But the challenge of the riding requires concentration. Long stretches in rain forest are barely ridable—pushing bikes up and down steep, muddy slopes exacerbates our edginess.

Then Keith forces a stop—a furious pain in his leg and swelling in his glands has us very concerned. We search desperately over his muddied legs for evidence of a snakebite but can find none. Keith never complains, so the pain must be vicious. We move on very slowly, observing him careful-ly. We should have realized that he had been whipped by the stinging tree. Our washing and wiping his legs probably extended the duration of his suffering. On the second occurrence, we are ready and use duct tape to rip away the invisible stinging needles. Lesson learned #1.

• Ascending and descending Bartle Frere, we still hold back on our pace. Though we know teams are chasing us hard, we don't react. We know that we move well on steep terrain—it plays to our strength. We're still moving with the same speed as we did at the beginning of race. Few other teams are as well rested as we are. It would be easy to sustain an injury on the tricky descent. We move quickly but unhurriedly. Another good tactical decision.

• More saltwater crocodiles force the rerouting of the next section. To the horror of every racer, we are now on roads—back roads, but roads nonetheless. And it is a long stretch of road. Faced with this unpleasant-ness, we do the only thing possible—*we pick up the pace*. Every team behind us detests this section as much as we do—we want to make the sit-uation worse for them. Knowing that we are running will increase the pressure on everyone chasing us. Strategic decision #2 and it works. We gain hours on every other team here.

• After a two-hour paddle with a strong following wind, we arrive at the first checkpoint of the kayak section. Stepping onto the beach, we dis-cover we do not have our passport. This tiny, unnecessary document is a relic of the Raid Gauloises—proof that we have been to each checkpoint. Evidently we left it at the kayak launch and we now have to wait until the race organizers can bring it to us. A minimum of three hours—this could cost us the race.

We look at one another and, to a person, relax. We know that we have performed excellently; we have harnessed our skills well and have over-come both the course and the other teams. If we are to be denied victory because of a technicality—so be it. *The rewards are within and we already have them.* We go to sleep while the organizers sort out the details. Best moment of the race.

• Later, the paddle turns nasty. The wind is strong and the seas grow-ing but that is okay. It is only when a squall blows through that we become concerned. We are a long way offshore, the rudders on both kayaks are only partially working, and we are tired. As the stars and then the main-land disappear behind the oncoming cloud, we raft up for safety. No telling how long this will last or how severe it will be. It isn't much fun. We are cold, wet, and miserable.

• Next morning, walking up the beach, we're pleased to have finished. Andrea is overwhelmed as her young son Charlie comes waddling out to see his mom. Another moment to savor.

We know we've made very few bad decisions and plenty of good ones. This is a prerequisite to doing well in adventure racing. Countless times during the event, we had to agree on issues major and minor. And as a team, we were excellent at it.

This is necessary but not sufficient. To be successful you also need the constant striving to keep four strong athletes operating as a unit. And the will to win has to be carefully harmonized with the many pleasures to be had from such an adventure. Finally, every adventure race involves its share of luck, good and bad.

These are the factors that allowed Team Eco-Internet to be first across the line at the most competitive international adventure race ever: The 1997 Discovery Channel Eco-Challenge.

Frozen PB&Js and 4:00 A.M. Hallucinations

NAME: ANNETTE BEDNOSKY
AGE: 38
RESIDENCE: JEFFERSON, NC
YEARS ADVENTURE RACING: 4

Photo courtesy of VHTRC.org

I was enjoying an early-evening run along the sidewalks of Boone, North Carolina when I heard my name called from a nearby stoplight. The voice was coming out of a shiny red Chevy pickup truck.

"Hey Annette. It's Mike Hallinan! Ya wanna do an adventure race?"

Of course I want to do an adventure race. They sound hard and cool and fun. The light was changing.

"Yes!" I shouted. *"My name is in the phone book!"* I waved and Mike and his red truck drove away.

Mike called that evening. He and his other teammate (also named Mike) were looking for a woman to join them for the 2003 North Georgia Adventure Race (NGAR). Mike Hallinan and I have been acquainted since our first meeting in the summer of 1992. We were both Outward Bound instructors for several years during the 1990s, and now we frequently bumped into each other at cycling events or outdoor shops in the Boone area.

"Who is this other Mike?" I inquired.

"Mike Wechter."

Wechter?!

Mike Wechter and I had also known each other since the early 1990s. We met as co-instructors during my first summer instructing at the North Carolina Outward Bound School. I'd come to NCOBS in 1992 after having spent the three years after undergraduate school working part-time jobs around the country and living out of my truck. During this "gypsy time" I'd been a tour guide in Yosemite, worked as a National Park Service ranger in Arizona, interned with the Voyageur Outward Bound School, and worked several seasonal residential outdoor education programs around the country. During my travels, trail running, rock climbing, and backcountry navigation became regular parts of life. I came to NCOBS looking forward to combining technical skills with the pillars of the program: self-reliance, physical fitness, craftsmanship and compassion. I was psyched to "change the world" and help young people to grow into courageous, strong, capable leaders.

At the Outward Bound School, we worked with ten boys aged fourteen to sixteen for three weeks—traveling on foot through the Nantahala National Forest backpacking, rock climbing, doing service projects, and paddling on the Chatooga River. Mike introduced me to new worlds as we traveled through the night, bushwhacking while sometimes dragging our packs through thick rhododendron at 3:00 A.M. I remember rain and wind, mosquitoes, and thunderstorms, and the windy day we spent together with our crew at a South Carolina climbing site while our students huddled miserably under a rock overhang and dreamed of transporting themselves to the comfort of home and the familiarity of Cap'n Crunch and Snapple.

This instructor role was new for me and I found it difficult to balance providing challenging opportunities that would help students grow and realize their potential, and providing nurturing support to these young people. During that course, I tortured Mike with my ignorance, idealism, and sensitivity. One of my greatest early lessons at Outward Bound was the first glimpse of learning what course director Skip Sickler reminded his instructors, "Compassion is important, but most people aren't as fragile as you think they are." I found this to be true as our ten students were challenged, learned, and unfolded in the North Carolina backcountry. This tough-minded compassion would later not only prove useful in my careers as adventure educator and school counselor but help set the tone for high-performance expectations of myself and teammates in ultrarunning and adventure racing.

Over the next few months, Mike, Mike, and I stayed in telephone touch discussing race details and gear and teasing each other with hard-core training stories. I never knew what to believe on the answering machine. For example, I arrived home one Sunday afternoon fairly wiped out after a challenging icy overnight backpacking trip in Pisgah National Forest to hear this on the answering machine:

"Hey Annette, it's Wechter. It's 8:45 A.M. Mike and I just finished a four-teen-mile run now we're getting ready for a sixty-mile mountain bike ride. Call us when you wake up."

Grrr . . . although I hadn't planned on working out anymore that day I wound up on an eight-mile run that evening, only to learn the next day that Wechter was just kidding about his multisport training on the answer-ing machine. It seems that the fear of being left behind is one of the things that motivates me to train harder!

On Friday afternoon January 17, 2003, I met Mike and Mike at the Woody Gap School in Suches, Georgia, for the gear check and race brief-ing in preparation for the 2003 NGAR. The three of us were Team En Fuego. It was a giddy reunion filled with reminiscing and much nervous anticipation of the weekend to come. The race was to be comprised of sixty miles of mountain biking, twenty-five miles of hiking and running and twenty miles of lake paddling to be done in thirty hours. The next morn-ing at 5:00 A.M. we would be given the maps and numbers needed to plot the coordinates of the checkpoints and create our route. Our support team—Steve and Mike Hallinan's brother, Jay—would meet us in the red Chevy pickup to assist us in the transition areas.

The temperature was rumored to be five below as we pulled into the schoolyard at 4:30 A.M. on Saturday and, along with seventy-eight other teams, began our last-minute preparations. There were three inches of snow on the ground.

Dumb Mistake

After an hour of plotting UTM coordinates and seventeen checkpoints on the five maps we jumped on our bikes and rolled out of the snowy schoolyard at a dark 6:00 A.M. Headlamps and moonlight reflecting on the snow, and blinking bike taillights from the teams, made things seem like a cosmic carnival. Our bike gears complained and we tried to coax them into working in the chilly morning air.

Like excited baby ducklings we followed the teams ahead of us, turn-ing out of the Woody Gap School and right onto the Forest Service road. After several minutes we noticed many teams turning around and ped-aling back up the icy hill. Alarmed we stopped, pulled out our maps, and decided we made a mistake. We turned around and again, like baby ducklings, followed teams back up the hill. We separated ourselves from the other teams—proud that we had discovered our error—and sped up another road! We pedaled up and up . . . only to stop for a very careful map check to discover that our original choice was correct. In mild frustration we backtracked and returned to the original route. As discouraging as this was, our "dumb mistake" was an essential reminder of what we already knew but had ignored: Carefully study the terrain and the map! Use your compass! Later in the race this practice would serve us well.

The first six checkpoints were over fifty-two miles of mountain biking on Forest Service roads and single-track. We even got to bushwhack with our bikes. At one point Team En Fuego was following tracks and following the crowd and the next minute we decided to be "pioneers" and pick our way down a ridge, bushwhacking to the trail that would bring us to the next checkpoint. This leaving the "safety" of the crowd and veering off from the trail was the first high point of the race for us. We found ourselves laughing as we pushed our bikes through the snow, and passed them around and under tangled rhododendrons and through the mountain laurel.

During the next several hours on the bikes we each took turns taking "diggers" on the icy roads and trails and more than once had to rescue one another from slipping off the trail and down the side of the mountain while still clipped into our pedals. We used our bikes as "walkers" to cross an icy double log bridge, stuffed our water bottles inside our jackets to keep them from freezing, and ate frozen PB&J sandwiches. We met spirited amazing people from all over the East and Midwest. We exchanged stories and experiences as we rode along. At CP5, we were told the paddle portion of the race was canceled due to two inches of ice that had formed on the lake. We would learn the new course once we arrived at the first transition area. We would also learn that it took the lead team five hours longer than expected to complete the first bike portion due to the icy and snowy conditions . . . and that Team En Fuego was in ninth place!

Good Consequences

Our lack of attention to navigation at the beginning cost us time and therefore made us militant about map and compass. At one point we found ourselves standing at a junction, all three of us in disagreement about our location. Wechter tried to persuade us where we were: *"The map doesn't lie!"* he insisted, as he thrust the maps into our faces. I thought he was interpreting the map to say what he wanted it to. Needless to say the map wasn't lying, and Wechter was right and we managed to move up into sixth place with his discovery!

Sometime in the night the wind picked up and the snow started coming down. It stung our eyes as we traveled to yet another checkpoint. Our route went between trails and off trails and Forest Service roads. As we came upon the third bushwhack of the race I began to inwardly and then outwardly whine: *"No. I do not want to travel uphill, up a steep ridge, to meet another trail to find this damn checkpoint!"* While Mike H. had demonstrated good skill and instinct with the navigation, I too had just enough experience to know better than to follow some random path and just hope for the best. Mike H. and I were keen on avoiding another bushwhack only to frustrate Wechter almost to the point of alienation. He continued to logically point out that the ridge was the clearest route to the CP. I came up with lame excuses and we walked on. But then I remembered early in the day our navigation error and Wechter's points about the map doesn't lie. "True," I thought for a second, "the map doesn't lie but I hope we'll get lucky." A few minutes later I realized my laziness and knew that I was acting like a loser rather than a team member and we wound up following Mike's lead. He was right, and after a steep several-hundred-foot elevation climb we successfully reached the ridgeline. In retrospect, the bushwhack wasn't nearly as painful as was the heated debate about the route.

We reached our final TA about an hour before first light, and ten minutes later we were back on our bikes with two more checkpoints to go. I fell on the ice three times within the first mile and at one point I was shaking so badly with fear that I could barely steer my bike. I was so scared to slip on the ice at eighteen miles per hour. I believe this hour before first light was the hardest of it all. I shook with cold and with the fear of falling, and felt dumb: like I was holding our team back. Mike and Mike supported me as I rode between them and slowly regained my wits. Wechter fell asleep for a split second on his bike, I saw a marble dog on the side of the road (which turned out to be a clump of snow), and Mike H. reported seeing a deer (we never determined if it was real or not!). Needless to say, we were all getting tired.

As the sky turned from black to dark blue to morning and our remaining miles ticked down, I felt so relieved and excited to be almost finished. Yet at the same time, I found myself blinking back the tears. They were tears of appreciation for my two teammates and our support crew, tears of pride, and tears knowing the impending letdown that always comes after experiencing something so intense. This was one of the best team experiences I had ever shared. I loved every minute of the physical and mental challenge, the giving and receiving of support, and the silliness and laughter that we shared out there. When we arrived at the finish line we learned that we'd placed third overall and second in the elite division with a time of about twenty-eight hours! We also learned many teams had withdrawn due to hypothermia or cold distress. At times the weather and course were brutal, but not as brutal I think as having to make the decision to stay or drop out. Many teams put months and months into training together. Combine this with the hundreds or even thousands of dollars spent on gear, time off and travel to the event, and the investments of time and money add up.

The conditions in north Georgia that winter were far icier and colder than any team or even the race directors anticipated. Many teams were very skilled in the disciplines yet had little practice with the weather we encountered. I couldn't help but wonder, *"Why did teams drop? Exhaustion, fear, lack of preparation, injury, because it wasn't fun anymore? What would it be like to become injured and have Mike and Mike go on without me? What if one of them became injured and couldn't or didn't want to continue? How would each of us fare if we needed to make the same decision to stay or leave?"* I shuddered and wondered if I could find the courage to do the right thing. Little did I know, we were only a year away from finding out.

The Next Year

A year later Team En Fuego was back for the NGAR 2004! We'd each had a busy year and although we'd not gotten together to train, we raced together in a couple of shorter events under a few different team names. Although these races didn't go badly, we didn't perform as well as we had during NGAR 2003 and decided to return to our original team name.

This year there was no snow, and the temperatures stayed above freezing. For most of Saturday and throughout the night the weather behaved just as one would expect in the Southern Appalachian Mountains: rainy, foggy, and windy, making for an even more interesting race. Race components included paddling on Lake Blue Ridge and mountain biking on single-track, fire roads, and some pavement. A long trek and a second mountain bike section completed the course. Like last year, this was a true adventure race. Teams had to make navigation and route decisions throughout the course of the day and long night. Pre-race activities were peppered with much anticipation and nervousness. Because of last year's extreme conditions many teams returned this year determined to complete the race. We were hoping to do as well as last year and qualify for nationals.

At the 6:00 A.M. race start, we began slowly. Starting slowly was a pattern we'd developed during the past few races. Although this was our fourth race together since NGAR last year, we hadn't really trained together. So we needed a little time to get "in sync" with each other—especially during the excitement of plotting UTM's and choosing routes.

Checkpoint 1 marked the transition from the mile-long portage to paddling. We reached CP1 in forty-second place out of seventy-five teams. After the rather straightforward boating section we moved up about ten places and were excited to change from our wet gear and get moving on our mountain bikes. After an hour or so of riding, the rain began to fall, as did the temperature. The bike leg ended with us riding the last forty-five minutes in the dark down a fast stretch of pavement to TA2. At the TA our support team, Katie Langley and Jay Hallinan, quickly refilled water and Gatorade bottles while we chugged hot cocoa and hurriedly changed our clothes. We left TA2 after fifteen minutes. We were in twentieth place.

We ran, hiked, and bushwhacked our way over many miles of the Benton MacKaye Trail. We were in high spirits as we approached CP15 around midnight and found out we'd moved to tenth place! After several more hours of bushwhacking and walking in the fog, and falling asleep on our feet, we moved up to seventh place at CP18! An hour or so after leaving CP18, the sky lightened and it became day. The race continued on, as did Team En Fuego . . . for the time being.

We came into the last TA after twenty-eight and a half hours on the course (about 10:30 A.M.). I had noticed Mike H. was slowing down over the last few hours, and he seemed to be hurting. I could feel the team's enthusiasm and competitive spirit waning. I didn't say anything, and tried to be patient with our situation, silently hoping it would pass. I figured we would get to the TA and would all be energized by warm clothes, and food and drink and be ready to jump on our bikes! I was wrong. Call me self-centered, tunnel-visioned, or "in denial," but I wasn't ready for what happened next. Both Mike and Mike announced to me that they had decided not to continue. Mike H. had bonked badly, while Mike W. was submerged in confusion over the fairness of continuing and leaving our friend behind. We'd never discussed this as a possibility and we were totally unprepared to deal with the reality of the situation.

I was overcome with disappointment and felt utterly powerless. I had been determined to finish even if it meant coming in as unofficial. Had it been permitted, I might have even gone on alone. There was nothing I could do, however, to fix the situation. So with tears in my eyes, I turned our passport in to the TA staff and told them we were done.

My world felt crushed. My first DNF: Did not finish. The dreaded DNF, which I couldn't at all imagine during NGAR 2003, was now staring me straight in the face. I asked myself, *"What role did I play in this? Why didn't I see it coming? Why didn't I say anything? Why didn't I do something to help? Is this the end of our team? Will Mike and Mike still be my friends? Will we ever race together again? Was I too harsh and selfish and not compassionate enough during the first part of the event?"*

Days after the race I was still self-absorbed in my confusion. I wanted to know what happened, how to prevent it from ever happening again, and how to come to terms with failure. Searching for some perspective on DNF'ing, I posted a message on the NGAR message board. What follows is just some of what was shared with me.

One veteran adventure racer, Neal Radford, who was at NGAR and competed in Eco-Challenge Fiji, responded:

"I've come to think of adventure racing as a way to temper the soul through a trial of fire. If we always finished a race and were never left with anything to deal with afterward how would we ever grow as racers, teammates, or even people?"

Guy Davis, an accomplished race photographer shared these thoughts with me:

"At the 2003 Subaru Primal Quest I noticed an interesting similarity in the interviews of all the top AR teams. They all acknowledged the importance of the team dynamic (and a good navigator). A common statement by the successful teams was that each team member must be able to recognize (or acknowledge) when they need help and accept assistance before it becomes a show-stopper.

"This race has clearly given your team the chance to examine your team dynamic and your racing expectations and make some adjustments or some hard choices. Ultimately, I think you'll end up being a better teammate and racer based on this learning experience."

I agree very much with their statements. I am reminded that one definition of *adventure* is "an opportunity with an unknown outcome." This race outcome was certainly unknown and unexpected! NGAR 2004 was over by 2:00 P.M. Sunday, but for me, En Fuego, and the other forty-nine teams who DNF'ed or finished unofficially it will be alive as a source of reflective material for a good long time. There is much to be learned from this experience.

Days after we DNF'ed I said I didn't want to adventure race again. I didn't want to deal with the disappointment and frustration again. Yet a week later, with a little time, perspective, and debriefing, my position had shifted. I am not afraid to jump back into the fire. I guess the words of Skip Sickler from that first summer at Outward Bound remain true for me: "Compassion is important, but most people aren't as fragile as you think they are."

Through my racing experiences and reflecting on those experiences I continue to learn that I can deal with and learn from situations and things that I initially feel will break me. Mike, Mike, and I are still friends. We are working through this experience and are deciding whether we will stay intact as a team or make some changes. In our debriefing of the event, Mike, Mike, and I have recognized what is now obvious:

We need to train together. Good relationships need to be nurtured with quality time and energy.

We need to be aware of each other's goals—individual and team.

We must anticipate problems and solutions before they happen.

We must carry more food and water.

We need to bring trekking poles and use them.

We must have more fun.

We need to be willing to ask for and accept help.

This way of looking at the world is applicable to all of life outside of adventure racing. Human beings are not that fragile. We can deal with disappointments, mistakes, and failures. It is our responsibility to learn and grow from them. After all, isn't that part of what adventure racing is:

an intense form of life experienced while playing in the woods? I don't know if Team En Fuego will continue in its original form or not. I do know that I have learned much from my teammates and have an obligation and the willingness to use our experience to improve future races and relationships of all kinds. Racing with Team En Fuego during NGAR 2003 and 2004 has been a celebration of life, fitness, and learning! Who says being an adult is boring?

Racing Blind . . .

Photo courtesy of Michelle Craig

L to R: Jeff Evans, Rob Harsh,
Cammy Ronchetto, Erik Weihenmayer

NAME: ROB HARSH
AGE: 34
RESIDENCE: CHICAGO, IL
YEARS ADVENTURE RACING: 5

It was just after midnight on Day 3 of the Arctic Team Challenge and we had been climbing for several hours toward a ridge on a steep section of the Mittivakkat Glacier. I was bringing up the rear, diligently minding the rope in case one of us broke through the snow into a hidden crevasse. Up to this point, though, the glacier had been pretty benign; we'd only punched through the snow in a few shallow spots where meltwater was running just below the surface. Still, we were all being a bit more mindful due to our tired state and the fact we were breaking our own trail up the glacier. After two thousand feet of climbing we finally crested the ridge and a huge crescent-shaped moon came into view. The moon completely dominated the eastern sky and was framed below by a huge plain of snow leading off toward several jagged peaks in the distance. Behind us to the west, the glow of the sun was making its way across the horizon and we could see the Greenland icecap rising from the sea across an iceberg-filled fjord. We stopped for a short rest and a moment to take in the view. It was the most incredible panorama I had ever seen, and as we looked out over the glacier, I was overcome by the fact that Erik couldn't see it. We stood there for a moment and described the sight to him, just as we had done at various other points along the course. Erik pondered our description, sensing the vastness of the glacier and the height of the surrounding peaks. I sensed that he would build these descriptions into mental images in his head, but I think in some ways it was his other senses that made the picture more accurate.

"How much farther?" Erik asked, turning his attention quickly back to the task at hand. "It's about sixteen more kilometers," I replied. "Can we still make it to the finish in time?" he asked. I knew it would be tight and the exhaustion on his face was starting to become evident. But if there was one thing I had learned about Erik over the past few days, it was that he could suffer more than just about anybody, and I knew it would take a lot for him to admit defeat. "Of course we can make it, no problem, we just need to keep moving," I replied, trying to stay positive. And with that, we quickly turned our attention from the view, gulped down some water and what little food we had left, and continued up the glacier.

Earlier that week we had arrived in Greenland ready to begin the 250-kilometer adventure race, and it was no secret that our team was very different from the rest. My teammate Erik Weihenmayer, who was well known for becoming the first blind person to reach the summit of Mount Everest, was now taking on the challenge of competing in and finishing an expedition-length adventure race. For Erik, adventure racing would be very similar to his experiences in climbing, although it would also provide many new challenges. The most obvious of which would be the fact that this was a race and there were time limits. Erik would now have to overcome many of the same obstacles he faced in climbing, plus countless new ones, all while racing against a clock. This would not be easy, and in order to finish, he would need a team that would be cohesive, flexible, and almost unrealistically optimistic.

That team had come together six months earlier after my longtime teammate Cammy Ronchetto had heard Erik speak in her hometown of Columbia, Missouri, and suggested we ask him if he was interested in joining us for a race. Cammy and I were both experienced racers, having competed in many of the big expedition races around the world, and we believed that Erik could apply the same success he had in climbing to adventure racing. Erik became excited by the idea and agreed to join us, bringing along with him his friend and Everest teammate Jeff Evans. Jeff was a skilled climber and mountain biker whose experience guiding Erik the past ten years made him the perfect choice as our fourth team member.

We now had the makings of a team that just might be able to pull it off, and aptly named ourselves Team No Boundaries. But the odds were still against us. We had chosen as our ultimate goal the 2003 Subaru Primal Quest, which was well known as one of the toughest expedition races in the world. Cammy and I had competed in this race before and knew the chances of finishing the ten-day, 450-mile race were less than 50 percent We were not your typical team, however, and when you consider the fact that this would be Jeff's and Erik's first adventure race and neither Cammy nor I had any experience guiding a blind person, our chances of finishing seemed even less likely.

We decided that if we were to have any chance of success, we would need to do a lot of training and compete in at least one practice race prior to Primal Quest. We began to train once a month in Colorado, getting together for long weekends, trying to simulate what it was like to compete in an adventure race. We took trips to Moab, the Collegiate Peaks, and Rocky Mountain National Park, biking, climbing, and paddling together as much as possible. In a few short months we had taught Jeff and Erik everything we knew about adventure racing, and they in turn taught us everything they knew about guiding a blind person. All we needed now was to experience a race firsthand and put our training into action.

The five-day Arctic Team Challenge seemed like the perfect practice race for our team. The fact that it was staged meant we would get the feel of an expedition race, but would also have the opportunity to sleep at night. The other thing that made it so appealing was the fact that it was comparatively short at only 155 miles, and that most of the race involved climbing and mountaineering, which would hopefully make Jeff and Erik's transition to adventure racing that much easier. Our goal for the race would be to simply finish and gain as much experience as we could along the way.

We left for Greenland just two months prior to Primal Quest and by the time we landed in Iceland the adventure was well under way. After sampling some of the local culture in Reykjavík, we boarded a small prop plane and flew toward Greenland, landing on a small dirt airstrip situated just below the Arctic Circle on the remote island of Kulusuk. Hoping all our gear was not far behind, we then boarded small speedboats captained by local fishermen and navigated our way fifteen-kilometers through the pack ice to the settlement of Tasilaq on Ammasalik Island. As we sped along we caught glimpses of whales, seals, and icebergs, describing everything to Erik as we saw it. Occasionally we would hear small pieces of ice hitting the bottom of the boat and held on tightly as we swerved back and forth avoiding the larger chunks of ice. After safely navigating through the pack ice we entered a magnificent harbor where we could see much larg-

er icebergs drifting along the shore and rows of small, multicolored houses perched on the rocky hillsides of the town above. It was late in the
evening and we could feel the warmth of the sun, which was still high in
the sky. This time of year the days were filled with twenty-two hours of
sunlight, and we were excited about the fact we weren't going to need our
headlamps during the race. Our joy soon faded, however, as we could now
see the ruggedness of the mountains that dominated the island.

We would begin the race a few days later with a challenging first stage
consisting of a five-lap, thirty-five-kilometer mountain bike, which would
start out on the steep narrow roads of Tasilaq and then wind its way up
into the trackless rocky foothills. There, the tundra-like terrain would be
incredibly difficult, but as it climbed in elevation, teams would be rewarded with views of stunning mountains and pristine lakes. The route then
led past an icy waterfall down technical single-track, and back into town.
After another steep climb on pavement, teams would then scream back
downhill through town and begin another lap.

As the cannon went off at the start, Erik was excited to be finally putting
his tandem mountain bike to the test. We started out well, towing each
other up the steep roads that led into the countryside. There the route
became quite technical, with lots of loose rock, and I was amazed how well
Jeff and Erik rode together, rarely having to get off and push. The tandem
was a much heavier bike and was very hard to maneuver, as the rear wheel
almost had a mind of its own and reacted slowly to the steering. By the third
lap, though, we weren't too far behind the other teams, but to no one's surprise, we were dead last. We had been hoping to at least keep pace with the
Ice Girls, an all-female team from Iceland who were back for their second
attempt at finishing the race, and we rode hard to try and catch them. By
the start of the fourth lap the lead teams had caught up with us, each
encouraging us to keep going as they passed—although I think they were
quite skeptical about our chances of even making it through the first day.
We finally finished the five-lap circuit one and a half hours behind the leaders and were now ready to transition to a twenty-five-kilometer trek, where
we would climb three peaks and gain nearly nine thousand feet in elevation before crossing the finish at the end of Stage 1.

We dropped our bikes and took off through town into the mountains.
We moved quickly, energized by the fact we were now nearly tied with the
Ice Girls. But as we left the flat ground of the town behind, the terrain

became incredibly rugged, dominated mainly by eroded rock, boulder fields, and scree. This was the worst possible kind of terrain for Erik and we now knew that we were in for a real challenge as we began the slow process of guiding him across the difficult rock. As we made our way, Erik would need to concentrate on every step, using a pair of extra-long trekking poles to feel for changes in the uneven ground ahead of him, then focusing on finding the best possible spot to place his feet. We would help keep him on track by describing the route and jingling a bell to keep him tuned in to which direction we were heading. As the travel became more difficult one of us would scout out the route ahead and choose the way that offered the least complicated terrain. This often ended up not being the shortest route distance-wise, but allowed us to move much faster. It was all very exhausting, and Jeff ended up taking on the brunt of the guiding, as he was much more experienced with Erik on this kind of terrain. Still, as hard as it was for us, it didn't even compare to the amount of effort it took for Erik.

As we neared the summit ridge of the first peak we found ourselves repeating this same process over and over with the route getting more and more difficult until we were finally cliffed out by a steep gulley that bisected the ridge. After a few grumblings from Jeff about my route choice, we ascended directly to the ridge and found the navigation easier. It was clear we were now starting to feel the pressure and that our team dynamics were going to be put to the test before this race was over. After another hour we made the summit and were afforded some spectacular views of the island's southern coast. We took a few moments to capture the moment and then descended the ridge toward the valley.

On the way down we encountered our first bit of snow and were able to glissade a good distance toward the valley below. For the first time we were able to nearly match the speed of some of the other teams, as Erik could move incredibly fast and he was definitely more at home on the snow than on any other kind of terrain. Once off the snow we continued to slowly descend more difficult rocky terrain until we reached a brilliant blue lake in the valley just below our second peak. Here we were faced with a route choice.

One route was obvious, following a long scree slope up to the ridge and then across to the checkpoint at the summit. The other climbed the southeast slope and then steeply around to the north, up to the ridge on a route hidden from our view. The map was really no help. With a scale of

1:100,000, there was very little detail, but it was clear that Jeff was lobbying hard for the steeper route. I greatly respected Jeff's opinion as he was very experienced in the mountains and knew Erik's limitations well. But as an experienced navigator I was confident in my decision, as the steeper route was full of question marks. We argued the point for several minutes and I hated disagreeing with him, as I knew it would put more of a strain on the team, but in the end we agreed to disagree, and decided on the obvious route.

We slowly started ascending and after a hard hour of crawling up the dirty steep scree slope, we gained the summit ridge. Off to the west we had our first glimpse of the mainland and could see the Greenland icecap rising from the sea. We turned and followed the ridge to the east, where we were greeted by some locals manning the checkpoint at the summit. We were informed that we were now well behind the rest of the teams and needed to get moving if we wanted to have any chance of finishing the stage.

We followed the ridge back down a ways and decided to try and make up some time by quickly descending to the snowfield below via a steep rock gulley. This was definitely the most technical terrain we had encountered thus far, but Jeff was confident Erik could handle it, and in some ways I was more worried about Cammy. It seemed silly as we had been in all kinds of races together before and I knew she was very capable of handling herself. Still, it didn't stop me from looking back occasionally to make sure she was all right. We proceeded cautiously, snaking our way down the gulley in a tight group. But as we made our way we found ourselves down-climbing sections of steep vertical rock and having to dodge small boulders as we became more spread apart. Eventually we were sucked in up to our shins by a river of rock sliding down the gulley toward the snowfield below. Surprisingly Erik seemed to take it all in stride and was much more comfortable on this kind of terrain than I expected. Once down on the snowfield we had another wonderful glissade down to the valley. Erik was definitely back in his element on the snow, and Jeff was able to take a good break, as Cammy and I were starting to become more comfortable with the guiding on all but the most technical sections.

After ten hours on the move we had made our way to the valley at the base of the third peak and were nearly home free except for one obstacle. We needed to cross a swift stream, which ran down the valley connecting two alpine lakes. We easily found the spot where most of the teams before us had crossed and a few photographers were on hand waiting to capture the moment. The stream looked fairly straightforward, but the water was nearly freezing and the current appeared quite strong in the middle. We hadn't practiced this with Erik before, but decided to go for it as the alternative was walking all the way down the valley and around the lake. We started to make our way across the fifty-foot stream, linking arms and forming a train, and we were nearly halfway when we realized we had made a mistake. Normally you would put the smallest person on the team somewhere in the middle to shield them from the force of the water. But as we had been so focused on Erik, we ended up putting Cammy at the back. Since Erik had to hold his trekking poles for extra balance, he had mistakenly assumed she would be able to lock her arm around his. Her grip quickly slipped, though, and she was eventually left stranded alone in the icy water with the full force of the current up to her waist. I broke free from Jeff and Erik, who were nearly on the other side, and made my way back out to where she was standing, frozen in the middle of the stream. As I fought the force of the current, Cammy lunged out to grab my hands, going for a brief swim before I was able to connect and pull her into shallower water. "You all right? I asked. "I'm fre-freezing!" she replied, her teeth starting to chatter. "I'm sorry, we messed that up pretty good. At least they managed to get it all on film," I said, trying to get a smile out of her. "Wonderful, I can't wait to see that again!" she replied, grinning and quickly trying to get into some dry clothes. It was a good lesson, however, and we now understood that we could no longer focus solely on Erik, and that each of us was vulnerable to the difficulties of the race.

From here we quickly made our way to the base of the third peak and started the climb to the summit. It seemed like a pretty straightforward route, but by the time we reached the top I sensed Erik was pretty trashed, although he certainly didn't let it show. Erik was cracking jokes left and right and I think we were all a little numb after an extremely difficult day in the mountains. There was no time to rest, however—we still had four more days of racing and we needed to make our way to the finish so we could at least grab a few hours of sleep before starting the next stage. I set a deadline of midnight, hoping to remind everyone that even though we weren't competing with the other teams, this was still a race and we needed to feel like we were racing. I think this seemed a little strange to Jeff and

Erik being their first adventure race, but they went along and by the time we made it back to town we were running toward the finish.

We crossed the finish line just minutes before midnight with a small crowd cheering us on as the sun dipped just below the horizon. The lead teams had finished almost seven hours earlier and would have the benefit of a full night's rest before starting again the next morning. We, on the other hand, had taken nearly fifteen hours to complete the stage, and by the time we grabbed some food and got our gear together for the next day, we would only manage about four hours of sleep. "Hey, I thought this was supposed to be a stage race," Erik said, with a big smile on his face. "Yeah, well, I guess we're going to get a little more practice with sleep deprivation than we thought," I replied, happy to see he was still in good spirits and not wanting to quit adventure racing just yet.

The next morning we received our next set of checkpoints and made our way to the start. Stage 2 would be another tough day, starting out with a thirty-kilometer mountain bike relay, followed by a paddle across the harbor and a thousand-meter ascent of one of the highest peaks on the island. As the cannon sounded, Cammy and I started out riding hard through town and then down a beautiful double-track road. We followed part of the course we had trekked the previous day and ended near a dam below a huge alpine lake. We then rode back down the same road, passing teams riding up from the other direction. Back at the finish Jeff and Erik were elated by the prospect that we weren't in last place. They took off on the tandem riding the same fifteen-kilometer route, while Cammy and I pumped up the inflatable four-person canoe and got everything ready to start the paddle. Not long after, Jeff and Erik arrived at the finish, and were just minutes ahead of the Ice Girls. We carried the boat down to the water's edge and pushed off thirty minutes behind the leaders.

We paddled hard trying to keep up, passing small icebergs and chunks of broken ice as we made our way across the harbor. Erik sat in the front of the boat and we let him set the pace. He was a natural paddler and I think he really enjoyed the feeling of being the guy everyone followed for a change. I sat in the back, occasionally calling out commands to switch sides and steering us around the sharp pieces of ice. The water was numbingly cold and a tear in the boat at this point would definitely not be a good thing. As we rounded the peninsula on the other side of the harbor, the mist cleared and the summit of Polheims Fjeld came into view. Polheims was a striking mountain that was dominated by an exposed ridge that rose two thousand feet to its summit and resembled a smaller, eroded version of the Matterhorn. After reaching the shore we would trek five kilometers across more rocky terrain to the base of a snowfield and then climb to a checkpoint at the start of the ridge. Here teams would be given the choice to climb to the summit untimed or climb back down to the boats without penalty. This was done mainly to ensure teams wouldn't be racing each other up the dangerous terrain on the ridge.

We arrived on the shore well in sight of some of the other teams and hurried to make our way to the base of Polheims. We again had some minor disagreement about the route, but by this time I had come to the conclusion that it really didn't matter which route we chose. If we went right or left we would still be in Greenland, and either way we would have to deal with the same difficult terrain. We reluctantly opted to go east and climbed up to a steep rocky slope to a col leading to the next valley. Erik wasn't too excited about being back on the difficult terrain, but he was looking forward to a fun climb on the ridge. Upon reaching the col, we traversed around the side of a smaller peak and slowly made our way down the valley. By this time we were again well behind the other teams and were starting to feel the sleep deprivation setting in. We discussed the possibility of skipping the final climb up the ridge in the interest of getting some sleep, but Erik was determined not to miss this part of the course.

After five hours on the move, we reached the ridge and set our sights on the summit. The race director was thrilled we had decided to go for it and cheered us on as we made our way toward a thirty-foot Chinese ladder that was bolted to an exposed section of vertical rock. The climb up was very airy, with thousand-foot drops off either side, and I could feel my chest pounding as we each ascended the ladder and then back onto the ridge. From here we continued to make our way toward the summit, carefully describing the route to Erik as we climbed the difficult fifth-class rock. Occasionally Jeff would throw out terms like "hospital fall right" and "pissed-off fall left" to describe the degree of danger. But it was the term "death fall," however, that really commanded the most attention, and meant that Erik was just a few feet from stepping off the two-thousand-foot ridge. We used this term more than a few times as we neared the summit, and each time the descriptions became more and more outlandish. And at one point Jeff even went so far as to say, "Step left and you'll never see your wife and daughter again." This of course really got Erik's attention, and as he negotiated the knife-edge, I was continually amazed by his climbing ability.

After three hours of climbing we safely reached the summit and Erik was elated to be standing on top. As we described the view, which literally looked out over the entire island, I realized the monumental effort it must have taken for him to climb Everest and I could now understand why he loved climbing so much. I only hoped that finishing an adventure race would give him that same sense of joy and accomplishment. After spending some time enjoying the summit, we turned back down the ridge and descended to the snowfield below. By the time we reached the boats and made our way across the harbor to the stage finish line, we had been going for fourteen hours, and we were again faced with the prospect of getting only a few hours of sleep.

The next morning when we received our maps for the upcoming stage, it was apparent that the race wasn't going to get any easier. Stage 3 would consist of one long forty-kilometer trek, which included a tough section of coasteering and a crossing of the Mittivakkat Glacier, before finally finishing on a beach next to the Sermilk Fjord. There teams would camp the night and start out the next day on the final 110-kilometer stage, paddling among the huge icebergs in the fjord, then trekking inland across two glaciers and more mountainous terrain, before taking on the final paddle to the finish line back in Tasilaq.

As the cannon sounded for the third time we made our way through town and into the mountains. Almost immediately we fell back into our slow groove, and the lead teams again disappeared from sight. Accepting our familiar place at the back of the pack, we continued our way up the valley, occasionally being swarmed by hordes of mosquitoes, until we finally climbed up and over a pass that led down to the island's southern shore. After the steep descent we reached CP2 and caught our first glimpse of the rugged coastline leading off to the west.

Earlier that morning the race director had described this section as the most difficult part of the course, and as we started our traverse we soon discovered that the entire coastline was essentially a maze of giant boulder fields, steep cliffs, and loose talus slopes. In many places the terrain was nearly impossible, and our pace soon slowed to a crawl as we fell farther behind the rest of the teams. This was definitely some of the worst terrain

I had ever seen in an adventure race, and at one point Erik even compared it to his experience in the Khumbu Icefall, a treacherous maze of ice boulders at the base of Mount Everest. After five excruciating hours, though, we finally managed to navigate our way the mere four kilometers down the coast, to the base of a steep snowfield.

We were now more than three hours behind the rest of the teams and feeling pretty trashed, but we knew we needed to keep moving if we were going to have any chance of finishing before the start of the next stage. We took a short rest and then ascended the snowfield to a pass where we were greeted with our first views of the Sermilk Fjord and a long glissade down the valley. After another few hours of trekking through some difficult, but wonderfully remote terrain, we reached the sandy shore then cruised along the coast a short ways to CP3. There we would begin our ascent to the Mittivakkat glacier, visiting three more checkpoints before descending to the stage finish line next to the fjord.

We made our way to the north and slowly climbed up a narrow valley along a river until we reached a spot about a kilometer from the glacier. By this point it had taken us nearly twelve hours to cover the first twenty kilometers and we knew we now needed to make up some time in order to finish. After some disagreement about the route, we eventually decided to take a shortcut, which would hopefully cut out a few kilometers of difficult rocky terrain. It seemed like a logical choice given the fact that we could move much faster on the snow, but it wasn't without some risk, as we weren't sure if we would be able to find a safe place to get onto the glacier.

As we began to climb north across the moraines and washes, things weren't looking too promising, and I started to think that maybe we had made a big mistake. The glacier had retreated significantly from its main lateral moraine, and there was now a huge ice cliff separating us from the gentle slope on top. We continued to work our way down, however, searching for a place that spanned the gap, until finally we made it to a point where we could see a small snow bridge leading to the foot of the glacier. We made our way down to the narrow bridge, and all breathed a huge sigh of relief as we stepped onto the hard ice.

We were happy to finally be on the snow where Erik didn't have to think so much about every step and he could finally take a break from the painful rocky terrain. We now hoped to make up some time, as we quickly slapped on our crampons, roped up, and started ascending. Erik was definitely back in his element, and after safely navigating around several small crevasses, we made our way to the east and began to climb a steep slope that rose two thousand feet toward the top of a ridge. As we made our way, the sun began to set behind us and we were able catch a glimpse of the Ice Girls slowly making their way down the other side of the glacier toward the finish. They were just five hours ahead of us, and it appeared at this rate our shortcut just might pay off. We pushed hard the rest of the way up the ridge and after a few hours and some incredible moonlit views looking back down the glacier, we made it to CP4. By this point our pace had slowed, but after convincing the checkpoint officials we could still make it in time, we were allowed to continue.

From here we had seven hours to cover the final fifteen kilometers to the finish and we slowly made our way to the north where we would find the last two checkpoints atop a pair of steep rocky peaks rising from the middle of the glacier. Over the course of the next few hours we crossed the heart of the glacier and watched as the sun made its way back across the horizon. By 3:00 A.M. the sun began to rise and as we neared the base of the first peak it suddenly became strangely silent. Erik was struggling to stay awake and after eighteen hours on the move it was apparent the long trek had taken its toll. We still had several hours to cover the final distance to the finish, but we were now concerned that if Erik pushed himself any farther we would have a difficult time making it safely off the glacier. His feet and calves were trashed after the past three days of trekking and he now faced thirteen hundred feet of climbing on more painful rocky terrain. Adding to this was the fact that we literally had no food left and just a bladder of water between us.

After three days and 140 kilometers of trekking, biking, and paddling, the choice was clear. Primal Quest was now just six weeks away, and rather than risk injury, we made the difficult decision to turn around and head back down the glacier, skipping the last two checkpoints. Our race was over and I think initially we were all feeling pretty disappointed. It never feels quite right to quit something after suffering toward a goal together for so long. We had definitely underestimated how difficult this race would be for our team, but as we slowly made our way down toward the base of the glacier, the disappointment began to fade and the realization of all that we had overcome started to emerge.

Four hours later we finally dropped out of a steep canyon at the base of the glacier and slowly walked up the beach toward the finish. It was the culmination of three of the toughest days any of us had ever spent in the mountains. We had many struggles along the way, and still had many more ahead, but we could now rest and reflect on the experience. In the days and weeks to come, we would realize that we had probably overcome more in these three days than all the rest of the teams in the race combined, and that our success couldn't be measured by whether or not we finished the race. For us, coming to Greenland was never about finishing. It was about coming together, bonding as a team, and gaining the experience we would need to finish an expedition race with a blind person. And whether we believed it or not at the time, we had achieved this goal.

The torture of Greenland had laid the perfect foundation, and reminded us that teamwork was more than just four individuals traveling together along the same path. True teamwork is about four people coming together with a common vision and a common goal, communicating with each other, lifting each other up, forgiving mistakes, and sharing the physical and mental demands of the race. We now were linked by this vision and had the experience that was needed for us to succeed. Jeff and Erik understood what an adventure race was all about, and Cammy and I had the confidence and experience to step up and guide Erik through even the most difficult kind of terrain.

Six weeks later we set off from the shores of Lake Tahoe at the start of the 2003 Primal Quest. Over the next 457 miles we would encounter an incredible challenge. The sixty thousand feet of elevation gain would be daunting, and the nonstop nature of the race would push each of us to our limits. With each leg of the race, Erik and Jeff would go farther than they had ever gone before. In all we would mountain bike over 240 miles, trek more than 100 miles, and encounter nearly 85 miles of whitewater and flatwater paddling. Throw in some caving, orienteering, and a climbing section with twelve hundred feet of ascending and seven hundred feet of rappelling, and the challenge for our team seemed mindboggling.

However, after eight days and twenty-one hours of racing, we defied conventional wisdom and stepped onto the beach and across the finish line. Of the eighty teams who began, we were one of only forty-four to make it across the finish line intact. Along the way we had endured a smashed rear cassette, five broken chains, a near race-ending mountain bike crash, a broken paddle on the whitewater section, and a grand total of sixteen hours sleep. It had taken a monumental team effort, but with Erik's will and our strong belief, we managed to push through that blurry line between what the world sees as impossible, and what we knew in our hearts to be fully possible.

A Surprise Finish at the Odyssey One Day

NAME: JEN BOXER
AGE: 28
RESIDENCE: CHARLOTTESVILLE, VA
YEARS ADVENTURE RACING: 3

Photo by Bill McGarrick

I've always had issues with self-esteem, especially when it involves anything where I would be put on the spot. I used to shy away from trying anything new (work, sports, etc.) because I was afraid I wouldn't live up to my, or others', expectations. This came into play before my first twenty-four-hour adventure race when a fear of not finishing almost kept me from even starting. This is the story of that race.

Growing up I was a swimmer. Then when I went to college I really focused on academics and for the first two years I hardly did anything athletic. I started mountain biking my junior year, and started racing mountain bikes the summer after I graduated. That led to some running and I managed to talk a friend of mine into doing a sprint adventure race with me. We had so much fun! I have always enjoyed pushing myself to the limit for long periods of time, so it just seemed natural that I would gravitate toward longer adventure races. The only problem is that at that time, I was having trouble finding anyone willing to do longer races with me, so I settled into sprint races for a while. I decided to volunteer at an Odyssey race, hoping it might help me meet new potential teammates. But then my self-esteem issues crept in, and I was actually so nervous to go by myself that I stopped at a gas station a few miles away from race HQ and almost turned around and drove home. I was afraid to go to the race and be surrounded by a bunch of people I didn't know in a situation I wasn't at all familiar with. But I managed to talk myself into going, and I'm so glad I did.

I ended up working at an assisted checkpoint and was talking to one of the support crew members of Team Lactic Addiction. I told her how I was hoping to find people to race with and she told me that the team she was supporting consisted of three guys who were racing as a two-person team and a soloist, and that they were actually looking for a woman to race with them so they could race together as a team. After the race I introduced myself to those guys and told them I was looking for a team to race with. Two of the guys were preparing for another race that was taking place near where I lived. I offered to let them stay at my place while they were in town, hoping that they might ask me to do a race with them in return. It turned out that one of them was going to be gone for most of the summer on business, and the other one was getting ready to move to Boston. But Jake, the guy moving to Boston, offered to come back and do a race with me—the Odyssey One Day, in July 2002.

I was living in Harrisonburg, Virginia, at the time, so Jake and I stayed at a friend's house in Charlottesville—a little closer to the race start. The race didn't start until seven o'clock the next night. I was nervous in the days leading up to the event, but I slept fairly well that night. I was super-nervous the day of the race, though. I was afraid I wouldn't do well enough, or live up to my or Jake's expectations. Jake had asked me about my goals for the race: Did I want to just complete it, push somewhat hard, or did I want to go as hard as I possibly could no matter what? I told him I wanted to push as hard as I could no matter what. He said he'd make sure that's what I did. So I was nervous that he would be disappointed in my performance. There were tons of reasons that I could justify why I might consider myself a failure at the end of the race. And if I did fail, then Jake might not want to race with me again. Then I'd be back where I started and I probably wouldn't have the confidence to try another race or even to try and meet more people to race with. I was driving myself crazy with thoughts like that.

Jake and I left the house the next day around 9:00 A.M. and stopped to grab breakfast. We arrived at the race HQ at about 11:30 A.M. Gear check began about an hour after that and around 4:00 P.M. we went to the pre-race dinner and briefing. Even as we were checking in and getting ready, I saw that I knew some of the people volunteering at the event and began to worry about what they would think if I failed to do well. In retrospect, Jake and all of the people I knew there are some of the nicest and most nonjudgmental people I've ever met so I have no idea why I felt the need to worry myself sick over this.

The Odyssey One Day adventure race consisted of mountain biking, trail running/trekking, orienteering, whitewater swimming and a ropes section. It covered about ninety miles and included more than fifteen thousand feet of elevation gain. It started off with a five-kilometer run, and then continued on foot for the first trekking portion where there were a couple of orienteering points. After that we were to switch to mountain bikes and about halfway through the bike section we had to stop at a natural swimming hole and locate something at the bottom of the pool. We would then continue on our bikes to the next transition, which would involve some whitewater swimming. After the swimming there was another trekking portion that included some rope work and a zip line. At the end of the zip line we were to get back on our mountain bikes for a long ride all the way back to the finish. There were seventy-two teams racing, a mix of soloists, two-person, and four-person teams, which at the time was the largest field that Odyssey had ever had for one of their adventure races. Then, to start it all off, there was a huge thunderstorm just before the race that dumped lots of rain and really drove up the humidity. The heat index was over a hundred degrees, and with the storm gone, the sun was shining bright. As we were waiting to start, Jake looked over at me and saw a look of fear in my eyes. He just patted me on the back and told me not to worry, that we were going to have fun no matter what. And we were off.

As for the terrain, it was definitely hilly. To put as much elevation gain in the race as they did, it felt like it was straight up and straight down without any flat spots. I'm sure there were some flat sections; I just can't remember them. The first trekking portion started on an old fire road and then we ended up turning off on some single-track trails and then followed the ridgeline on some grassy trails. I started to feel what I thought was a hot spot on the side of my heel, but when I looked into it at the first transition area I discovered that it was actually a big blister. Argh! And the worst thing was, it could have been prevented. I was wearing the same type of shoes that I usually wear trail running, but my old pair had worn out so I bought a new pair and had only done one short run in them before the race. I knew I should not have done this, and I felt bad about it. But what could I do now? We eventually got back on a gravel road and the last portion was downhill on the gravel road until we got to the transition to the bikes. This provided some relief from the blister pain.

We started the first bike leg around 11:30 P.M., and would continue on the bike until around 5:30 A.M. There was a good mix of gravel roads, fire roads, and single-track. There was also a ton of climbing involved. A lot of the single-track was too steep to ride, and there were a lot of fallen trees in the way. Parts of the trail might have been ridable during the day with fresh legs, but at night, after a long running/trekking section, it just wasn't very ridable at all. And if the terrain wasn't enough, the blister on the side of my heel was absolutely killing me! The skin on top of the blister had peeled off so I had this raw blister more than an inch in diameter rubbing on the side of my bike shoe (which aren't the most comfortable things to hike in even with healthy feet) as we hiked our bikes. We had tried to put some moleskin around the blister at the previous CP, but it just didn't stick very well. The pain in my foot forced me to alter my normal walking stride, which was leading to problems elsewhere—most notably in my left knee. About halfway through the bike portion we had to jump into a swimming hole and swim to the bottom to find a mannequin. The water was *really* cold, which caused my knee to stiffen. Shortly after we got back on our bikes, I started feeling a dull pain in my knee. It hurt with every pedal stroke, and hurt even worse when I had to walk with my bike.

This is when things started to get bad. It was around 3:00 A.M. and we were doing a ridiculously steep climb up some double-track through knee-high grass. I was already at a low because of the time of night. According to my bike computer I was hovering between two and three miles an hour and it was hurting me to go that fast. Eventually I faced the fact it would be more energy efficient and just as fast for me to get off and push my bike. It didn't hurt my knee too bad to walk up the hill, but I *really* didn't want to walk anymore in my bike shoes because of my blister. Jake had looked at the map and estimated that it would be about three miles of climbing until we got to the next CP, which would then be followed by a big down-hill. So of course in my head I was expecting to get to the CP in exactly three miles, and not one step farther. Well, three miles came and went on my bike computer, and there was no sign of the CP. I was getting really frustrated because I had convinced myself that I wouldn't have to do this for more than three miles. Jake kept looking ahead, pointing out what he thought were chem lights marking the CP ahead, but of course it never was. The CP was probably only about a half mile farther than we had expected, which really isn't very far. At the time, however, it felt like it took forever. And it just about put me over the edge.

As soon as we reached the CP, however, things quickly turned around.

We started what would be a six-mile downhill ride. That perked me up a lot. Then, a couple of CPs later, at the top of a long gravel road climb we found out that we were in first place! We had been near the front of the race all day, and had really only seen one other team. We knew we were doing pretty well, but we had no idea we were in first! I was so excited; I just focused on so badly wanting to stay in first place that although my knee and heel were killing me I just accepted them as a part of the race, dealt with the pain, and pushed on as hard as I could.

The next section of the race was the whitewater swimming section. We got there while it was still a dark zone and had to sit around for a little bit before we were allowed to get in the water. We finally got started at 6:00 A.M. and the water was so cold. It probably felt even colder because the sun wasn't out yet to warm us up. It was during this section that I noticed that the blister on my foot was starting to get infected. We were required to wear a personal flotation device, kneepads, elbow pads, and closed-toed shoes. We also had to use a boogie board and kick our way downstream. I couldn't do a freestyle kick because it hurt my blister too badly, so in the flatter water sections (about three hours!) I kicked breaststroke. This also bothered my blister (albeit less than kicking freestyle), but it did make my left knee hurt even more.

After the swim we transitioned to a trekking portion that included some rope work. By this time my knee hurt to the point that I could hardly walk without it giving out on me. The blister on my foot was also hurting badly and by now it had stuff oozing out of it because it was infected. Needless to say, I looked pretty funny trying to walk and run without bending my knee. I really wasn't in a very good mood at this point. To make matters worse, every little rock and root that I stepped on would cause a pain to shoot through my knee or rub my heel bad enough that I would quickly jump to my other leg, which would once again send pain through my knee. There were a few times that we had to hike downhill into the ravines. I just sat on my butt and slid down the hills because it was way faster for me to do that then it was to try and walk down them. It was less painful too. I knew I had to suffer through it, though, since we were still in first place.

The last section was a biking section that included a bunch of climbing, but fortunately it was mostly on gravel roads, and it was midday. Physically I was beat up. My heel was blistered; my left knee was swollen and hurt like hell every time I had to bend it past thirty degrees of flexion (which was every time I pedaled). To top it all off, I had fallen on the previous bike section and rammed my other knee into the brake lever, causing it to swell up quite a bit, but it looked worse than it felt. In the whitewater swimming section, even though I was wearing kneepads, my knees banged against rocks a bunch of times, which caused them to swell up even more. My shins were bruised and scraped from hitting them on the rocks in the white water section as well. So I looked and felt pretty awful, physically. Mentally, however, I was feeling great. The sun had come up and given me a renewed sense of energy. Plus, it was in this last section that we realized that we were most likely going to win the race! Needless to say, we were both feeling good about that. Jake had done a few races before and had finished well, but had never won any of them, so he was really happy, and I was just ecstatic over how well we were doing.

The last climb felt so much easier then I thought it would because I knew that was it. I was not going to have to deal with any more climbs for a long time. I was superrelieved because my knee and heel were killing me and I knew that once I crossed the finish line I wouldn't have to force myself to keep going any longer. Of course I would pay the price by not being able to ride or run for the next two months.

We finished first in eighteen hours and thirty-seven minutes. I felt so good after we finished, despite the physical pain I was experiencing. In order for me to get around after the race, I had to walk on the toes of my right foot and keep my left leg straight. No matter how funny I looked when I walked and how badly I was hurting, I still had a huge smile on my face because I felt so good about what I had just accomplished. This race was such a rewarding experience in many ways. It taught me how amazing our bodies really are, and how much we can accomplish if we put our minds to it. It also taught me not be so afraid to try new things, even if I do fail at some of them. I still have some self-esteem issues when it comes to selecting and entering races, but I no longer worry about finishing. I know I can. Jake and I are now racing together regularly. We have won another race, and placed highly in others. It's a good thing I didn't turn around at that gas station.

Crossing the Line

Photo courtesy of Nic Stover

NAME: NIC STOVER

AGE: 27

RESIDENCE: BOISE, ID

YEARS ADVENTURE RACING: 2

L to R: Brad Acker, Jen Garretson,
Nic Stover

Some folks aren't ready to create their own adventures. Putting them in a real adventure would be like letting your prize chihuahua go play with the coyote pack at sunrise. —Brutus of Wyde

In April 2002, I lay on the couch watching this crazy endurance event called the Eco-Challenge. A torn MCL and about twenty pounds overweight, I made the determination right then and there—without owning running shoes, or even a fraction of the gear required for an adventure race—that I was going to do a race in 2003. I wasn't always chubby, but college had put me in touch with pizza and beer, and the proverbial beer gut was the result. It was time to make a change.

Mountain biking and climbing were all I really knew, so I had a lot to learn. I bought my first-ever pair of running shoes and joined a running club, the Boise Hash House Harriers. This self-proclaimed "drinking club with a running problem" is where I met Jen, a full-of-life woman who had just done her first adventure race. She was preparing for an Ironman triathlon, so our initial interest in each other focused around training and adventure racing. It wasn't long before we realized we shared so much more, so we started dating. We formed Team Simple Pleasures and set our sights on an adventure race in March 2003.

That first race was a twelve-hour sprint in Moab, Utah that went pretty well. Our biggest problems involved getting off course and a little cramping. We emerged in twelfth place with one thing becoming very evident: We were hooked. After returning home, we elected to apply for a worldwide adventure race known as the Raid X-Adventure. We were shocked when we were accepted and spent the next four months preparing for a two-day race in central Idaho. We dove in headfirst and found some teammates. We had no idea what we were getting ourselves into.

Less than a week before the race, one of our teammates (Mike) dislocated his shoulder and we were forced to scramble for a replacement. A soft-spoken South African (Clint), stepped to the plate having never done an adventure race before. On Friday, August 8, we arrived in Stanley, Idaho, home of the gorgeous Sawtooth Mountains. Instead of the usual RVs and screaming kids, the park was chock-full of gearheads from all over the world. Jen and I soon realized we would be one of only a few amateur teams in the entire race! Kind of like putting a weekend golfer up against Tiger Woods at the Masters.

At the 7:00 P.M. briefing, our route was revealed. Over the next two days, we would encounter forty-eight miles of trekking, eighty-nine miles of mountain biking, ten miles of canoeing, and eight miles of inline skating. Three members would race at a time while one got to sit out and prepare for the next section. Nervous and unsure of what lay ahead, we grabbed our maps and sat down for dinner. We ate quickly and headed to the hotel room where we took to packing and repacking our bags, trying to determine what gear and food would be needed and when. Our adventure started earlier than expected as Brian, while attempting to cut the fingers off his gloves, almost cut his real finger off instead. We remained calm as we determined that an hour drive to nearby Ketchum for medical attention was our next adventure. At midnight, just six hours before the start of the race, we wrapped Brian up and sent him to get medical attention. Brian returned at three thirty and got a mere thirty minutes of shuteye before the dreaded alarm went off signaling the start of our journey.

We set out at 6:00 A.M. riding on some excellent single-track as the dawn of a new day entered. This particular section was twenty-eight miles of mountain biking, and included four thousand vertical feet of climbing. After finishing the first big climb we started our descent, which was chockfull of stream crossings, technical sections, and short steep hills. Given Brian's complete lack of sleep and painfully cut-up finger, he struggled to keep on the trail and make the climbs. Then the really steep stuff hit and Brian's dodging of obstacles turned into a misfit balancing act as he would begin to go over the handlebars or off the bike and would hop on one leg to avoid crashing too hard while dismounting the bike. Emerging from the single-track, Brian and I kicked it into high gear and unknowingly left Clint behind. I had to backtrack and find Clint who had patiently waited where the road had forked. This would turn out to be the only navigational mistake we would make on the course the entire weekend.

Arriving at the checkpoint after over four hours of biking, we recharged and picked up Jen for the eighteen-mile hike and another forty-five hundred feet of climbing. After about an hour of running the flats and trekking the uphills, Jen started to feel sick, and our pace slowed instantly. I was still feeling energetic, so we hooked a bungee from her front to my pack and Clint grabbed her pack. We reached the summit of Custer Lookout in last place, which eliminated any stress over staying ahead of other teams. The descent was brutal, and we tried to run what we could. The effects of the day, however, were already taking a toll. As we battled the heat and the approaching cutoff, we somehow managed to find another gear, and blazed the last bit of that section in record time.

Brian, Clint, and Jen shoved off for the ten-mile paddle looking a little wobbly, but riding a healthy tailwind that provided them with a much-needed push on the flatwater. I was trying to rehydrate and load up on food as fast as possible. Then it happened: cramps! They struck first in my quads, before quickly moving to my hamstrings and calves. I would move to stretch one part of my legs, and another would cramp up. It was pure pain that reflected the abuse we had already put our bodies through, with plenty more to come. I continued to suck down sports drinks, tea, and water in an effort to restore life to my legs. My teammates completed the section in about two hours, only fifteen minutes off the best pro time. They even managed to pass several teams in the process. We tended to blisters as the sun began to set and geared up for the ropes section and a supposed "eight-mile trek."

As we started the trek, I was beginning to feel the nausea that Clint and Jen had been experiencing for a while. Then it got worse. Deep breathing, walking, nothing was helping. I knew I was in trouble, and it wasn't long before I was puking along the side of the road. Brian and Jen were so patient and after a few minutes I began feeling a little better. Discussions opened immediately into why do we do these races. Conclusions varied from "ego," to "being different," to "testing limits," and so on. We finally decided that we do it simply because "it is fun." Just then, our attention quickly shifted four hundred feet above our heads to the zip line that would soon send us sailing across the canyon. You call that fun!?

Moments later I was clipped in to the zip line, and I gazed far across to the other side. I received my instructions, said my final words ("What the hell am I doing?"), and let it rip. In no time at all I was sailing across the valley at an astonishing rate of speed. *Wow!* What a rush. Fueled with adrenaline, I unclipped from the zip line and headed down to the rappel. Lowering off the edge, I began my rappel and found it to be nowhere near as thrilling as the zip line. After becoming entangled in some other ropes on the descent and pelted with small rocks, I was happy to have the anti-climactic rappel behind me and have my feet back on solid ground.

As the darkness crept in I knew I was in trouble. The nausea was gaining strength with each bite of food or sip of liquid. As Jen and I struggled up the mountain, Brian took Jen's pack and bolted ahead. In an effort to slow him down we loaded him up like a pack mule with my pack on one side and Jen's on the other. We then started over a series of false summits. I felt horrible, but I was still able to enjoy the scene as the almost-full moon rose over the landscape below.

Bobbing and weaving and struggling a little more with each step, we pushed on. Jen stopped to fix her shoe when she was hit with some serious cramps. Her calf cramped up like a tennis ball, and the pain showed on her face. At the next checkpoint, Gerard, who was working for the race, joined us and he said he would guide us off the mountain. We figured he knew where he was going and we could just follow him down. Wrong! He led us up and down and back and forth before finally finding the correct route. When we detoured from a well-established trail and began bush-whacking I openly questioned his logic and was simply told we had "dropped into the gulch too early." Later I found out there was a short and much more efficient route, and the ironic thing is, it is the route that we would have taken had we not been guided otherwise. Living and learning was the story of today.

By this time Jen and I were digging deep, focusing on our steps, and trying to keep the cramps and nausea at bay. Brian was caught between keeping up with the "guide" and staying back with us, which sometimes gave us a feeling that we were out there alone. Before hitting the road I saw some rocks that looked just like steaks. I'm not talking about hallucinations here. These were red rocks with white marbling that looked just like New York strip steak. Despite the nausea, it seems I was quite hungry. We tried to jog some when we hit the road but had nothing left, as we arrived at the transition at almost 2:30 A.M. The supposed eight-mile trek had taken us the better part of seven hours. We had missed the bike cutoff by three hours and we were content with piling into the cars and heading for the camp area.

Arriving at the camp area at 3:30 A.M., teams were already stirring, getting ready for the 4:00 A.M. trek. Thoroughly exhausted, we elected to take the slowest team's time plus a one-hour time penalty, and laid out a tarp to settle in for a few hours of shuteye. We awoke at 6:30 after sleeping through our alarms and quickly packed the car and headed to the transition. Jen, Brian, and Clint loaded up and set out at 8:00 A.M. for the fourteen-mile bike leg, hoping to make it by 9:30 for the twenty-mile hike and bike. Arriving at 9:40, they had missed the cutoff but we were relieved to discover that only three teams had actually made it, so we would lose little time.

The drive over turned out to be another adventure, as we had to contend with losing a paddle off the jeep, and then a flat tire. All in a day's work, right? Passing through Ketchum we stocked up on essentials: Pepsi, coffee, and a newspaper. Thinking we might find a blurb about the race we were blown away to find ourselves on the front page! The article focused on the recent passing of Brian's wife, and what draws athletes like us to adventure racing. I think it was about that time that we all realized what we meant to each other and had an even greater understanding of what Erin had meant to Brian. We all got choked up and vowed to finish this race—no matter what.

Arriving at the much-dreaded death sticks section (in-line skating), Jen was really nervous and Brian and I were not exactly pumped either. We baked in the sun and contemplated strategy for the rolling hills. Two weeks prior at an adventure race in Colorado we had gotten bruised and battered in a skate section, so we were all very reluctant to strap them on again. But we did. From the beginning of the skate section, Jen was doing fine on the downhills, but was struggling on the uphills. At the turn-around it became evident that if we wanted to make the final stage we would have to rig a tow system—something we had never practiced before. Our chosen system involved Brian and I holding a rope on each end while Jen grabbed the rope in the middle. This allowed us to pull her on the uphills, and was really paying off until she reached the point where she could not skate any longer. The cutoff for the final leg was 3:00 P.M.,

but we figured that since they had started it ten minutes later than originally scheduled, we would have till 3:10 to get in. When we saw Clint running down the road, our hope of an extended cutoff evaporated. He
announced that we had just seven minutes to make it to the transition and
clock in for the next stage. We were drained. None of us had what it took
to make it. But we pressed on.

Then came the turning point—that point in time that defined the
entire weekend for us. We were nauseated, fatigued, hot, and searching for
that last little bit of desire and energy to get us to the checkpoint. The
steady pace that we had been maintaining all along was thrown into complete upheaval as we struggled to get Jen up the hill by whatever means
possible. At the base of the last big climb, we dug once more and in our
state of fury Brian accidentally clipped Jen's skate, and she went down.
While trying to miss Jen, I also went down. Lying on the hot asphalt with
no time to spare, I got up and calmly encouraged Jen to dig just one more
time. Jen said nothing, just rose from the ground and gave it all she had.
Fighting back tears and frustration, we pushed and pulled her up the hill.
Reaching the top, I collapsed on the asphalt and went into spastic dry
heaving, in desperate need of air. But I could not stay down. No, it was not
over! We still had to check in and then subsequently get on our bikes and
get out of there before the cutoff.

Clint was looking strong, Brian was eager to redeem himself from his
previous ride, Jen was done, and I was dead to the world. I must have
looked horrible because people kept asking, "Are you okay?" I tried my
best to pull myself together and prepare for the final eighteen-mile ride.
Fastening into the bike, I let out a thundering belch and we were off.
Pedaling along, I tried to shovel down some food. Before long the wide
gravel road that we are enjoying gave way to narrow, unrelenting single-
track. At one point I had to stop, stretch, and breathe to control the nausea. Then we hit a slightly steeper section and I totally lost the ability to
ride. I had entered into an area where physical strength no longer mat-
tered; mental toughness was all that was going to get me through. Clint
resorted to shuttling his bike ahead and then coming back for mine. For a
guy who didn't know me very well, he sure was taking great care of me:
making sure I was hydrating and regularly asking how I was doing and
offering assistance. I had developed a sense of kinship with Clint that usually takes years to build.

Pushing the bike up the single-track proved a test of pain and tolerance as branches continually caught the pedals and sent them careening into my shins. At one point I asked Clint to "Make the pain stop" and he calmly replied "I got a penknife in my pocket, but I promised your girl I'd get you home." Reaching the CP at the top of the hill, I glanced at the map and confirmed that we still had another ten miles to go. Off we went, sure that the downhill would allow me to recover and be settling to my system. A crash within the first three minutes, however, indicated otherwise. I decided to rely on a time-tested technique and started praying for no more falls. We made it to the asphalt and started our final ascent, before exiting onto more single-track. This is where I came unraveled. I stopped to control the nausea, but nothing was going to stop it this time. I started dry heaving, and then the dreaded cramps returned to my quads and calves. Having come too far to quit, I limped slowly, needing to call on every last ounce of energy I had in my body to complete the journey. Usually I get a burst of energy as I near the finish line. This time, however, knowing we were nearing the end did not help, simply because I had nothing left to give. I fell again and again. And instead of lying and collecting myself, I had to get up quickly and move to keep the painful cramps at bay.

The final push involved one final hill of about thirty feet that literally took me several minutes to climb. I could see the flags at the finish line where our friends and medical attention anxiously waited. I finally got to the top of the hill and crossed the finish line. I posed for a quick group picture, then immediately headed to the ambulance. They started an IV drip and tried to test my glucose levels, but I was too dehydrated for them to get any blood. Mentally and physically drained, the emotion took over as I tried to talk. The immense feeling of accomplishment coupled with the devotion I felt to my teammates was incredible.

We had been out there far longer than almost any other team, and had endured much pain and suffering. After three IV bags, I got some of my color back, and was ready to move to the car. It was over! We had finished second to last, which was something we could all be proud of.

The acknowledgment of what we had accomplished would take time to completely set in, but for the time being I reflected back on what I had accomplished in the past year and quietly said to myself, "You did it." The dream I had while sitting on the couch, hung over and overweight, to someday do something like this had been realized. I had changed my lifestyle and was a completely different person.

After enduring extreme mental and physical stress I was free to return to my desk and the relative peace and quiet of everyday life. Thirty-eight hours of gel, vomit, tears, sweat, pain, cuts, expectations, failures, and successes were behind us now. We had chosen to put ourselves in situations that most human beings would never want to venture into—situations that would cause most people to fail. But not us. We had succeeded.

Racing Under the Midnight Sun: Explore Sweden Airborne Expedition Race

NAME: SCOTT COLE
AGE: 27
RESIDENCE: VANCOUVER, WA
YEARS ADVENTURE RACING: 5

Photo courtesy of Vytenis Benetis

L to R: Vytenis Benetis, Jodi Zwicky, Tim Pearson, Scott Cole

Team Discovery/The North Face participated in the first airborne expedition race, organized by Swedes Mikeal Nordstrom and Helene Lind. The five-day, three-destination event (each stage twenty-four to thirty-six hours) was a high-paced multiday expedition race. Only the top elite teams completed the full course, with the remaining teams choosing (or being forced into) shortened versions to ensure continuation at subsequent destinations. Team Discovery/ The North Face included myself, Vytenis Benetis and Jodi Zwicky, winners of the 2003 Beast of the East, and Tim Pearson, from the winning team of the 2003 Southern Traverse.

Ornskoldsviks, Sweden (six hundred kilometers north of Stockholm) —"Oh . . . Ohhh . . . Ohhhhhh—O—Got it!" We were in-line skating down (hill) into town to grab some dinner on our first night in-country and I safely grabbed hold of a telephone pole split seconds before reaching an uncomfortable acceleration. Cruising was my forte; stopping was not. But for this race that was bound to be an asset. Speed was the only way to cover the 180 km of expected skating. Regardless, I knew I had a challenge ahead; combining the distance of this evening's blade session with my total previous blading experience, it very likely didn't add up to 180 km.

We were forewarned about the unique nature of the event. Besides the unconventional airplane component and critical checkpoints (you miss the cutoff, you miss the plane, you're out of the race) there were a number of nontraditional disciplines like in-line skating, mountaineering, coast-eering and the conspicuous absence of kayaking (instead, canoes and restrictive canoe paddles). Horseback riding and sailing were on the original agenda, but were nixed prior to the start. But not before Jodi and I had an "eventful and painful" horseback riding lesson in western Pennsylvania. Regardless, this was likely to be more than a "slog it out" run, bike, paddle event and for this I was psyched. I've heard plenty of racer opinions about disciplines that should and should not be in an adventure race, but I reckon a true championship team should be one that not only trains hard and races well together, but also sports a myriad mix of outdoor skills. If you're only doing what you're good at, doesn't it take the adventure out of adventure racing?

Hampnas: The Olympic Village

Hampnas, a small dormitory college served as an ideal "Olympic Village" for the athletes and volunteers and provided all the comforts we'd forgo in the days ahead—warm food, accommodation, and mechanized transport. For two days under an omnipresent sun, we completed gear checks, skill tests, and packed our gear crates for drop-off at secret destinations throughout the course. To prove our "skills," we had to capsize our whitewater raft on the lake to simulate an involuntary swim in the rapids. We also had to rope up for the mountaineering section, complete with crampons, butterfly knots, and self-arrest practice. Of course a lot of teams spent their downtime tooling around on their (oftentimes brand-new) in-line skates. In what would be one of the more fortuitous events for the team, Tim Pearson's North Face gear showed up via overnight courier only an hour before our scheduled gear check. Tim, the easygoing Kiwi, was restricted by luggage requirements and was counting on the new gear upon arrival. Unfazed by the ordeal, he pulled his mountaineering boots out of the box to receive his mandatory gear check-off (How 'bout them blisters, Tim?).

Race directors Mikeal Nordstrom and Helena Lind did an outstanding job of organizing the event, from the unique accommodations leading up to the race, which created a lot of camaraderie among the competitors and race staff, to the handling of last-second mishaps. For example, the night before the race started, someone broke into the building containing all the teams' gear and stole in-line skates and other miscellaneous items, leaving a number of teams without mandatory equipment. Mikeal stepped up and took responsibility and chartered transportation to town to buy the necessary equipment, even picking up the tab. Of course, this was minor compared to the real fire Mikeal had to put out about a month before the race when the main sponsor of the event—the Swedish Air National Guard—had to back out of their promise to provide the cargo plane to transport racers among the three course destinations. It turns out there was a (governmental) paying customer that needed the aircraft in Kosovo. Realizing the race must go on, Mikeal figured out a way and chartered a private plane.

By far, most of our pre-race time was spent packing, repacking, and debating the best items to put into each of our four gear crates. From our vague instructions (e.g., "Box one should have ten to twelve hours of food and skate gear" "Box two should include swim googles and wetsuits and thirty-six hours of food"), we speculated on what else may be in high demand when we come across each box—extra socks? Dry shirts? Salty food? Chocolate? Tums? Vaseline? The winning team was going to be not only physically superior, but logistically experienced.

Game Time: Destination 1

Wednesday 8:00 P.M.: Our bus departure from Hampnas brought us to a 10:00 P.M. boat launch that would eventually bring us to secret Destination 1, where the race was scheduled to start one minute after midnight. We were told to have our wetsuits and swim fins ready for the start. We arrived on Hogbonden Island, a picturesque archipelago island amid Sweden's Highcoast, and the scene was surreal. We motored out of a quiet fishing harbor at 11:00 P.M., with the sun just on the horizon, the clouds glowing pink, and our destination fast approaching. We saw a path full of candles leading us to the top of a rocky island, as if we were about to embark on a *Survivor*-like adventure. The teams hiked a trail to the top of Hogbonden along the candlelit path, and stumbled upon a party at the top—music was playing, volunteers were scurrying about setting up a pre-race BBQ (which was clutch for those of us who didn't pack enough food on the bus!), as photographers captured the midnight twilight.

Before long, the gun sounded and we raced down a couple hundred meters to CP1 where we received our instructions and maps. The objective was to coasteer—that is, hike up and over and swim between—four rocky islands en route to the mainland, following bonfires and our own navigation through the trail-less islands. With our full wetsuit gear on, we were dripping with sweat almost immediately as we clambered along the rocky coastline under a magnificent full moon rising from the east. In the southwest, the sun remained just below the horizon, providing a stunning three hours of dusk. The air and water temps were both hovering at ten Celsius (low forties Fahrenheit), providing a strong incentive to keep moving—as if the "don't-miss-the-plane" race pace was not enough.

An adventure race is not complete without an unforeseen challenge of your own making and we cooked up a few early on. During our first cross-island swim, Tim lost a swim fin and had a tough time keeping the other one on. It was only twenty-five minutes into the race and we quickly dropped back a number of spots as Tim and I teamed up to find the most efficient way to carry our packs, boogie boards, and bodies across the channel with the aid of two and a half fins. We finally got it together and pulled ashore in last place, with Jodi and Vytenis waiting onshore wondering whether we had enjoyed the swim so much we just didn't want to get out. We quickly made up time bushwhacking across the islands and plunging ourselves back into the icy water to repeat the process all over again from island to island. Jodi is the type of person who rarely complains but she mentioned a few times that her pack was feeling heavier than normal. We didn't think much of it, but by the time we reached the coasteer-to-bike transition two hours later, her pack was noticeably heavier than when we stared. It turns out she forgot to close the air valve on her dry bag, which contained all of her mandatory equipment and (previously) dry clothes. Unfortunately, Vytenis had also made the same mistake. Their ultralight North Face sleeping bags were wasted—they would carry water-laden gear for the next four days.

The challenges always provide an opportunity to critique and improve your approach to race preparation, particularly with unique disciplines like coasteering. Who knows, maybe in a pre-race run-through Tim might have realized his fins didn't fit over his booties when kicking hard across a channel? Maybe one of us would have made the stupid mistake of failing to close our air valve before our midnight race start. Perfect example of the benefits of preparation: In November 2003, I had competed with Team Nomad at the Southern Traverse (New Zealand) where coasteering was a key discipline. With the luxury of a week of pre-race preparations (not always feasible, I admit), we all donned full wetsuits, packs, swim fins and trail shoes and plunged into the icy waters of the South Pacific for a "trial run" of coasteering. We had identified a number of things that did and didn't work and optimized our distribution of gear and the transition between swimming (fins) and rock scrambling (trail shoes). It worked!

Days later we were five hours into the race and were passing teams during the coasteering leg, which put us up front going into the night trek. You can never underestimate the benefits of proactive race preparation (though race experience is a good alternative for teams with less time to prepare).

Two hours of coasteering brought us to TA-1, our bike boxes, and a new set of maps. In thirty minutes, we assembled our bikes, stuffed our wetsuits into our bike crates, and were ready to go. Vytenis managed to gash himself with a knife while opening his bike box—a stubborn cut that refused to stop bleeding during our ride and required three stitches a day later from the race docs. The sun was back up a little after 2:00 A.M., but as we would learn over the next few days, the air temperature rises stubbornly until the more traditional hour of 8:00 A.M.

Our pace was brisk for the rest of Destination 1, which brought us a seventy km bike ride (mostly paved), a thirty km canoe (with a plethora of portaging), a forty km in-line skate (with a handful of intimidating hills), a thirty km orienteering trek (with great views, lots of vertical, and very few trails), an eight-hundred-foot rock climb via Ferrata, and another mountain bike (Via Ferrata is a type of rope-assisted rock climbing practiced much more in Europe than in the U.S. Essentially, you're traversing or scrambling up cliff faces while clipped into a secure rope.) The pace was much faster than we would have followed in a normal six-day expedition race—but this race had something that others lack, a do-or-die cutoff time to catch the plane. This race was more like a series of three high-paced thirty-six-hour races strung together, rather than a "slog-it-out-pace-yourself" expedition race.

The key cutoff for Destination 1 was called the critical checkpoint (CCP) and followed the second mountain bike section. It had to be reached by 8:00 A.M. Friday, at which time teams had to decide whether to continue on the course—completing a bridge rappel with swim, canoe, and another mountain bike—or "cut bait" and hightail it to the plane. We stumbled into the via Ferrata with glum faces, expecting to be told that we were unlikely to reach the CCP in time, thus dropping out early. Instead, we were given a second life when racer-turned-volunteer Nigel Aylott greeted us: "Good news—the CCP has been moved to the end of this via Ferrata in order to allow more (that is, almost all!) teams to make this cutoff." Ahh, our nicely packed mountaineering gear box (for Destination 2) would not go unused!

Part of the problem in not making the "original" cutoff was the challenging course, but it was also related to Jodi's sickness. During our thirty km trek over hot and dry terrain (yes, it can be quite hot in Sweden), Jodi rode the vomit-comet, unable to keep liquids down and sporting unstoppable diarrhea and dizziness. The team was forced to stop for over an hour in the shade for rest/recovery, during which time Jodi spent more time sprinting into the woods and making explosive noises than actually resting. Miraculously, she bounced back and was ready to give it a second go despite her disagreeable stomach. In the meantime, however, we had called the race doctors from our mandatory cell phones for their opinion, given her symptoms (unlike some races, we were allowed to use the cell phones to get the doctors' advice without risking disqualification). After Jodi recovered, the doctors insisted we take an hour to slowly walk over to the road for them to drive by and confirm her status as "good to go." They concurred, but as expected, Jodi never came back to 100 percent. In some types of expedition races, this could have been a bump in the road, but given the time pressure to make the critical cutoff, we simply couldn't afford to give her the complete rest she needed. So we pushed on.

After the via Ferrata we pedaled about thirty km to the airport to catch our plane. We arrived with about an hour to spare and went straight to our gear box to dig out some much-needed food. As other teams lay motionless asleep on the concrete floor of the hangar, we quietly munched on cold pasta, canned ravioli, and peanut butter and jelly as we packed the bikes into our crates. Our sleep would wait until we got on the plane.

Mountaineering: Destination 2

We slept soundly on the plane (go figure) and awoke to the jolt of the landing and the purposely ambiguous voice of the flight attendant: "Good afternoon and welcome to . . . somewhere." We didn't know where we were, but we knew it had to smell better outside our plane than it did in. We rubbed our eyes, stretched our legs and lumbered over to the buses waiting to take us to start line 2. Another hour of wonderful sleep awaited on the bus, interrupted only by race director Mikael Nordstrom screaming something about a pack of reindeer in the middle of the road.

Our buses pulled us into a treeless valley in what appeared to be a national park. Though we didn't know our precise location, the surrounding snowcapped peaks and a seemingly nonexistent treeline told us we were "somewhere" north of the Arctic Circle.

After a short pre-race meeting under the surprisingly warm Arctic sun we were awed by a short chant from an indigenous nomadic reindeer herder, whose voice literally echoed off the steep rock walls around us. At the starting gun, we ran down the short hill to CP1 and gathered our maps/directions. Our large-scale 1:100,000 maps pointed to an epic fifty-five km trek with lots of vertical and an ascent of Sweden's highest peak—Mount Kebnekaise (6,929 feet).

The helicopter hovered overhead to get views of the teams as we scrambled up to the first checkpoint thirty-five-hundred feet above the valley floor and a couple of miles from the start. Virtually every team had made the flight, so the field was full and quite competitive, setting a fast pace up the hill. I remember looking downhill and seeing a lake still frozen, unaffected by the twenty-four hours of sunlight, as the hot sun and steep climb forced us to peel layers of clothing. We reached the top of the first milestone and saw in front of us a deep glacial-carved valley, patches of snow and rock, a bright blue sky, and the glimmering peak of Mount Kebnekaise far off in the distance. Awesome! It was one of those moments when you forget you're racing and think, "Damn, this is one of the greatest vacations I've ever planned!"

We followed the snowless patches of loose rock and footprints in the snow, ultimately changing to snowshoes—the only solution in the winter landscape, which was rapidly turning to mushy applesauce. We crested and descended a five-thousand-foot pass, reaching the base of the main glacial route up Mount Kebnekaise. That's when I realized I had drained my one-hundred-ounce. water bladder hours ago and hadn't replenished it. Though I didn't realize it for a couple more hours, I was rapidly descending into the dehydration/nausea that was plaguing many teams. My natural high would be short-lived.

About eight hours into the trek, we passed through the next checkpoint, where we were told to strap on our metal crampons and attach ourselves together as a mountaineering rope team. By now the tables had turned: It was Jodi's turn to lead. Just as I had done for her twenty-four hours earlier, she traded off carrying my pack and coaxing me to eat and drink, but by then it was too late. While being too preoccupied with the scenery to drink, I was now serving a painful punishment. We'll probably never know exactly what caused Jodi's and my sickness. It may have been simple dehydration—as the race doctors suggested—but it seemed odd that so many other teams had symptoms more often correlated with stomach bacteria.

Everybody has a high and low point during a race and I had mine simultaneously. It climaxed about an hour after losing my stomach as I stumbled toward the summit ten minutes before midnight. The sun was holding stubbornly at an angle more reminiscent of a typical six o'clock summer evening as snowcapped peaks stretched as far as you could see. I barely had the strength to "top out" on the short steep climb to the snow cone. The memory is vivid, perhaps because of the conflicting emotions, debilitating weakness enveloping my body, and the pure magic of the Arctic summer. Only forty-eight hours before, we were swimming in Sweden's icy coastal waters, and now we stood atop a harsh and unforgiving landscape during a rare moment of calm. A light breeze reminded us that even under these ideal conditions, seven thousand feet above the nearby Barents Sea was not a good place to stop. We still had a lot of walking to go, so the checkpoint volunteer snapped a photo for us and we pushed on.

Destination 2, north of the Arctic Circle, also included a seventy km inline skate back to the tiny airport in the mining town of Kiruna (where we had arrived). As was the case with Destination 1, only the lead teams were able to complete all the disciplines in this section of the race. Most teams opted out of the skate realizing that either (a) they were unlikely to make the airport in time or (b) six hours blading on "chip and seal" pavement was not the team's strength. One team started out, but turned back after only a few kilometers.

As for Discovery/North Face, we were battling just to complete the return half of the trek. I was unable to eat, yet still demanded mountains of energy to put one foot in front of the other. Jodi was dealing with a golfball-sized blister on her foot and still not her normal self, and Vytenis managed to drop his crampons off his pack, making our rappel/descent of the icy gulch a time-consuming affair (we had to belay him slowly while we stood atop an exposed ridge and shivered uncontrollably). After gaining the valley floor, we were still facing eighteen km to reach the "do-or-die" cut-off for the bus ride to the airport. We passed by a hut that had become a first-aid stop for the race and told Mikeal Nordstrom over the race radio that we would make the bus departure. After all, we had three hours. We lied.

A meager jogging pace would have been plenty, but with sleep deprivation, sickness, and blisters it became survival. Vytenis and Tim—the team horses—took the heaviest packs and charged ahead to try and hold the bus. I remember giving no second thought to the "stay-within-a-hundred-yards-of-your-teammates" rule. In my own mind, my disregard for the rules was the result not so much of race survival as an apathy driven by my sleep-deprived haze. It felt like Tim and Vytenis were leading Jodi and me along like reluctant children. They were insisting on urgency; we were doped up and unable to respond. The race pace of two days ago seemed forgotten, as Jodi and I plodded along with our governor set well below what it should have been.

Toward the end of the trail, Jodi and I found stick-written notes in the dirt, informing us of the distance remaining and pleading for us to "Hurry"! As we neared familiar territory and recognized landmarks from the starting line, Vytenis came running at us. Still in my fog, I was thinking, "Oh, good, we finally caught up to them." But he quickly jerked me out of my hallucination when he started screaming about a van. We had already missed the bus, but a couple of race volunteers were holding the last race vehicle just for us. We had about an hour until the plane was to take off, crates of gear to load, and seventy km to drive; it didn't look good.

We chucked the boxes, backpacks, and gear in the van's trailer and launched ourselves toward the airport. Luckily, our race saviors were equally as determined to make the plane as the trailer fishtailed all the way. We pulled onto the runway tarmac as the last race staffers were walking up the stairs to the plane. Just in time for another nap.

The Last Leg: Destination 3

Our second flight to "somewhere" turned out to be Umea, the biggest city in northern Sweden. Getting off the plane, teams were instructed to catch one of two buses—those that completed the mountaineering trek got the green bus to the start of destination 3 (that was us); teams that failed to complete the mountaineering trek, got the white bus back to the race finish and their race was done. The one-hour nap on the plane did little to alleviate the fatigue, sickness, sluggish feet, dehydrated bodies, and red eyes among racers and volunteers alike. One race volunteer even caught pneumonia.

The bus brought teams to the banks of the roaring Class V Vindeln River for the start of the final destination. As rain came crashing down, teams poured into the adjacent restaurant/home and claimed spots on the floor. We sat down to a wonderful café meal of cake and orange soda. The sugar brought my body back to life, and the prospect of the upcoming whitewater rafting and long mountain bike (my strongest and most comfortable discipline) brought my spirits up. We spent the next five hours sleeping on a gloriously comfortable plank-boarded living room floor. A total of twelve teams survived to the start of Destination 3. In what seemed like a cruel incentive for a strong performance, the lead teams that had completed the full skate section at Destination 2 were rewarded with a four-hour head start. Nobody on our team was complaining about the extra rest.

One of the best feelings in adventure racing is the second wind brought on by rest—a new life that engenders a contagious enthusiasm among teammates. Our pace quickened as Vytenis led us through a short orienteering leg to reach the rafts. We blasted through some good-sized rapids interspersed with long stretches of flatwater. It seemed to me that Jodi was still not back to her normal self—unusual for someone with so much stamina. She hung on through the rapids, but the last mile and a half was classic race director torture—an upriver paddle through a muddy tributary that became a "get-out-and-walk" affair. Jodi was shivering uncontrollably while wading through the stream. For a well-fed racer, the exertion of dragging a heavy raft through a muddy swamp would have generated ample heat, but Jodi's body was out of fuel and vulnerable to the elements. She needed dry clothes and sustained movement, but without keeping her food down, she could only last so long.

The next leg was the crux of the Destination 3, a 224 km mountain bike ride (almost all paved) toward Hampnas and our finish line, attained only after another coasteering and orienteering leg. Jodi pushed on like a trouper, but when she wasn't falling asleep on her bike, she was pulling off the road to dry heave. She looked miserable, yet refused to quit. After forty km, Vytenis, Tim, and I faced a difficult decision. While it's nice to have a stubborn, never-give-up attitude in a teammate like Jodi, the downside is that we have to make rational and critical decisions for her. On the one hand, we didn't want to pull the plug on our unhappy teammate if she simply needed some encouragement to push through her comfort zone. On the other hand, we didn't want to be responsible for potentially permanent damage occurring to her kidneys because she was severely dehydrated and ignoring the body's signals to rest. Just a few months earlier, Vytenis had pushed through the same types of signals in the Cal-Eco Adventure Finals in California, where he led Team Earthlink to a first-place finish, but at a high cost. He spent a few days in the emergency room as a result of severe kidney failure. His medical tests showed him on the verge of complete shutdown. It was with this experience in mind that we made the final decision to pull Jodi out of the race.

We called the race doctors and they came to pick her up. Confirming that we had made the right decision, she took three bags of IVs on the car ride back—a sign of severe dehydration. Tim, Vytenis, and I continued, finishing the bike leg, but didn't have the inspiration to finish the remaining course unranked. We had reached our goal, which was to make both critical cutoffs and saw an incredible variety of Sweden's terrain. As we pedaled toward the finish-line banner, we swung left at the last second; we weren't an officially finishing team.

Ceremonial Burning

We never found out what caused both Jodi's and my sickness, though we weren't the only ones to suffer. At least eight other racers had similar symptoms (e.g., vomiting, nausea). In fact, two of the four racers on the local Swedish team who raced hard at the front of the pack throughout the race found themselves in the hospital with severe symptoms. Race doctors insist it was simple dehydration; others believe we may have been better off treating the water despite suggestions to the contrary by locals.

At the post-race BBQ on a picturesque lake near Hampnas, we partied alongside bonfires under a never-ending dusk. Team Nokia received the winner's check for thirteen thousand euros, having completed the entire course in about seventy-one hours of actual race time. The highlight of the evening was Team Seagate's Christina Strode-Penny's ceremonial burning of her in-line skates in the firepit. The sentiment against the skates seemed almost unanimous, as the burning of toxic rubber elicited a universal chorus of agreement.

Why I Race

Photo by Dan Campbell Photography

NAME: REBECCA RUSCH
AGE: 36
RESIDENCE: KETCHUM, ID
YEARS ADVENTURE RACING: 8

What is it like to quit your dream job, cast aside all social expectations of what you're supposed to do, and jump in with both feet into the cauldron of the unknown? Seven years ago, after doing a couple of Eco-Challenges, I decided to find out what it was really like to commit to full-time adventure racing. The journey didn't start that way. I did not have any intentions of being a professional athlete or even doing adventure racing for very long. I just decided that I wanted to take advantage of the unique opportunity that was unfolding before me. I did my first adventure race on a whim and an invitation from some friends who needed a woman who could do more than one sport. I excelled in two sports, rock climbing and paddling, so I was the most likely candidate. Honestly, the main reason I agreed to join the group was to have something to motivate me over the winter months. In the summers, I climbed outdoors every week and raced outrigger canoes with an internationally renowned team. However, winters in the climbing gym were leaving me feeling out of shape and uninspired. I needed something new and challenging to get me excited and feed my competitive nature until the climbing and paddling season rolled back around.

That first race was a twenty-four-hour qualifier for Eco-Challenge Australia. I knew nothing of the sport and had no intention of doing another race after that one. In fact, I nearly backed out of the race the week before. I was in tears as I tried to visualize what the experience would be like. I was certain that I'd be the weak link, not be able to stay upright on the bike, and struggle to survive athletic activity for twenty-four hours straight. I cursed myself for agreeing to something that seemed utterly impossible and ridiculous to me. The only reason I did not back out was a sense of responsibility toward the team. I knew they would not be able to find another woman on such short notice.

The race was incredibly hard and incredibly eye-opening for me. We ended up winning, and despite my massive insecurities, I was one of the stronger members of the team. I had no idea how it had happened, but I was able to keep up with three very strong, athletic men who had a lot more endurance sport experience than I did. After that first race, things began snowballing and I started to be invited to more and more events. Soon, I began forming my own teams and drumming up sponsorship. I eventually realized that in order to keep traveling to races, I would need to quit my job. At the time, I was managing a large, successful rock climbing gym in Los Angeles. The job was fantastic, but didn't allow me enough flexibility to be away for weeks at a time. I also found that Los Angeles wasn't the ideal training environment for me. I did not want to pass up the opportunity of a lifetime. So I calculated my expenses, weighed the options, and figured out that if I wanted to quit my job and pursue adventure racing, I would have to be homeless for a while. The potential rewards and my curiosity seemed to outweigh the risks.

I've always been a bit of a nomad, so the idea of hitting the road excited me. I had some vague plans and locations I wanted to visit, but generally, my agenda presented no constraints. The only specifics that I knew were that I had to fit myself and my belongings into my truck and I had to keep expenses low. I also knew that I would stay out west in the mountains and deserts where I could climb, kayak, trail run, and explore. The places that inspired me the most from my past climbing trips were Yosemite, Moab, the Sierras, and the Rockies. I could spend a lifetime in those areas alone and still not see everything.

So the tedious process of condensing my life, boxing up and storing possessions, and packing my gear began. It was a torturous process to decide what I would need for an open-ended trip with an unspecified destination and an unknown agenda. I pored over each article of clothing and each piece of gear, trying to decide which would make the cut. Over a period of weeks, I slowly sifted through my belongings, attempting each time to simplify my life and free myself from so many possessions.

My only mode of transportation was a 1975 Ford Bronco named Betty. I had rebuilt and restored the truck myself. She was fairly reliable, but old, small, got lousy gas mileage, and was a bit finicky at times. Just driving hundreds of miles in that truck was going to be an adventure itself. After weeks of packing, repacking, consolidating, putting gear into storage, Betty was jammed to the ceiling with climbing gear, paddling gear, cycling gear, repair tools, a computer, a cell phone, personal files, books, cooking gear, camping gear, cameras, a can of Mace, journals, CDs, and even a little cactus glued to the dashboard to keep me company. The truck looked like a traveling sports store. It was so full that I couldn't see out of the windows or fit a passenger. Christmas gifts from my family that year were things like a file box to keep important documents, a travel diary, a travel toiletry kit, a road atlas, and phone cards. My friends and family supported my unscripted wanderlust 100 percent.

I had informed friends, many of them new adventure racing friends, that I'd be on the road a while in search of good places to stay. Invitations came flooding in. I expect some of those people never really thought they'd hear me knocking at their front door. My best friend in Arizona offered a room, a friend in Utah offered an empty trailer in Moab, and another acquaintance offered up a guest room in Truckee, California. Of course, there were invitations from my family members in Michigan, Texas, Illinois, and Washington, DC, but they obviously didn't meet the travel criterion of staying out west. My climbing and adventure racing friends lived in more intriguing places, so I hit them up first.

Moab, Utah, was the first stop. I went to live in a friend's doublewide trailer and it seemed like heaven. A washer and dryer inside, a place to park and work on my truck, space to unload a bit of gear, a real address and lots of other dirtbag climbers and cyclists roaming around town. I quickly registered my truck in Utah, got a driver's license, changed all my bills to automatic debit, and got a P. O. box as sort of a home base to collect mail every once in a while. The anticipation of leaving California and setting out on my adventure was now behind me. The reality of my situation began to set in. I was alone in an unknown town with no plans, no friends around me, and the responsibility of creating a new life for myself weighing heavily on my shoulders. I did not regret taking this giant step, but I was scared and unsure of where to start or what I wanted for myself. I hoped that opportunities would present themselves, but I also knew that I couldn't sit around inside the trailer, waiting for opportunity to knock on the door.

Over the next five years, I settled into this lifestyle and became a professional nomad and a professional adventure racer. I traveled to fifteen different countries, raced a raft down the holy Ganges River in India, rode camels in the Moroccan desert, hosted parasites from Borneo, walked across the Himalayas from Tibet into Nepal, soloed multiday climbing walls in Yosemite and Utah, spent countless hours under the hood of my truck, and became a connoisseur of canned tuna and gas-station food. I could never have predicted that either title—adventure racer or nomad—would have suited me for so long. At one point, I had keys and an open-door policy to four different homes in four different western states. My cell phone and e-mail became the only modes of communication where my family, sponsors, and friends could find me. Filing taxes became an interesting prospect because I had no official residence and no official income. I did do a smattering of work as a climbing and adventure racing instructor, worked at a cross-country ski center, helped frame a couple of houses, and did some motivational speaking for extra income. But the work was far between and at the end of the year was never in the same state. My accountant had a hell of a time justifying my "business" as an adventure racer.

My family became used to the fact that I was lousy about writing holiday letters, remembering birthdays, sending cards, and all the kinds of things that one always intends to do but usually doesn't. It seemed I was always off in some other country doing another race. I think it was hard for everyone to keep track of me. My mom became the official team correspondent and was responsible for informing friends, family, and sponsors of my whereabouts. All I had to do was drop an e-mail or phone message to her and the international communication tree was in effect. Even though I was well into my thirties, my mom was still looking after me and making sure that everything was under control.

What I remember most from those years is the generosity and understanding of my friends and family. I can't believe how much I mooched off other people for so long, yet they were happy to give, happy to see me on their doorstep, and happy to help me achieve what I was working toward. During that time, I was racing as much as possible, building a team, working with sponsors, and essentially creating a life. I had not dreamed or envisioned this life for myself. It just seemed this path was being defined for me by circumstance, ability, and desire. I definitely struggled with bouts of loneliness and uncertainty. There were times that I longed to unpack my truck and have a sense of place and belonging. The month just after a long race was always the hardest. Coming back from such an intensely emotional and physical overload always left me feeling depressed, lost, and lacking stimulation. I had no savings plan, no home, no specific five- or ten-year plan. I lived from race to race, recovering, training, and traveling in between. Despite being homeless and broke, I was free and seeing the world. I knew this wouldn't last forever, so I accepted the difficulties in order to take advantage of the unique experience.

Eventually things began to come together. My team and teammates evolved over many years and many races with a host of different people from all over the globe. I am grateful for every single person I have raced with because I have taken something from each of them and created my team and my racing style around all of that input. I can remember every race and can think of something from each race that I would change and would take to the next race with me as a lesson. One race that was a highlight in my career was the Patagonia Eco-Challenge in 1997. Due to the nationality rule and unbelievable circumstance, I was able to pull together the best three-woman, one-man team ever assembled. As a pretty new racer, I ended up as the captain of a team that consisted of Cathy Sassin, Robyn Benincasa, Ian Adamson, and me. These guys were all friends of mine. I had met them at the climbing gym, at adventure racing camps, and at other races. I knew they were big names in the racing scene with a lot more experience than I had, but the stars aligned for this race and I asked them all to race with me. They agreed, we raced in the top of the field for the whole race, and became the sweethearts of the race. All along the race-course, we were known as The Divas or Las Diosas by the locals. Only two hours behind the winners, we finished fourth to a huge crowd chanting "Las Diosas!" We had made history.

That race left me heady with emotions. Our performance instilled me with confidence in my abilities, and the rush of racing in the top of the field provided me with a new sense of purpose with adventure racing. It was the first time I was able to compare myself with other women in the sport and the first time I was able to travel alongside visionary leaders in the sport like John Howard, Keith and Andrea Murray, Team Nokia, and Team Buff. It was also the first time in the history of racing that a mostly women's team was gunning for the lead and finished among the top in the world. The powerful message we sent regarding female endurance athletes resonated around the world. The message the race sent to me personally liberated me from years of programmed female stereotypes. For the first time, I realized that women were not the weak link, that endurance sports suited women, and that I was very good at adventure racing. I was elated, shocked, and excited about racing among the best in the world.

By this time, I started to notice people out there looking at my lifestyle with envy because they were thinking that all I do is go out into the hills each day and train. It's true that even now, seven years later, I don't have to punch a clock nine-to-five. But the commitments and expectations are in many ways more demanding than a traditional career. I love what I do, but it's also not an easy lifestyle. Gone by the wayside are some of the passions that brought me to adventure racing in the first place. I no longer have much time to go on long climbing trips, race outrigger canoes in Hawaii, or race on the U.S. women's whitewater rafting team. Instead, I give up those opportunities in order to adhere to the commitments of my adventure racing. When I started this journey, I was dropping commitments I had in order to be able to travel and race. Now I have come full circle. I am passing up different opportunities because my professional adventure racing has taken the front seat.

Sometimes I long for the lazy days of climbing with my friends on the weekends, going to Yosemite to solo a wall or disappearing for a week or so in the backcountry. However, I can look back on the last seven years with amazement. If I look at a world map and start to list the places I've been able to race, my jaw drops. Whenever someone asks me what I do for a living and I answer sheepishly that I'm a professional adventure racer, a silly, proud grin comes to my face because I still can't believe it myself. When I bought my condo in Idaho and started to decorate my walls with trinkets from Kyrgyzstan, Borneo, Tibet, Argentina, and Morocco, I was amazed at the memories I had collected. And when I look at the pictures of my teammates on my refrigerator, it brings tears to my eyes thinking of the miles we've covered together. I realize today that more than our successes, it has been the years of trials and hardships that have made us as close as siblings.

After our glorious race in Patagonia, The Divas headed back to their respective teams and I dreamed of sculpting a team of the strongest and best racers in the sport—a team anchored by a powerful competitor like myself. I knew I was strong enough to captain a mostly male team and once again prove the field for women racers everywhere.

From Day 1, my credo with teammates has always been that I must enjoy their company. This sport is such a strain emotionally and physically that I find it imperative to surround myself with teammates who not only are good racers, but also make me laugh and care about me as a person. It all sounds simple and cliché, but you would not believe how many people race with teammates whom they do not like or respect. Over the years this credo has not changed, but instead has become even more crucial. Slowly and meticulously, I began to find racers who inspired me and fit my criteria. Patrick Harper was the first core teammate who joined me on a long-term basis. He joined our team in Tibet as a last-minute replacement. His experience of growing up in the Idaho wilderness, competing as a cross-country skier, ultrarunner, and paddling first decents in many Idaho rivers gave him the perfect combination of athletic prowess and wilderness knowledge. Patrick is thin, wiry, and much stronger than he looks. Novak Thompson was next to join the team. I raced with him in Vietnam and was blown away by his navigation skills and hard-core attitude. Nothing seemed to faze him physically or mentally. He is a man of few words and he does not put up with any crap. His background in the Australian military taught him how to navigate and suffer efficiently. His triathlon racing had honed his lightning-fast speed and living on the beach had sculpted him into an incredible paddler. Like Patrick, Novak's lanky, thin physique belies his true strength. The final addition to our core group was Australian kayaking legend John Jacoby. John had been adventure racing for longer than any of us and had raced with the best in the world. He is big, strong, levelheaded, and extremely easygoing. He seems too big to move quickly and appears to lumber along ungracefully, but still posts extremely fast marathon times. He is never fazed by other teams, difficult situations, or personality conflicts. Although it had taken years, my dream team has evolved. We have a couple of strong alternates that rotate in and out depending on schedules, but this core group has been our most successful team.

As we've moved into higher and higher rankings, the strain on training, sacrifice, and commitment have become even more of a challenge. We had steadily improved our performance as a team and regularly finished near the very top end of each race that we entered. In recent years, adventure racing has evolved into faster, more competitive, and more cutthroat events. No longer are there just one or two teams who are gunning for the lead. Now there are seven to ten top international teams who could win any event. Granted, the basics are still the same. These teams are all still friends of ours. However, the stakes are higher. Our sponsors are expecting us to deliver results and we are all attempting to make a living at our sport. We are competitive by nature, so we want to keep up with the ever-increasing speed, and we all still love to win. My commitment has been forced to increase and shift as the level of racing has increased.

The year 2003 was a highlight year for me. Our core team of Patrick, John, Novak, and I won the prestigious Raid Gauloises in Kyrgyzstan. It was the first race that I entered where I knew in my heart that we could win. That subtle sense of confidence gave us an edge. That race was not perfect by any means. Patrick was suffering from gastric problems and was unable to eat. On the morning of the second day, we had to stop and allow him to recuperate as we watched the lead teams breeze by. The time stopped paid off and we were able to catch and pass the field by the fourth day. As we traveled past groups of nomadic Kyrgyz in their yurts, we were able to maintain our lead and win the race. The Raid was definitely the pinnacle race of the year, but the rest of the season was a glowing success as well. It felt wonderful to be respected in the sport and finally be comfortable in my abilities and at home with my team.

As we transitioned into 2004, I was expecting the tidal wave of success to continue. However, it was not to be the case. This recent year of racing has been the least successful, most disappointing, and most devastating for our team since we began. From the first race of the year to the last, we were plagued. The strain of unsuccessful races and injuries took a toll on our income and even our team morale began to suffer notably. We bickered, stressed about finding teammate replacements, and worried about our sponsor commitments. Yet we all still shared the desire to race well, we all still believed in our abilities, and we knew that we had the foundation for world-class race results. We had already proven this to ourselves multiple times in the previous year. But the results just never fell into place. It felt like we were constantly fighting an uphill battle just to get to the start line. Our racing career definitely became more like a job than ever before. Much of the joy of racing was slowly being eroded. It was incredibly disheartening to be at races, watching teams finish as we stood on the sidelines knowing that we should be among them.

All the injury and illness during this year paled in comparison to the devastating experience our team went through at the 2004 Primal Quest. In a financial sense, this race was the biggest one of the year. It hosted a massive amount of prize money and the best teams in the world. In the two previous years, we had finished second and DNF due to a teammate injury. We wanted to win this race and felt confident that we could. Although it had been a rough season, we had three of our core team members and a strong alternate. Finishing well in this race would have also meant financial security for us for the remainder of the year.

By the third day, we were racing comfortably at the front of the race. More importantly, we were having a blast traveling with Team AROC, learning Australian drinking songs, basically competing against each other, but still traveling together, sharing stories, and having a wonderful time while we suffered through the course. I was the lone American in the group of eight and was enjoying the laid-back attitude, colorful commentary, and generally great camaraderie. Just after wandering through a beautiful alpine meadow and climbing a slippery, difficult peak with a ton of loose rock, the accident occurred. What transpired in the next few moments and days would change me forever.

Suddenly time stood still as a huge rock in the steep gully dislodged. Both our teams, all eight people, were strung out at various points in the rocky gully. The experience was surreal. Time seemed to stand still as I heard the panicked cries of "ROCK" from my teammates above. My instinct as a climber served me well. I did not hesitate for an instant to look around for the falling rock. Instead, I dove headfirst behind a tiny outcropping on my right. I buried my face into the rock, covered my head with my arms, and waited for what seemed like minutes. The sound of rocks crashing and falling seemed to last forever. I tell could from the sound that there was a lot of rock fall very close to me. When the sound finally stopped, there was a moment of heavy silence, then Alina McMaster's guttural screams. Alina's screams and the look on Novak's face were all I could register for a few moments. I had never heard or seen these types of expressions from my friends. The next thing I heard was my teammate Guy's voice over the satellite phone calling in two major injuries. The largest rock had hit my teammate John Jacoby, breezed right by me and Alina, eventually hitting Nigel Aylott from Team AROC, killing him instantly. As we regrouped, my teammate Novak was the person I gravitated toward. He was strong and calm in the face of this nightmare and also the person that I felt closest to. He looked me straight in the eye and told me how close I had come to being hit. He had seen the whole accident with his own eyes. His piercing expression clearly depicted his anguish and the severity of the situation.

The next few hours consisted of getting everyone off the tiny, loose summit. Alina, Tom and Matt from Team AROC joined with Guy and were able to climb five hundred feet down the peak to an organized helicopter landing zone in the meadow. Novak and I remained on top of the peak with John. He'd been struck by the rock and cut to the bone on his calf. I did not know the extent of the injury because John had had enough awareness to instantly pull out our team first-aid kit and tightly wrap the wound as his shoe filled with blood. What I did know is that his blood was everywhere, he was getting cold, and he definitely could not walk. John is always the pillar of strength on our team. In the four years I've raced with him, I've never seen him use first-aid materials, complain about any sort of pain, or drop out of a race. The combined facts that he broke out the first-aid kit and asked for help were blaring signals to me that his injury must be very severe.

We were still perched on the treacherously loose rock at the head of the gully. The only place the helicopter would be able to evacuate us was from the very top of the peak fifteen feet above us. Those fifteen feet were slippery, loose climbing with devastating exposure. Novak and I managed to assist John as he crawled to the summit. We laid him down on packs, insulated him with our space blankets and extra clothing, and elevated his leg while we waited hours for a helicopter to negotiate a landing. Just at dusk, a helicopter managed to hover unsteadily on the peak while John and I climbed in. There was not enough room for Novak, so he made the descent alone in the dimming light.

As the evening unfolded and reality set in, our two teams bonded together in sadness, shock, and despair. I have never felt that I needed people around me more than during that time. During our "official" debriefing from a psychologist a few hours after the accident, we were told that in order to stave off depression, we should all hydrate well, avoid alcohol, and do some light exercise. In the true Aussie tradition, we piled into the car and drove one block to the nearest pub.

Despite the psychologist's order to avoid alcohol, the Aussie "piss up" seemed to be just the therapy we all needed. We were joined by the film crew, our support crew, and others who were affected by the incident. We closed down the bar and we all camped together under a big tarp in the transition area. I felt such sadness about Nigel's death, but such closeness to my teammates and friends. I have never felt two conflicting positive and negative emotions so strongly in my life. I oscillated between love and hate, joy and despair all evening.

The next few days were as surreal as the accident. Time seemed to have no meaning and my memory from those days is disjointed and jumbled. As all the teams were gathered from the racecourse and a memorial service was held for Nigel, discussions began about how to handle the remainder of the race, and people's true colors became apparent. Overall, I was quite impressed with and thankful for how the racing community responded. Unfortunately, there were a few ugly events that will forever color how I view adventure racing and some of its participants. Despite the tragedy, the enormous amount of prize money seemed to have tainted the hearts of some of the individuals. Many teams were in disagreement among themselves about whether or not to continue racing, how to award the prize money, and how to honor Nigel and Team AROC's performance at the time of the accident. I felt like some teams viewed the accident as a way to move up two places in the rankings.

During this time of mourning, I was grateful to be surrounded by friends and fellow racers who seemed to understand and sympathize. On the other hand, I also felt like an intruder in my own sport. No one except our two teams could really understand what we had suffered through. After this race, I was struggling to keep the wonderful things about adventure racing from being overshadowed by the prize money, race results, and the overly competitive nature of some of the athletes. I am extremely competitive and am also trying to make a living at the sport that I love. However, I do not race to risk my life or watch my friends die. That is just a price that is too high in exchange for winning an adventure race.

When I got home from this race, I plunged into a self-imposed hermit lifestyle. I stayed home, communicated very little with anyone, didn't train much and searched my soul for why I raced. I was depressed and needed to process the feelings I had experienced. I had to decipher if I still wanted to keep racing and taking part in the sport that I loved, but had also caused me so much grief. My career and passion for the past seven years had swiftly been compromised and I felt lost and alone. My sense of purpose was gone. Most of my best friends in the world are adventure racers. They are people whom I see only a few times a year at gear checks, along the trail, and at race parties. I barely know what they do with the rest of their lives, but still we share a deep friendship and respect because of our common interests and struggles in racing. I knew that I cherished those connections and didn't want to lose them. However, I also knew that I never wanted myself or anyone that I know to have to go through such a difficult drama again.

All my soul searching led me to evaluate why I got involved with adventure racing in the first place and why it had kept drawing me back for so many years. When I first started racing, the attraction was the travel, the seemingly impossible goal, and the team kinship. Never did the dangerous aspect of it appeal to me or excite me. What was exciting about the sport were the unknown courses, the long, intense journey with your team and the physical journey you go through in yourself. When I think back to my favorite races, it is not necessarily ones that we won that grace the top of the list. Instead, the races where we overcame, worked together, and grew closer are the ones I am most proud of. For example, I finished the Moroccan Eco-Challenge unranked and nearly dead last, but it was the first race that I captained and actually crossed the finish line. The Patagonian Eco-Challenge was amazing because we finished fourth with a predominantly female team and broke down major gender issues in the sport. The Raid in Tibet was my hardest race ever. I was plagued with bronchitis at seventeen thousand feet and was nearly pulled out of the race by the medics. We dropped from third place to twenty-seventh, but my team stood by me, we kept moving forward, and we ended up seventh overall. In the Kyrgyzstan Raid, we won the race, but only after having to stop, nurse a sick teammate, and then work our way back up through the field. I knew that if I intended to keep adventure racing, I must find a way to return back to those core attractions that had fueled my desire for so many years.

After the drama with Nigel, I was at home in Idaho. Our team still had two small races and two big races left in the season. Because of sponsor commitments and because I didn't know what else to do, I went to the two short races with my team, went through the motions, and finished well, but I was uninspired. I did not go to Mild Seven Outdoor Quest because

I knew that my head was not in the game and did not want to subject my teammates to my dark, depressed mood. I stayed home and pondered whether or not we would still go to the Raid in Argentina. We waited eagerly to see if John's calf injury from Primal Quest would recover quickly enough to race. Unfortunately, he developed a blood clot from his injury and would not be able to race for the remainder of the year. I was faced with the difficult decision of whether or not to take the team to Argentina with two replacement teammates.

Because of the strict qualification rules, our team had to include two women and two men. As defending champions of the Raid, I knew there were expectations on us to perform well. I had looked forward to this race for the entire season. The original team that we'd qualified for Argentina would have given everyone a run for their money, and I knew the course would have suited our original team *very* well. It was rumored to be a long course with difficult navigation, in high mountain terrain with a huge amount of paddling. It was just the type of course that we normally excel at. However, that dream team was no longer intact. Instead, Novak and I were the only two original team members who had made it through the entire season. Our other two racers were strong athletes, proven in other expedition races, but relatively unknown to us.

Just three weeks before the race, Novak and I decided that we would participate in the Raid. I was excited about a team with two women and the possibility of once again proving that women are not the weak link in endurance sports. We also felt strongly that a positive finish to the year would improve morale, keep sponsors interested, and end our rough season on a high note. I also was coming to the conclusion that I did not want to be labeled as a quitter. None of our peers in the sport would have been surprised if our team succumbed to all the difficulties of the season and just thrown in the towel. I knew the racing community would not criticize me, but in my heart, I would have felt like I turned down an amazing experience just because we were no longer favored to win the race. I would have felt like I had not done everything in my power to keep our team together. As my own harshest critic, I would have labeled myself a quitter.

The moment I stepped onto the plane to San Martin de los Andes and saw friendly, familiar faces smiling at me, I knew I had made the right decision. After two months of relative isolation from my friends, it felt like a weight off my shoulders to see all my racing friends who still loved me, respected me, and were excited to see me despite our lousy season. Things such as race results don't change who you are in your friends' eyes. Our race in Argentina again did not turn out as planned. We arrived at the start line as a modified team with a different goal than defending our title. Our race was unfolding smoothly and the course was amazingly beautiful. Novak and I were enjoying the race, feeling strong and looking forward to the experience. However, our replacement teammate Elina Maki-Rautila was suffering from a bronchial infection. Climbing Lanin Volcano at twelve thousand feet in cold, windy conditions had taken its toll on her. She was coughing excessively and struggling with limited lung capacity to get her breath. Her condition seemed very similar to what I had experienced crossing the Himalayas in the Tibet Raid. After hours of deliberation, resting, and multiple medical evaluations, the race doctors decided that Elina's condition was too serious to continue racing. They ordered our team to drop out of the race.

When we were first told to stop, I went through the all-too-familiar emotions of anger, disappointment, and embarrassment. I sat by the river as other teams paddled by, wishing like crazy that I was still out there paddling and racing. I thought about our whole season and how brutally hard I had worked for such a poor outcome. We'd made very little prize money this year, we'd had very few good race results, and our team was not intact physically or emotionally. I also feared that we'd lose our sponsorship for next season. I sat at the river trying to figure out where I'd gone wrong as a team captain. What could I have done to make things work out better? Why was I working so hard with so little reward? Just at that moment, my teammate Novak came up to me, sat down, and put his arm around my shoulder. He let me cry on his shoulder and listened while I finally let all the frustrations from the whole year come pouring out. Novak is generally unemotional and a bit rough around the edges. He has a heart of gold, but it doesn't always shine through unless you're looking quite hard. The simple, monumental act of him coming to me when I needed a friend is just one shining example of why I've raced with him for four years in a row.

After we officially withdrew from the race and Elina was transported to the hospital, Novak, in true Aussie style, commandeered a bottle of red wine. We sat alone in the empty field among our smelly, wet race gear. All the other crews and race organization had packed up and moved on to the next transition. Novak opened the bottle and we toasted to our lousy season, to our great friends, and to a much better season in 2005. As we waited for teams to finish for the next few days, we drank many more bottles of wine, went on a hike together and got stuck in some bamboo, went shopping for gifts, shared meals, stayed up till 6:00 A.M. dancing one night, and overall had a fantastic vacation. I still harbor disappointment about not finishing that race, but mostly because the course seemed so beautiful and I missed being a part of it. Thoughts of prize money, reputation, and sponsor obligations were the last thing on my mind at that point. I was just enjoying being in a wonderful place with my friends.

Three months after the worst experience of my life and a serious challenge to my motivation, I had returned to adventure racing. I had discovered that I still loved it, was still inspired and challenged by it, but with a different perspective than in the past couple of years. In a way, I had come full circle in my race experiences. Initially, I was just racing for the love of the sport without much thought over placing or prize money. The steady rise in performance, sponsor commitments, and expectations that occurred over the years had clouded my perspective. It took Nigel's death to bring me abruptly back to reality and to reassess my values and goals. I needed to be able to answer the question, Why do I race? In my reevaluation, I have realized that I am still 100 percent committed to the sport of adventure racing. If our team can survive a year like this one, I know we have cemented a bond that can never be broken. I now know why I return again and again to this sport. I am still willing to work extremely hard and pour my heart and soul into adventure racing, even for very little perceived return on investment. Perhaps it's the rewards you cannot see that are the most precious.

As I look forward to next season and a new year of racing, I am surprised and overjoyed to find myself again filled with anticipation of what the races will be like, what countries I will be able to visit, how I will perform, and which friends and teammates I will be able to see again. Seven years ago, I jumped off a cliff into this unknown lifestyle. As the years trickled by and my life has defined itself, I have grown physically and mentally stronger than I ever would have imagined. I have traveled to the corners of the world and experienced different cultures and lifestyles. I have been challenged as a team leader and have never stopped learning from each experience. I have created a respectable career in a difficult field. The bottom line is that I have grown into an adult. Not the kind of adult who forgets what it's like to explore, play, and discover new things. Not the kind who is so overwhelmed with responsibilities and commitments that they forget to have fun. Despite being a homeowner now, my wanderlust and childlike desire for exploration are just as alive as the day I steered Bronco Betty away from the climbing gym. The difference now is that I have a new appreciation and respect for myself and for what people are capable of accomplishing together. I have a career and a lifestyle that I love. I can easily identify the precious things such as friends and family that motivate me and make my life feel purposeful. I cherish looking back on past excursions that have pushed me to the limit and know that they have made me a more complete person. I have very few tangible rewards that I can identify from my years of wandering and racing. However, the intangible life lessons, lifelong friends, and piles of unforgettable memories will always grace the front of my refrigerator and the core of my personality.

In the Face of Tragedy: Helpers vs. Stampeders

Photo of Patti Lynch courtesy of Suzanne Yack

NAME: SUZANNE YACK,
   PRIMAL QUEST VOLUNTEER
AGE: 51
RESIDENCE: JACKSONVILLE, FL

Some people read tea leaves, others study palms. I observe faces.

When I travel around the globe, I make it a game to study the faces of the people around me. At airports, in crowded elevators, or on the top floors of a tall building, I sort people into two groups: helpers and stampeders. If an emergency arose—a bomb, a fire, an earthquake—who in this crowd will reach a hand back to help others, and who will stampede for the exits?

I look for character, selflessness, caring, and resolve in their faces.

As a volunteer at the 2004 Subaru Primal Quest, I played the same game. But where at most places I can count ninety-nine stampeders to every one helper, at SPQ every last person landed in the helper group.

Adventure racers, from all walks of life, have in common the traits of courage and willpower. They are the people who you can count on in a tight spot, the ones who will strive, until every last alternative has been explored, to save the life of a fellow traveler, whether it be a another adventure racer or a mother struggling to free her child from a burning car.

As I started meeting the racers, I discovered that, indeed, many of them are in the helping fields: Marines, state troopers, guides, and even a few massage therapists and chiropractors in the mix.

The helper category could not have been more proven than by the swift actions by Patti Lynch, who was the race official at checkpoint 21 on an exquisite fall day, when tragedy struck.

A volunteer, Lynch is also a seasoned adventure racer who was recovering from a climbing accident that resulted in a broken back and left her in charge of a checkpoint instead of charging up a mountain.

She is a Santa Clara police officer, and when the call came in that a racer had sustained extreme injuries on Mount Illabot, Lynch relied on her eleven years of police experience. Familiar with the language and protocols of rescue operations, she moved seamlessly from leisure into action. Her previously relaxed disposition grew determined and focused and I could practically see the gears turning in her head, spanning the territory of what possibilities needed to be considered in this emergency that was still unknown and still unfolding. Her face told the story: She would rise to the occasion, doing whatever it took to bring the teams down from the mountain safely.

She also knew that Team Nike/ACG, coming up the fourteen-mile mountain bike ride from two thousand feet below, would be required to pause indefinitely at checkpoint 21 and wouldn't be able to continue on to the orienteering portion of the course until the situation on Mount Illabot was resolved. She knew that at some point their delay, too, would become an issue, as it would for the teams behind them.

Helicopters passed overhead—first one, then another, then another. Team Nike/ACG, arriving at the checkpoint, noted their presence and sensed the situation was serious. All that Lynch could say was, "There's been an accident. It's being assessed."

Nike/ACG members conserved their energy, spoke quietly among themselves, speculating about the injuries they knew must have occurred, trying to make sense of it. And as reason overcame optimism, they still expressed hope for the teams on the mountain. There was no whining, even as these racers, who were dressed for aerobic activity and not for napping, curled deeper and deeper into body-heat-protection positions to ward off the chilly air. They lay on the cold ground, their core temperatures dropping as quickly as the sun.

Rules are rules—they knew no assistance could be rendered, nor comfort given by race officials. And yet, the evening sun was soon behind clouds and Nike/ACG didn't have clothing for forty-degree temperatures. Their faces were tensing from the cold and their lower jaws began to chatter. They started jogging in place to stay warm.

Lynch saw that pivotal point coming and made the call to remote headquarters at Rockport, where she received the answer she sought: The four athletes were hurried into a race vehicle, the seat warmers were turned on, and the heater was dialed to high.

The faces of the athletes, having learned that they would be sent back down the mountain on their bikes, a fourteen-mile retreat in the gathering darkness, showed no bitterness or angst, just quiet resolve and a few squinting glances off into the distance that revealed their concern for their friends on Mount Illabot.

There were others who brought steady, swift competence to the moment. Winslow Passey, a mountain guide familiar with the Cascades, happened to be at checkpoint 21, and stayed on the scene to be available to render aid. The crackling voices from the makeshift headquarters telegraphed the quick, reflexive response of a seasoned and mountain-savvy crew, moving swiftly into action.

Tragedy sometimes happens in all outdoor sports, just as it does at NASCAR or the neighborhood pool. Whenever we venture out of the safety of our houses, tragedy can strike, and sometimes we don't even have to step out the door.

Adventure racers have qualities the rest of us mere mortals just hope for: courage, undeniable resolve and extraordinary endurance. But, as Nigel Aylott's death on that autumn afternoon illustrated, they are not superhuman. Their faces—often dirty, sometimes scratched, always ruddy—reveal their character well: Sure, they all want that finish line, but in the end none of them is a stampeder.

They're the people you can count on when all hell breaks loose.

Suzanne Yack, longtime Alaskan and former editor of the Juneau Empire, *is vice president of FreshMinistries in Jacksonville, Florida, where she works to alleviate poverty in the United States and prevent the spread of AIDS/HIV in Africa. Suzanne volunteers at adventure races simply because she enjoys the people.*

The Finish Line

In the chill of predawn darkness, you and your teammates gather at the starting line, surrounded by people with varied backgrounds, levels of experience, abilities, goals, and fears. You have spent months planning, training, and preparing for just this moment. Are you ready? Probably not. You could never be fully prepared for what you will face out there.

Then before you know it, there is a loud bang and you are off. The race director's final words of wisdom resonate in your ears: "Carry plenty of water, prepare for afternoon thunderstorms, and as always navigation will play a critical role." You look ahead and see the elite teams already opening up a gap, while you stay true to what you have planned—slow and steady, gaining strength as you go. Somewhere between the thousands of dollars of gear flashing around you, and the nervous excitement, you realize, "Hey, I am making this happen. I am competing in an adventure race." No matter if it is your first race or your fifty-first race, some things are certain: The challenges you will face will be unknown, the journey will be a challenge, and the end result will be a reward you have truly earned.

Throughout the race, you will experience moments of pure joy and elation, and times of utter pain and despair. It will seem as though you are experiencing a lifetime's worth of emotions packed into just a few days. You will undoubtedly learn what you are truly made of. You will discover strengths you never knew you had, and gain insight into your weaknesses and limitations. And the beauty of the sport is that you will share all of these experiences with your teammates. You will help them learn more about themselves and push themselves to new limits. Together you will do things you never dreamed possible, and whether things go right or wrong, it will be an incredible bonding and learning experience for everyone.

We hope that you have enjoyed the tales from these athletes about their adventures and experiences. As many of the contributors have shown, the lessons learned during the course of a race are often more valuable than the race itself. We can take those lessons and apply them to the next race or, better yet, to life itself. After all, it's not the destination we are after. It's the journey.

See you at the races . . .

About the Editors

Neal Jamison, editor of *Running Through the Wall: Personal Encounters with the Ultramarathon* (Breakaway Books, 2004), is a freelance writer and middle-of-the-pack ultrarunner. Although relatively new to the sport of adventure racing, Neal is passionate about all sports that require athletes to dig deep and push beyond "normal" limits. Neal says writing a book and running a hundred-miler are similar. "They can both hurt real bad," he says. "But about a week after I'm done with either one, I can't help looking for the next one." Neal lives in Roanoke, Virginia, with his wife and son.

Maureen Moslow-Benway is an experienced adventure racer who has successfully completed numerous races, including two Eco-Challenges. She is also an avid trail runner, mountain biker, backpacker, and adventure traveler who has hiked, biked and paddled her way through thirty-four different countries. Maureen has written about her adventures for several regional and local publications. She lives with her husband Bob, their three children, Matthew, Connor, and Mikaela, and a menagerie of animals on a hobby farm in central Virginia.

Nic Stover works as the director of contracts for Tamarack Resort and proudly resides in Boise, Idaho, with his girlfriend and adventure racing teammate, Jen Garretson. Nic is an avid peak bagger, skier, adventure traveler, mountain biker, and adventure racer. Recently, Nic broke the speed record for climbing the nine 12,000-foot summits in Idaho and has completed a number of adventure races for Team Tamarack Resort. Nic and his team look forward to another quality season as they set their sights on completing their first expedition-length race.

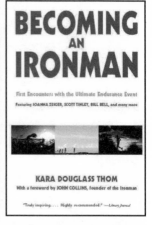